AQA Media Studies

A2

Exclusively endorsed by AQA

Maggie Andrews

Elspeth Stevenson

Series editor
Julia Burton

Nelson Thornes

Published in 2009 by:
Nelson Thornes Ltd
Delta Place
27 Bath Road
CHELTENHAM
GL53 7TH
United Kingdom

09 10 11 12 13 / 10 9 8 7 6 5 4 3 2 1

A catalogue record for this book is available from the British Library

ISBN 978 0 7487 9816 2

Picture research by Annabel Ossel
Cover photograph by Alamy
Page make-up by Pantek Arts Ltd, Maidstone, Kent
Illustrations by Redmoor Design

Printed in Spain by Graphycems

Contents

AQA introduction

Nelson Thornes and AQA

Nelson Thornes has worked in collaboration with AQA to ensure that this book offers you the best support for your A2 or A Level course and helps you to prepare for your exams. The partnership means that you can be confident that the range of learning, teaching and assessment practice materials has been checked by the senior examining team at AQA before formal approval, and is closely matched to the requirements of your specification.

Blended learning

Printed and electronic resources are blended: this means that links between topics and activities between the book and the electronic resources help you to work in the way that best suits you, and enable extra support to be provided online. For example, you can test yourself online and feedback from the test will direct you back to the relevant parts of the book.

Electronic resources are available in a simple-to-use online platform called Nelson Thornes learning space. If your school or college has a licence to use the service, you will be given a password through which you can access the materials through any internet connection.

Icons in this book indicate where there is material online related to that topic. The following icons are used:

Learning activity

These resources include a variety of interactive and non-interactive activities to support your learning.

Progress tracking

These resources enable you to analyse and understand examination questions (On your marks...).

Research support

These resources include WebQuests, in which you are assigned a task and provided with a range of weblinks to use as source material for research.

Study skills

These resources support you as you develop a skill that is key for your course, for example planning essays.

Analysis tool

These resources help you to analyse key texts and images by providing questions and prompts to focus your response.

When you see an icon, go to Nelson Thornes learning space at www.nelsonthornes.com/aqagce, enter your access details and select your course. The materials are arranged in the same order as the topics in the book, so you can easily find the resources you need.

How to use this book

This book covers the specification for your course and is arranged in a sequence approved by AQA. The book is divided into two Units. Unit 3 covers critical perspectives, exploring in detail various media issues, debates and theories, which are essential to your understanding in both your examination and your coursework. Unit 3 goes on to model approaching texts and topics critically to help you in responding to the questions in your examination. Unit 4 is written to provide you with specific and detailed guidance on your coursework.

Learning objectives

At the beginning of each section you will find a list of learning objectives that contain targets linked to the requirements of the specification.

The features in this book include:

Key terms

Terms that you will need to be able to define and understand. These terms are coloured blue in the text book and their definition will also appear in the glossary at the back of this book.

Investigating media

Activities which develop skills, knowledge and understanding that will prepare you for assessment in your Media Studies course.

Media in action

Information on key events, products, companies, and points of interest which enhance your understanding of media.

Links

Links to other areas in the textbook which are relevant to what you are reading.

Case study

A study of a specific company, genre, platform, etc.

Thinking about media

Short reflective activities that extend your understanding of key ideas.

Technical tip

Useful suggestions and reminders.

AQA Examiner's tip

Hints from AQA examiners to help you with your study and to prepare for your exam.

Examination-style questions

Questions in the style that you can expect in your exam.

Chapter summary

A summary of what has been taught in the chapter.

Weblinks in the book

Because Nelson Thornes is not responsible for third party content online, there may be some changes to this material that are beyond our control. In order for us to ensure that the links referred to in the book are as up-to-date and stable as possible, the websites provided are usually homepages with supporting instructions on how to reach the relevant pages if necessary.

Please let us know at **webadmin@nelsonthornes.com** if you find a link that doesn't work and we will do our best to correct this at reprint, or to find an alternative site.

AQA examination questions are reproduced by permission of the Assessment and Qualifications Alliance.

Introduction to Media Studies A2

What will I be doing on this course?

You have completed AS Media Studies and have already got to grips with studying media in a critical way, drawing upon the core concepts to analyse how texts from a wide range of media platforms are constructed and convey meaning. Although core concepts will still inform your study at A2 Level, there is also plenty of new material for you to learn for your A2 course.

A2 Media Studies requires you to:

- engage with media debates and issues
- understand and utilise media theories
- understand the significance of the context in which media texts are produced and consumed
- undertake independent learning, research and production.

You will already be aware of the vast array of different media products that we consume in our everyday lives and there is much to think about, discuss, research, study and debate about the power, influence, use and significance of media texts. A2 Media Studies asks you to study and engage with issues and debates taking place about the dynamic relationship between media and society. In studying media you are therefore also studying the context in which media is produced and consumed.

One of the most exciting challenges that A2 offers is for you to undertake case studies, independent research and learning; focusing on areas, issues or debates that particularly interest you for both practical and analytical work. Importantly you will make links between what you learn when you are analysing media and what you learn when you construct media texts. This is both exciting and a little scary. This book is here to help you through the course.

In order to do this you will need not just to engage with the core concepts, but also to encounter a number of theories and critical perspectives utilised in contemporary media studies. Many of these critical perspectives, debates and theories try to explain why media texts are constructed and consumed in particular ways. You will be introduced to critical perspectives, debates and theories in Chapters 1 and 2.

Theories, debates and critical perspectives do not however provide easy answers, rather they offer tools to help you engage more analytically when both consuming and producing media texts. It is not enough merely to encounter theories, debates and critical perspectives, you need both to think about them and discuss them in order to develop your own opinions based upon your studies.

An exciting element of media studies is that your understanding is developed by undertaking practical work, and at A2 this also occurs. You will produce a practical project that is informed by and informs your understanding of debates about media and is linked to a research project.

How will my work be assessed and examined?

- Fifty per cent of the A2 marks are assessed by the Unit 3 examination, which will usually be taken in the summer term (although some of you may decide to take it in January). The examination lasts two hours and is marked by external examiners. It assesses your knowledge of media concepts, contexts and critical debates and how you use them to analyse media texts, processes and issues. In the exam you will be expected to demonstrate an understanding of how media texts produce meanings and responses.

- Fifty per cent of the A2 marks are assessed by the Unit 4 coursework component. Again you will be assessed on your knowledge and understanding of concepts, contexts and critical debates but also how you plan and present research and construct media products using technical and creative skills. This is internally marked by your school or college teachers and lecturers. A sample is then sent off to the exam board for checking and moderation.

The units at a glance

Units 1 and 2 were covered in the AS Media Studies textbook.

Unit 3: Critical perspectives

In preparation for the examination you will be given two pre-set topic areas on which to undertake case studies that will form an important basis for your writing in the examinations. The exam has two parts: in Section A there will be two unseen media texts, which act as stimulus for three short questions; in Section B you will write an essay from a range of options drawing upon your case studies.

 Link

You will be given guidance on how to undertake a case study in Chapters 3 and 4.

Unit 4: Media: research and production

Unit 4 involves critical investigation of a theme or text in some depth and linked media production, which reflects this research and investigation. Both the critical investigation and media production will be marked and the relationship between them must be clear.

 Link

Chapters 5 and 6 provide guidance on how to undertake the Unit 4 coursework.

Pathways through the course

Do not expect to undertake your course or read this book in a linear fashion. Most of you will undertake coursework preparing for Unit 4 and the necessary learning and case studies for Unit 3 alongside one another.

The reading, learning and engaging with debates required for A2 study requires a deep level of engagement and topics will need to be visited more than once. Aim rather to undertake chunks of Chapter 1: Media Issues and Debates or Chapter 2: Media Theories at a time. Dip into this material and consider the case studies that are provided and then explore the issues, debates, perspectives and theories in relation to media that you are studying, and/or consuming.

Chapters 3, 4, 5 and 6 give you guidance about exams, case studies and coursework: you will need both to read through initially and to keep returning to them for guidance on preparing for exams and undertaking coursework.

Expect to return to Chapters 1 and 2 to support your revision and independent study. You will find this easier to do if you really make the book your own, writing notes on it, underlining or highlighting points and adding sticky notes. This way the book will become a resource for your revision.

E-resources can also be used on a pick and mix basis to help you engage with ideas and debates and deepen your understanding. Remember, learning should always be active – it is easy for all of us to find out that although our eyes are scanning a page of text our minds are elsewhere!

A2 Media Studies is both challenging and exciting; it gives you the opportunity to really think critically and gain a greater understanding of the media-saturated world in which we live – so enjoy the experience.

Acknowledgements

The authors and publisher would like to thank the following for permission to reproduce photographs and other copyright material:

1.1 Universal Pictures/The Kobal Collection; 1.2 News International: photo Corbis;1.3 More Magazine/Bauer London Lifestyle: photo Peter Pedonomou/ Camera Press; 1.4 Guardian Syndication: photo Phil Mingo, Pinnacle;1.5 Bebo.com, permission to use look and feel of website;1.6 Solo Syndication: Photo PA; 1.7 Express Syndication; 1.8 News International: 1.9 Corbis; 1.12 News International: photo Getty Images; 1.13 News International: photo Claudio Onorati/EPA;

2.1 Brittany Ferries; 2.3 News International; 2.5 The Advertising Archives; 2.6 The Hospital Group; 2.7 Getty Images; 2.8 Corbis; 2.9 The Advertising Archives; 2.10 Guardian Syndication: photos Dan Smith; 2.11 Pride Magazine;

3.1 News International: illustration Blouzar Ltd; 3.2 Guardian Syndication; photo Getty Images; 3.3 Mirrorpix; 3.4 Solo Syndication: photo courtesy Keith Bernstein/TWC 2008; 3.5 News International: photo Corbis; 3.6 Courtesy of Optomen Television Ltd/Channel 4; 3.7 Paramount Pictures/Ronald Grant Archive; 3.8 Heat /Bauer Media; 3.9 Heat /Bauer Media; 3.10 Heat /Bauer Media; 3.11 Mirrorpix; 3.12 Guardian Syndication: photo Murdo McLeod; 3.13 courtesy Right Honorable Ann Widdecombe MP; 3.14 Liveleak.com;

4.1 Look/IPC Media; 4.2 Guardian Syndication; 4.3 Express Syndication; 4.4. Viewpoint: the learning disability magazine published by Mencap; 4.5 News International: photos M.E.N. Syndication; 4.6 Solo Syndication; 4.7 Guardian Syndication: photo Reuters; 4.8 News International; 4.9 News International; 4.10 News International: illustration Corbis; 4.11 www. childhamandhambrook.info; 4.12 Solo Syndication; 4.13 Solo Syndication: photo Alamy; 4.14 News International: photos Manchester Central News Ltd. (Terry Adams), M.E.N. Syndication (Dessie Noonan), Bare Films Ltd. (Dominic Noonan), Mercury Press (Curtis Warren and George Bromley Snr.); 4.15 News International; 4.17 That's Life/H Bauer Publishing; 4.18 The Casting Suite; 4.19 Crown Copyright; 4.20 Guardian Syndication: photo Win McNamee/Getty Images; 4.21 Crown Copyright; 4.22 Guardian Syndication: photos AP/EPA; exam questions: AQA 2008, exam text articles Solo Syndication;

5.1 ABC TV/The Kobal Collection (Ugly Betty), Rex Features (Ross Kemp); 5.2 Elspeth Stevenson; 5.3 Elspeth Stevenson; 5.4 Elspeth Stevenson; 5.5 www.bbc.co.uk/filmnetwork; 5.6 Channel 4/FourDocs;

6.1 Filmed and Directed by Dom Phillips, Blue Lagoon Media; 6.2 © Optimum Releasing 2007; 6.4 Torchwood magazine is published by Titan Magazines, under licence from BBC Worldwide Limited: Torchwood © BBC 2006; 6.5 Tony Fisher/BBC; 6.6 to 6.10 Elspeth Stevenson; 6.11 Freeverse Inc./Felt Tip Software (Sound Studio).

Note from the publisher: Some applications made for permission to reproduce texts received no reply or were refused; in some of these cases an artist was commissioned to give an impression of the text. Students should refer to the original source before undertaking detailed critical work based on these images.

Every effort to obtain permission to reproduce images and text has been made, and any ommissions will be rectified at reprinting.

3 Critical perspectives

1 Media issues and debates

At A2 Level, examiners are looking for you to take a much more critical attitude towards the media texts that you encounter. You need to discuss not just *how* these texts are constructed, but also *why* and *with what influence*.

You need to begin to engage with many of the debates that surround the place and potential power of media in our society. These are hotly debated topic areas and therefore you need to consider some of the critical perspectives taken by different media theorists.

Media texts convey our understanding and knowledge about the world and this is why the representations that they present are considered powerful. Arguably many of our values and ideologies also come from media representations. Think of stories in the news, celebrities, most sporting events or politicians: what we know about them comes from media representations. We will begin this chapter by focusing upon texts, representation and realism.

If media texts are influential in constructing our understanding of the world then this leads to questions about the power of the institutions that produce media texts, and this is what will be explored in the second section. Media producers might argue that they only produce what audiences want to watch, listen to, read and buy, so audience power over media texts will also be considered in this section.

Finally the last section will explore three contemporary areas of debate in media studies:

- media effects
- moral panics
- censorship.

These debates are all concerned with the power of the media.

Representation

You have already encountered representation during your AS study and will understand that it is a difficult concept. Representation can be understood as how groups, events, places and experiences are represented in media texts. It can be a depiction or description of something, someone or an event. It may involve symbolising or standing in for what is being represented, for example, red roses or hearts are used to symbolise love and romance.

Many debates about representation are couched in terms of **realism**. These debates explore the degree to which media is realistic or to what extent it is a version of the reality presented. Significantly the term 'realist' is most often used about fiction texts, such as soap operas (*EastEnders*, BBC 1985–) or sitcoms (*The Royle Family*, BBC 1998–2006), rather than about news or documentary shows.

Key terms

Realism: a media text or representation that seems credible to an audience, in terms of events, people, emotions or experiences as opposed to a text that is seen to be merely fantasy.

■ Key terms

Reflective view of representation: understands media representations as a reflection of lived reality.

Constructionist view of representation: an understanding that our knowledge of the world is constructed by media representations.

Cultural concern: an issue, concern or paranoia that a society or culture becomes preoccupied or worried about.

News and documentary programmes are assumed to be realistic and based on factual information. At AS Level you learnt that all media texts are constructed texts. This means that they always convey a version of reality that is inevitably selective and biased towards the people who created them. For example, the televising of the England team's final football match in the 2006 World Cup shows how the reflective view of representation works – the images selected often showed the England manager Sven-Göran Eriksson's reactions to English penalties. His facial expressions along with the commentators' dialogue interpreted the events for the audience. A **reflective view of representation** suggests that while the media does reflect reality, it also mediates it through media language and narrative to give a certain perspective.

The **constructionist view of representation** is a more complex understanding of representation. You have already encountered this approach at AS. This approach suggests that our understanding or knowledge of the world is constructed by representations, found in a range of media texts utilising media language and narrative. Sometimes a constructionist approach is clear to see, for example, the British media coverage of the final Rugby World Cup match in Paris in October 2007 focused on the penalties, the 'disallowed try' and how 'bravely or impressively' the England team played. This version was constructed through the media process of representation. The South African media, naturally, focused on the positive aspects of South Africa's game – portraying a different version of reality to a different audience.

■ Thinking about media

Think for a moment about the war in Iraq; most of us have almost no first-hand experience of Iraq or the war. Our knowledge of events is constructed through language using terms such as 'invasion' and 'liberation' from Saddam Hussein and the 'fight against terrorism'. The use of different terms such as 'civil war' or 'freedom fighters' would alter our perception and therefore our opinion of the events.

Representations are influenced by the cultural, political and social contexts in which they are produced. A reflective approach to representations will see media representations as reflecting the values, ideologies and political and **cultural concerns** of a particular historical moment. For example, the film *Charlie Wilson's War* (2007) showed how a fun-loving Texan senator Charlie Wilson channelled American funds and weapons into Afghanistan in response to the Soviet Union's invasion of that country in 1979. This film can be seen as a reflection of the growing public opposition to American foreign policy in the Middle East and the American involvement in wars in Afghanistan and Iraq. Alternatively, a constructionist approach would suggest that the film constructs audience knowledge and understanding of the history of American involvement in Afghanistan and so contributes to the development of anti-war sentiment. (You can look at a number of extracts from the film online on YouTube.)

Fig. 1.1 *Publicity poster for* **Charlie Wilson's War**

Thinking about media

A similar debate around whether media simply responds to changes in cultural, social and political environments, or in fact influences those changes, can be framed around the women's magazine *Cosmopolitan*. The magazine remodelled itself in 1965 to become a more sexually aware and 'sassy' publication in line with changing attitudes to sexuality and the beginnings of the feminist movement.

■ Was this change a reflection of the cultural attitudes of the era or did it contribute to changing those attitudes?

Investigating media

Explore an interesting example of the new version of masculinity (see Chapter 2 for further discussion of gender) by looking at the popular BBC2 programme *Top Gear* (2002–), the accompanying magazine and websites.

■ Do you think these texts reflect contemporary versions of 'laddish' masculinity or do you think these texts contribute to contemporary constructions of masculinity?

Both reflective and constructionist perspectives on representation are concerned with power. A reflective approach focuses upon the relationship between texts and reality and the way in which reality may be distorted or changed in the interests of powerful groups. A constructionist approach is concerned with who has the power to ensure that their version of reality is the accepted and dominant one.

⁊ Reality TV

In recent years there have been a number of television programmes that seem to blur the lines between fact and fiction. For example, the BBC series *Walking with Dinosaurs* (1999) used computer-generated images of dinosaurs to show scientists' impressions and understandings of how dinosaurs lived thousands of years ago.

Another media genre that blurs fact, fiction and realism is reality TV. Reality TV is hard to define as it is a hybrid genre that is continually shifting and developing. It was initially understood to present everyday life as entertainment; however most contemporary shows place participants in highly constructed situations. Reality TV now involves presenting a range of very structured scenarios, heavily edited to provide audience entertainment.

The genres that reality TV draws upon are:

■ *documentary* – using real footage of real people (not actors)
■ *soap opera* – using a multiple **enigma narrative**
■ *game show* – with a prize for which participants compete
■ *voting* – such as talent shows.

Recurring elements of reality TV include:

■ *transformation* – of an individual, group, workplace, object or even pet
■ *symbolic violence* – when experts or other contestants criticise participants or the show's format involves humiliation.

Although not all reality TV contains each of these elements, it has become hugely popular in recent years even on prime-time TV (between 8 and 10pm).

Key terms

Enigma narrative: a narrative that involves the audience by setting questions or puzzles for them to solve.

Case study: *Driving School*

There are many debates about whether it is justified to include reconstructions in reality TV. One of the earliest popular reality TV programmes *Driving School* (BBC1, 1997) featured a woman called Maureen Rees who had failed her driving test numerous times. The programme included scenes of Maureen waking up at night and going over her Highway Code. When people realised that these scenes were reconstructions it caused a controversy. Producers argued that the events had taken place, just not when the cameras were there, so realism and authenticity were not compromised by reconstructing these events for the cameras. However, many of the 12½ million viewers did not agree.

Investigating media

How popular is reality TV? Examine TV schedules for a particular day and identify all the reality TV shown.

■ At what times and on what channels is reality TV popular?

■ Who do you think the intended audiences of these programmes are?

■ What do you think is the appeal of these programmes?

Look at the Broadcasting Audience Research Bureau website and examine the top 30 programmes in a recent week, for each channel.

■ How significant is reality TV to the schedules?

■ Is reality TV more important to some channels?

■ Is reality TV more popular at particular times of the day?

Media in action

Different critical perspectives explain reality TV's popularity in different ways. A focus on production emphasises the correlation between the increasing numbers of reality TV programmes and changes in the broadcasting industry, including:

■ the growth in the number of TV channels through cable, satellite and digital television networks, which produce very little of their own programming

■ reducing revenues for commercial TV channels in the competitive multi-channel environment of contemporary television

■ these changes in the industry have resulted in pressure to produce popular, accessible and cheap television. Reality TV fulfils these criteria as while it is produced cheaply it gains gravitas by adopting current affairs techniques. Reality TV is thus ideal for independent production companies.

Other critical perspectives explain the rise of reality TV based on the entertainment value that these texts offer their audiences. Corner (1996) suggests the popularity of reality TV rests upon the dynamics of 'anxiety and security'. In some texts, such as *I'm a Celebrity ... Get Me Out of Here!* (2002–), audiences enjoy experiencing risk, danger and then relief at successful outcomes in the programmes. In other programmes the audience, who are usually guaranteed a favourable outcome, enjoy the excessive drama, pain and trauma that the emotionally or physically vulnerable participants experience.

Case study: *Ramsay's Kitchen Nightmares*

In *Ramsay's Kitchen Nightmares* (Channel 4, 2004–), celebrity chef and Michelin starred restaurant owner Gordon Ramsay visits failing restaurants and orchestrates the restaurant's transformation. In the process, those working in the restaurant are subject to humiliation, violent verbal abuse and an emotional roller-coaster that nevertheless always ends successfully.

The first episode of *Ramsay's Kitchen Nightmares* involved a young, inexperienced chef serving Gordon Ramsay rancid scallops. This scene was voted 2005 TV moment of the year. The owners of the restaurant tried to sue Gordon Ramsay as they felt that the editing of the documentary grossly misrepresented them, thereby ruining the reputation of their restaurant.

Case study: *Supernanny*

Supernanny (Channel 4, 2004–) involved a TV nanny Jo Frost visiting struggling families and guiding the transformation of both parents' and children's behaviour in order to create a harmonious household. The transformation usually occurred after the parents experienced an emotionally violent humiliation when shown videos of their own incompetent parenting. Part of the pleasure for the audience lies in the illusion created that there are easily attainable solutions to the common scenarios and problem of parenting children.

■ Media in action

It is important to be aware that the popularity of any reality TV programme rests upon its inter-relationship with other media texts, for example:

- ■ tabloid newspaper cover stories about participants
- ■ celebrity and television magazines discuss the participants and the judges or experts in the programme
- ■ chat show programmes give further media attention to reality TV programmes, to the participants and their lives off-camera
- ■ spin-off programmes on digital TV networks with smaller audiences
- ■ websites provide a range of extra information and gossip about the programmes and the participants
- ■ audiences can discuss, gossip and speculate about the shows and the participants on Internet chat rooms
- ■ spin-off books, videos, CDs and DVDs
- ■ updates of information, results, reminders and ring tones provided through mobile phone networks.

AQA Examiner's tip

When discussing reality TV, try to refer specifically to the range of critical perspectives on reality TV you feel are most convincing and relevant. For example, refer to symbolic violence, transformation, realism or entertainment values. Try to convey your wider awareness of the significance of other inter-related media texts when discussing a reality TV text.

■ Key terms

Voyeurism: gaining pleasure from watching, especially secretly, other people's behaviour and bodies in sexual, intimate or emotional behaviour.

■ Investigating media

Select any reality TV programme. Through an internet search find out how many of the above inter-related media are connected to that programme.

■ Case study: *The Apprentice*

The Apprentice (BBC, 2004–) is a reality TV programme in which 12 to 14 men and women live and work together over a period of two to three months. They compete to win a job with wealthy entrepreneur Sir Alan Sugar. Each episode is structured around a business-oriented task with two teams competing to win. Past examples are producing and selling sweets at London Zoo, selling flats on behalf of an estate agent or selling cars for a second-hand car dealer. One member of the losing team is fired each week, in a dramatic and verbally violent showdown with Sir Alan Sugar in the boardroom.

The text offers the audience a range of pleasures as they **voyeuristically** watch the contestant experience extreme emotions and try to cope with the pressure, stress and humiliation of eventually being fired. Between episodes audience members are able to share their speculations and predictions with friends and family as they gossip about the show. *The Apprentice*, Sir Alan Sugar and the contestants are heavily reported on in a wide range of media texts and extracts are shown on online media such as YouTube, all of which adds to speculation and hype around who will be 'fired' from the next show.

Through programmes such as *The Apprentice*, the BBC sees itself as fulfilling its public service remit of informing, educating and entertaining the public about business, entrepreneurship and interviewing. Thus it can be seen as assisting the general public to do well and to succeed in their working lives.

A more careful analysis of the representation of the text of programmes such as *The Apprentice*, however, raises questions about the degree to which it conveys and promotes a particular ideology around capitalism – that the rich deserve their wealth as they work hard, cope with stress and are uniquely talented. These ideas are conveyed through the use of specific media language and a particular narrative structure, for example:

- ■ commentary – the commentator's voice-over
- ■ views of various locations in the city of London verify the reality of events
- ■ dramatic music is used to convey a certain atmosphere during the introductions, tasks and in the boardroom
- ■ low camera angles emphasise Sir Alan Sugar's superiority and power by looking up at him from below
- ■ the length of each series emphasises the hard work and struggle needed to succeed
- ■ the weekly threat of elimination and the fear of failure justifies the £100,000 a year salary of the winner.

Grumpy Garden Gnome starts on fresh cull

Television
BBC One
★★★★

Tim Teeman

Hang on: is this a reality show or a haircare advert? Have you ever seen men with such overstyled barnets? Sir Alan Sugar may claim that *The Apprentice* is about business, but the beauty parade and combustible personalities of the contestants make a mockery of claiming a higher purpose for this ratings-winner. That recalls the hopeless vanity of the television soap operas which for years demanded to be called – if you don't mind – "continuing dramas".

The fourth season of *The Apprentice* returned with its customary, coloured-up, panoramic views of Canary Wharf and thunderous classical music, both of which are utterly misleading. For one, Sir Alan Sugar's HQ is in Brentwood (here's a challenge, BBC: we want swooping shots of Brentwood), and for another *The Apprentice* is really Big Brother clothed in the drag of "business". Many business people must watch it askance – ineptitude and bullying almost always supersede teamwork and professionalism.

The Apprentice is about watching beautiful egomaniacs squabble, exhibit delicious hubris and eventually get skewered by Sir Alan in boardroom confrontations so tense that they are best watched with a cushion to clutch as the buck-passing and insults reach, with clock-ticking inevitability, that final growled: "You're fired!"

If TV shows – and reality shows in particular – survive to their fourth season, they lose their way. Too many tricks. Not *The Apprentice*. It is masterfully conceived and tightly directed. At the outset we have the contestants' grandiloquent claims: "The spoken word is my tool," said Raef Bjayou, with a dangerous quiff and vowels so plumy he made Noël Coward seem a chav.

There was a cavalcade of impressive-sounding jobs. Sara Dhada is an "international car trader"; what is that? She has a short fuse and is already complaining about being interrupted. Lucinda Ledgerwood, in purple beret and well versed in Greek, seemed to be an extra from *Midsomer Murders* rather than a thrusting young executive.

Fig. 1.2 *Newspaper article about* **The Apprentice** *(The Times, 27 March 2008)*

A reflective perspective focuses on the selectivity of the text's representations of the contestants, Sir Alan Sugar and capitalism. A constructionist approach emphasises how such programmes contribute to our knowledge and understanding of capitalism. This approach could suggest that the knowledge gained from *The Apprentice* shapes the audience's own experience of capitalism, big business and industry. It could be seen to have a powerful influence framing the way in which audience members understand wealth and big business, contributing to the programme's structure being seen as a 'natural' and fair reward for hard work. If an individual's life experiences do not measure up to this learnt knowledge, he or she may blame him or herself rather than question these powerfully transmitted values.

It could be argued that *The Apprentice* is an unrealistic and constructed view of the world of business, entrepreneurship and wealth creation. However, it may have what Gledhill (1998) described as 'emotional realism'. The emotional experiences that the show's participants face, such as insecurity and failure in the workplace, antagonism and irritation with work colleagues, competitiveness and a lack of honesty, are recognised by audience members. The emotions are real, hence the term emotional realism.

 Thinking about media

Think of a reality TV show you have seen recently. What scenarios and experiences in them seem emotionally real?

AQA Examiner's tip

When analysing specific media texts try to consider whether they have been constructed to convey particular values and ideologies. Link this to debates about the power and influence of the media in contemporary culture.

JADE

'Jack Told Me I Was Huge'

But blimey, look at her now. Jade Goody opens up about her weight, Jack's cheating and getting drunk on £3,000 bottles of champagne...

Q *Was it hard to get back with Jack after you split up late last year?*

A I wanted to get away from Jack, because I didn't want to be with him any more. I felt more like his mother than his girlfriend. But when I wasn't with him, I wanted to be. It was easy to get back with him, but I'm waiting for more stories to come out from girls saying he's cheated.

Q *Are you going to get engaged?*

A There's no engagement and there won't be. All the hype in the papers has spoilt it really.

Q *That's sad Jade. Let's talk nicer things, you're starting up Jade's Fit Camp, how come?*

A Well, I went to a fit camp myself, and lost just under 2st in two weeks. But it's unrealistic. At the end of the week they said to me, 'This is what you have to eat.' It's in packets, it costs £200. If you don't eat it, and don't train 12 hours a day, you'll put the weight back on. And I have. I'm not as fat, but still. I've always struggled with my weight. I've even been on slimming pills. So I need to set up something for normal girls like me.

Q *We're in. Tell us more...*

A We've got four trainers – military and non-military – a nutritionist and a chef. There'll be a hot tub too. You'll lose a dress size in a week.

Q *Do you like the way you look?*

A I've put on weight, but I do like the way I look. I'm confident naked, and I don't mind Jack seeing me naked.

I think if you haven't got a naked relationship with your partner, then you haven't got one at all. I couldn't lie there and have sex with the lights off.

Q *Did Jack notice that you'd put on weight?*

A Jack said, 'God! You're the biggest you've ever been. The biggest I've seen you.' But he still makes me feel sexy.

Q *Do you want more surgery?*

A I was going to have a tummy tuck, but I thought that there are so many women out there who are like me, I'd be sticking my fingers up at them, saying that's the only way you can lose weight. And that's not true.

Q *Do you compare yourself to thinner celebs?*

A I joke with my mates. I get called 'The Bear', and we call my other mate 'The Tank'. That's how we deal with being bigger. But I don't compare myself to celebs like Danielle Lloyd.

Q *Do you see Dani much?*

A People who want to be famous and papped are up their own arse.

Q *Did you go out in New York when you were out there?*

A Oh yeah, we drank a lot. I bought a £3,000 Cristal magnum. It came in a locked wooden box with its own bodyguard – it was like being Britney.

Q *Talking of expensive gifts, did the Prince of Brunei give you a £3m ring?*

A Yes. He's a brilliant mate. He's mad though. He was like, 'Come back and play hide and seek in the palace.' So I did. And I broke his £500,000 table. I felt sick. I thought I was going to have to remortgage my house to pay for it.

And with that she heads off with a film crew in tow. For more on Jade's Fit Camp visit www. jadegoodyfitcamp.com.

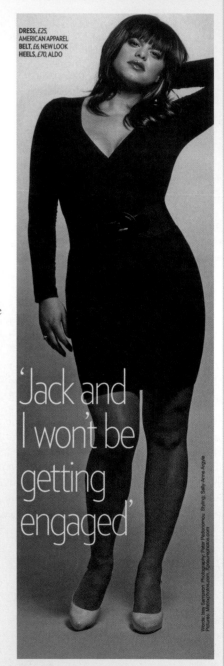

DRESS, £25, AMERICAN APPAREL
BELT, £6, NEW LOOK
HEELS, £70, ALDO

'Jack and I won't be getting engaged'

Fig. 1.3 *Magazine article about Jade Goody (**More**, 31 March 2008)*

Celebrity

Reality TV has been seen as contributing to the rise of the celebrity. Contestants receive heavy media exposure on television, in popular newspapers and magazines and on the wide range of internet sites that complement all reality TV. For the general public an intimacy and insight into the private life of a celebrity is created through interviews in many media texts such as tabloids and magazines such as *Hello!*, *Chat* and *OK!*, personal websites or the blogs that celebrities produce on their websites, or radio and television chat shows.

The attributes of celebrity are that they:

■ are well known for being well known
■ focus on gossip
■ are frequently seen in magazines and newspapers (especially tabloids)
■ are informal and intimate
■ are seen as familiar, down-to-earth and 'someone like us'
■ are often flawed in their private life, as displayed through a range of supposedly spontaneous actions.

Celebrity is not a new phenomenon. Politicians, royalty, sportspeople, singers and actors have all courted celebrity status. Queen Victoria had photographs of her and her family in posed domestic family settings, distributed to improve her public image. Early Hollywood film stars such as Douglas Fairbanks and Mary Pickford allowed themselves to be filmed in their mansions for promotional purposes in the 1920s, producing a set of images that would not look out of place in *Hello!* or *OK!* today.

Some critical perspectives see celebrity as an example of cultural decline. They argue that celebrity status was once based upon skill, expertise and achievement and it is now based upon luck, being discovered and creative marketing and public relations (PR) campaigns giving celebrities valuable media exposure.

A more positive interpretation of the contemporary celebrity points to the wider range of social groups (in terms of class and race) from which celebrities now come. While it could be argued that celebrities in the first half of the 20th century were predominantly white and often middle class, contemporary celebrities such as Lewis Hamilton (as a black motor racing sportsman) and Jade Goody (as a working-class girl contestant on a reality TV show) indicate a more democratic and inclusive representation of society.

> ### Thinking about media
> ■ Try and think critically about three celebrities that are frequently seen in the media. Is their fame based on being famous or do they have unique skills and attributes that account for their fame?
> ■ Do you see contemporary celebrities as an example of a more inclusive and democratic society?

The 'intimacy' between the public and celebrities can be argued as being a carefully constructed representation. Creating this representation involves a media performance, constructed by a wide range of media professionals: PR agents, managers, stylists, photographers and promoters. The task of constructing a celebrity is made easier by a range of media outlets, including:

■ the growth in the last 5 or 10 years of celebrity magazines such as *OK!*, *Heat* and *Now*

■ tabloid press – arguably 'soft' celebrity news has taken over from 'hard' news

■ chat shows and reality TV

■ radio and TV channels that need cheap programming.

Gamson (1994) argues that 'celebrity is produced, and constructed by concerted, co-operative action of media industries for profit'. The way in which a celebrity's representation is constructed is explained in the biography of 1940s and 1950s Hollywood film star Cary Grant. He claimed: 'Everybody wants to be Cary Grant. I want to be Cary Grant'.

For producers of media products, celebrity may help to control uncertainty in a competitive marketplace. For example, featuring a well-known celebrity on the front page of a newspaper or tabloid increases sales. Advertisers use celebrities to endorse products, hoping the status or aura associated with them will be transferred to their product.

A major criticism of the celebrity phenomenon is that it has led to the trivialisation of 'hard' news and politics. In a media-saturated society this has apparently resulted in politicians being judged on their media image rather than their ideas, messages and competence.

Critical perspectives of celebrity

The following case study looks at the rise in popularity of celebrity chef Jamie Oliver. It is used to illustrate the critical perspectives of media theorists Stacey (1994), Dyer (2004) and Adorno and the Frankfurt School (1991).

Case study: Jamie Oliver

The TV chef Jamie Oliver rose to fame through a BBC2 TV series called *The Naked Chef* in 1999. Other TV series followed, along with a lucrative advertising campaign for Sainsbury's, columns in a range of magazines (including *Marie Claire*), the publication of a number of books, his own website, appearances on chat shows and attention from the tabloid press.

Stacey (1994) argued that the meaning audiences place on celebrities is linked to the pleasure gained through fantasising about escaping from the confines of their own lives. The fantasy involves being part of the lifestyle that celebrities are perceived as living. For example, this includes owning luxury homes and clothes, travel, staying in hotels, eating in expensive restaurants and being the focus of lots of attention. Following this critical perspective, Oliver's popularity can be explained through the appeal that his constructed world and lifestyle had for his audience. The world constructed for Oliver, by his producers, presented him as living in a trendy London mews house (affordable to only the very rich), with a bachelor life of entertaining friends, playing in a band and shopping, drinking and partying. Oliver's constructed lifestyle is to many of his viewers a fantasy or dream world; it is aspirational.

An alternative critical perspective is put forward by media theorist Dyer (2004) who suggests that a celebrity must resonate with the ideas, values and spirit of the time – even the moment. Dyer's critical perspective links Oliver's popularity to the re-emergence of the new lad in the new millennium, evidenced in TV show *Men Behaving Badly* (ITV 1992: BBC 1994–8), and magazines *Nuts* (IPC 1996–) and *Zoo* (Bauer 2004–). In his first ever programme, Oliver was portrayed cooking for his sister and friends, and the episode finished as he kissed goodbye to a queue of thin, attractive young women. Oliver, however, was a softer version of the 'new lad'; he could cook, was nice to his family and worked hard. A constructionist perspective would explain these celebrity representations as contributing to our knowledge and understanding of masculinity in the new millennium.

Adorno and the Frankfurt School (1991) looked at both the positive and negative influence celebrities can have on the general public. They argue that the general public might identify with charismatic celebrity individuals, with negative outcomes. For example, connecting the rise in incidences of anorexia in young girls with the popularity and endorsement of thin supermodels and celebrity WAGS (the acronym for footballers' wives and girlfriends). Alternatively the potential power of celebrities can be harnessed for positive effects, such as the way in which Oliver's celebrity status has been managed to encompass his more mature status as a family man with two children, including his campaign to highlight the problems of nutritionally poor school dinners in his television series *Jamie's School Dinners* (Channel 4, 2005).

Another example of the positive power of celebrities is that of Bono (the lead vocalist of the Irish rock band U2), who has tried to alleviate poverty and debt in Africa by raising money and awareness, for example through the Live 8 concerts in 2005. However, criticism has been aimed at the involvement of musicians, such as Madonna, in the 'environmentalist' Live Earth concerts in 2007, as they arrived in fuel-guzzling planes.

Fig. 1.4 *Oliver has also been involved in opening two training restaurants in the UK under the brand name '15'. This still conforms to Oliver's earlier 'laddish' image, but the associations of '15' and* **Jamie's School Dinners** *construct him as both mature and socially aware (enlarged text shown below,* **Observer Food Monthly***, March 2008)*

Investigating media

Select one contemporary celebrity to research. Look at online newspapers, the celebrity's websites and the websites of celebrity magazines such as *OK!* or *Heat*. Consider the following questions.

- *Production* – through what medium did this celebrity gain their celebrity status and how is it maintained?
- *Text* – what is ordinary and extraordinary about this celebrity? How can they be seen as being symptomatic of the context or culture in which they are produced?
- *Audience* – who consumes the media coverage of this celebrity; what meaning does it have to them, do you think?
- Do the various media theorists' critical perspectives on celebrity help to explain the popularity of the celebrity that you have researched?

News and different realities

The news is often perceived to be the one area of media text where fact and realism are guaranteed. However, presenting, writing and documenting news is a selective and partial process that utilises specific media language and narrative, which both reflects the perspective and bias of the creator and can influence the audience's perception of the events portrayed.

News is provided through newspapers, via broadcast, digital and satellite television and radio, the internet and even mobile phone messages. Despite the competition between news producers there is a significant level of overlap between the various news outlets.

WINNER
Fifteen, Cornwall
A non-stop cabaret of sea, sand, sky, deranged surfers and dog walkers unfolds outside the huge windows that stretch the length of this laid-back restaurant. Surfers breakfast there on a first-come, first-served basis, and from then on it's book in advance. This admirable gaff has been a runaway success since it opened and ticks all the boxes: the 15 trainees come from disadvantaged backgrounds; the profits go to charity; they operate a stringent recycling policy... and the food is absolutely delicious. At our last visit they were doing a brilliant set-lunch menu for £24 and had a pile of the most delicious herb bread for sale for £3 a loaf. Service is at Cornish speed (slow) and the only indication that there were students in the open-plan kitchen was when one of them dropped an entire pile of plates.
Fifteen Cornwall, Watergate Bay, Cornwall, 01637 861000, www.fifteencornwall.co.uk
★ **WIN** A TASTING MENU WORTH £120 WITH WINE SEE P29

Thinking about media
- Where do we find out about 'news' in contemporary society?
- Do you think you utilise different sources of news from those of your parents and grandparents?

Key terms

News agenda: the topics and issues focused upon by media news.

News values: the relative importance of certain stories over others.

One of the ways in which the media can exert power over its audience is by setting the **news agenda** – choosing topics and issues that create a certain focus. This is done by focusing on some areas of news, while silencing and marginalising other aspects. The case of Madeleine McCann, who was just under four years old when she went missing, exemplifies how this is achieved.

Case study: Madeleine McCann

The narrative of events presented by Madeleine McCann's parents, both medical doctors, is that Madeleine disappeared from their holiday apartment in a small Portuguese seaside resort called Praia da Luz. Madeleine had been put to bed with her two younger siblings on the evening of 3 May 2007, while the parents went out to supper with friends to a nearby tapas bar. Six months after the event there was no sign of Madeleine despite a huge publicity campaign orchestrated by her parents, paid for by a fund of contributions from the public.

As time went by and in the absence of any verifiable information about the case, a frenzy of rumours, gossip and speculation began to surround the story. This was exacerbated in September 2007 when both parents were named as official suspects by the Portuguese police. Two competing versions of reality emerged. One version speculated that Madeleine was kidnapped, perhaps by a paedophile who, because of police incompetence, was not caught. An alternative speculation claimed that Madeleine's parents had unintentionally killed her and then disposed of her body.

For over six months Madeleine's story was continually in the news, dominating the tabloid press, discussed on a number of internet blogs and becoming the subject of documentaries on both BBC and ITV. During that period of time, other children who went missing received either no, or very little, media coverage. Similarly, hundreds of children who were in pain, ill or dying as a result of war, famine, disease and natural disasters received very little media attention.

As tragic as the events around Madeleine's disappearance were for her family and friends, a critical perspective on the media needs to ask why the Madeleine case received so much news coverage and other stories of vulnerable children did not.

One way of understanding the focus on Madeleine's story is in terms of **news values**. Although there are debates about what elements of a story make it newsworthy, there are identifiable aspects of the Madeleine case, which make it particularly likely to be selected for media attention:

- *it is a negative story or bad news* – disasters, tragedies, fears and crime all interest audiences of news, where good news rarely does
- *personalisation and human interest* – the story follows in detail one family and their pretty daughter Madeleine
- *shock value* – either version of reality is equally shocking: that Madeleine was taken from an idyllic, carefree holiday resort; or that her own parents might have killed her
- *creation of celebrities out of people to whom the general public can relate* – although Madeleine's family was previously unknown, their media campaign and exposure has turned them into celebrities

Fig 1.5 *An artist's impression of the kind of website that played an important part in the publicity around the Madeleine McCann case*

- ■ *continuity* – the heart of the story is now an enigma narrative with speculation and theories around what happened to Madeleine that can continue on and on
- ■ *proximity* – Portugal is not far from Britain and its popularity as a holiday and retirement destination gives the story the sense of close proximity.

Such explanations on their own are not sufficient; the representations involved in the Madeleine McCann story had particular resonance because they linked with other issues and debates that were already circulating in the media. For example:

- ■ paranoia about paedophiles that has been prevalent in Britain since the Sara Payne case in 2000
- ■ distrust of medical doctors following the Harold Shipman case and other high-profile legal cases where medical doctors have been shown to have made mistakes, such as the trials of Sally Clarke and Angela Canning, together with an assumption that medical doctors are well or over-paid
- ■ distrust and criticism of foreigners as evidenced in this case by the condemnation of the actions of the Portuguese police.

Investigating media

Use the Internet to research the cases mentioned. Look for elements and themes that can also be seen in the Madeleine McCann case.

Exactly six months after she vanished, prayers and a new clue in McCanns' hunt for their 'ray of sunshine'

Does this remote mountain town in Morocco offer hope at last of finding Maddie?

Fig. 1.6 *Newspaper headline about a possible sighting of Madeleine McCann (**Mail on Sunday**, 4 November 2007)*

Key terms

Cultural concern: an issue, concern or paranoia that a society or culture becomes preoccupied with or worried about.

Media in action

Perhaps the most significant **cultural concern** articulated in the media around the Madeleine McCann case concerns parenting, specifically mothering. Many bloggers and some journalists, even if not accusing Madeleine's parents of killing their daughter, have been quick to criticise their parenting. This links strongly with the heavy media coverage and debates about parenting skills in recent years, evidenced by TV programmes such as *Supernanny* (2004–) and *Honey, We're Killing the Kids* (2005–6). So virulent has been the criticism of Madeleine's parents on some websites that these chat rooms have been closed down, for example:

How dare the parents, highly paid as they are, go out and have a drink, leave their child behind, don't bother to pay for a babysitting service or crèche facility and then open a fund for the general populous (sic) to fund the finding of their daughter

Source: Microsoft Access 24 May 2007

Arguably public speculation around this particular story rests upon the audience's perception of how genuine the media performance of either Madeleine's parents or the Portuguese police is. Public distrust of both parties and their versions of reality continues and is couched in issues such as Madeleine's mother's lack of public emotion in the media. The behaviour of both parties is judged against versions of 'realism' gleaned from a range of other factual and fictional media texts.

Following legal action by the McCanns a number of tabloid papers including the *Daily Star* and the *Daily Express* printed an apology to the McCanns and made a donation to their campaign (Fig 1.7). The internet is not of course so easy to control.

Kate and Gerry McCann: Sorry

The Daily Express today takes the unprecedented step of making a front-page aplogy to Kate and Gerry McCann.

We do so because we accept that a number of articles in the newspaper have suggested that the couple caused the death of their missing daugher Madeleine and then covered it up. We acknowledge that there is no evidence whatsoever to support this theory and that Kate and Gerry are completely innocent of any involvement in their daughter's disappearance.

We trust that the suspicion that has clouded their lives for many months will soon be lifted.

As an expression of its regret, the Daily Express has now paid a very substantial sum into the Madeleine Fund and we promise to do all in our power to help efforts to find her.

Kate and Gerry, we are truly sorry to have added to your distress.

We assure you that we hope Madeleine will one day be found alive and will be restored to her loving family.

Fig. 1.7 *Newspaper headline with apology to the McCanns (***Daily Express***, 19 March 2008)*

Investigating media

Select a current news story that has been prevalent in the media in recent weeks and consider what elements have made that story particularly newsworthy. Look at examples of its coverage in the press, magazines, on television and across a range of websites.

■ Why do you think it was selected to receive such heavy coverage?

■ Look in recent newspapers for the stories that were consequently sidelined and try to understand why.

💡 Violence and the media

If we accept a constructionist approach where media representations help to construct our understanding of the world, then it is not surprising that representing violence in the media causes much controversy.

Defining media violence is difficult, but the following may be useful:

> Media violence is evident in a text when there is violation that causes actual physical or emotional harm and there is intentionality behind this violation.

Author's own definition

The extent to which media violence offends an audience is connected to the acceptability of that violence. For example, cartoon violence is not always intentional, rarely violates, and any harm caused is momentary. This explains why cartoon violence, as in *Tom and Jerry* (1940–67), rarely offends viewers. In the ritualistic killing of 'Kenny', in all the earlier episodes of *South Park* (1997–), the audience knew that no long-term damage was done as Kenny always reappears in the next episode. In 2007, the National Society for Prevention of Cruelty to Children (NSPCC) used cartoon violence to represent a father's violence towards children. The use of cartoons enabled the NSPCC to depict violence in mainstream television schedules where they hoped to trigger a widespread and emotive response.

The acceptability of violence is linked to considerations of:

- ■ *realism*
- ■ *seriousness* – if violence is constructed as a joke or game this is more likely to be criticised whereas a serious topic, such as war discussed on the news, is not
- ■ *whether violence is unpunished or not* – there is greater concern about the portrayal of violence that goes unpunished in the media
- ■ *whether violence is fun or heroic* – violence enacted by a hero in pursuit of a noble end is unlikely to cause the same level of concern as violence that appears to occur for fun.

More realistic fictional violence causes greater controversy than cartoon violence, such as that in horror, action or gangster-type movies. In many films, violence is usually punished, for example, super-heroes experience some degree of punishment – they may suffer considerable pain or are marginal and lonely figures with few real friends. In cases where violence is represented as going unpunished, this is considered offensive and shocking.

It is acceptable in some media genres, such as the news, to show graphic violent images without evoking criticism because they are seen as serious or factual representations of 'real' life. Alternatively violent computer games have been castigated as unacceptable as they often contain violence that is fun and provides pleasure.

Ultra-violent releases will test guidance to the limit

Two events in the computer games calendar will provide important tests for the regime envisaged by Tanya Byron: the arrival next month of *Grand Theft Auto IV*, and a court decision last week to overturn a ban on the ultra-violent *Manhunt 2*.

The latest *Manhunt* game will be released imminently after a nine-month legal battle by its producers, who opposed its ban by the British Board of Film Classification for gratuitous violence and "sustained and cumulative casual sadism".

The game puts the player in the position of a scientist who is subjected to terrifying experiments and escapes from a menacing asylum. An edited version, in which some of the most violent scenes were excised, was also rejected by the board. The ban was overturned, permitting the game, published by Rockstar, creators of the controversial Grand Theft Auto series, to be sold with an 18- certificate.

Games publishers said last night that they were prepared to live with plans for rigorously enforced ratings if it averted censorship and kept the £18 billion industry on track.

Violent games account for one in ten of the 2,000 new games produced every year. Less than 3 per cent of games carry 18-certificates in Britain.

The most eagerly awaited game of the year is *Grand Theft Auto IV*, the latest in the 65-million-selling series set in the criminal underworld.

Six of the worst

Manhunt 2
Developers Rockstar recently won a nine-month battle to sell this ultra-violent game in Britain despite the British Board of Film Classification objecting that the action, set in a psychiatric hospital for the criminally insane, "encourages visceral killing and focuses on stalking and brutal slaying". The original Manhunt was blamed for the murder of a boy, aged 14, in Leicester in 2004.

Grand Theft Auto IV
In the latest instalment, players run over pedestrians, kill police, visit prostitutes and are encouraged to drink-drive.

Bully: Scholarship Edition
Features a shaven-headed schoolboy who terrorises other pupils and teachers at his school with pranks including dunking children's heads in lavatories and firing catapults at teachers. Criticised by anti-bullying campaigners and teaching unions for "glorifying" school bullying.

Resident Evil 4
Player is a special forces agent who is sent to rescue the President's kidnapped daughter. Images include a woman pinned to wall by a pitchfork through her face.

50 Cent: Bulletproof
Loosely based on the gangster lifestyle of the rapper. Player engages in shootouts and loots the bodies of victims to buy 50 Cent recordings and music videos.

God of War
A warrior hunts the gods who tricked him into killing his family. Prisoners are burnt alive, victims torn in half.
Source: Times database, *Family Media Guide*

Fig. 1.8 *Newspaper article about ultra-violent computer games* (**The Times**, *27 March 2008*)

Thinking about media

Consider any computer games that are currently popular. Think about one that uses violence as part of its appeal or game plan, such as *Counter-Strike* (1999). Is the violence:

- cartoon style or realistic
- punished or unpunished
- serious or fun?

Do you think there should be limitations on violence in computer games or limits on who they are sold to?

It is interesting to consider that the introduction of more realistic, fast-action violence in games like *Famicom* (1983), *Grand Theft Auto* (1997) and, more recently, *Reservoir Dogs* (2006) have been credited with turning round what had been an ailing market for computer games.

Violent computer games have triggered much disapproval, possibly because of the scope for violence to be seen as unpunished, heroic and fun.

Potter (1999) suggested that in order to take a critical perspective of media violence it is important to consider how a violent incident is represented in that media text. He asks the following questions when looking at a violent text.

- Who is the perpetrator of violence?
- Who is the victim of violence?
- Is the violence presented as justified?
- Are the consequences of violence portrayed?
- Is the violence represented as normative or as abhorrent?

These are important questions to think about when considering the potential power that media representations of violence have and how this can contribute to our construction and understanding of the world.

Thinking about media

Consider a film you may have seen that contains violent imagery (most violent imagery will take place in films that have been given a rating of 15 or 18, but milder violence can also be found in films rated 12A). Think about Potter's questions.

Case study: *The Bourne Ultimatum*

The above elements are clearly exemplified in the film *The Bourne Ultimatum* (2007). The violence shown in this film earned it a 12A rating. The narrative focused upon a CIA agent, played by Matt Damon, who is searching to discover his identity and to free himself from corruption within the CIA. There is a **binary opposition** between the hero and corrupt CIA operatives. The hero's violence is justified by either his service to his country or a need to defend himself. Any unjustified violence by those chasing him is punished either by their death or by them being brought to justice. Much violence takes place in urban areas and the mechanics of this violence and some fights are the subject of close visual attention by the cameras.

Media in action

Concerns about violence on the internet and in computer games have led to the development of filtering software and ratings on computer games. It is also important to try and understand why this area of media violence is appealing. Some critical perspectives suggest that playing violent computer games is a response to feelings of lack of control in life more generally, hence their appeal to younger players. Other critical perspectives suggest that violence is intrinsically tied up with a sense of masculinity in Western society – not being squeamish about violence is part of asserting manhood. This perspective explains why many media texts aimed at young men often contain gruesome images of violence, such as magazines like *Nuts* and *Zoo* and films like *Saw* (2004).

Key terms

Binary oppositions: when a text is divided into two clear groups of characters, situations or values, for example, police and criminals.

■ Media in action

Police series on television and crime films have developed their own conventions that represent violence in particular ways. Some of the following are common in these texts:

- a narrative structured around the clear binary oppositions – 'goodies' and baddies'
- chase elements in the narrative or in particular sequences
- '*mise-en-scène*' – crime taking place in dark, cramped urban areas
- heavy visual focus on the instruments of violence, such as guns.

Cameron and Frazer (1987) claim that representations of sexual violence are endemic in our society. Media texts often portray women and the elderly as victims of crime.

Yet statistically, in Britain, the group most at risk of violence is young men. These media representations have however constructed a perception of the world that makes many young women nervous when they are out at night on their own and some elderly people scared to leave their homes.

Fictional violence is, as Gitlin (2003) points out, an easy target for criticism. However, he suggests that careful attention is also paid to what representations of violence are selected and what is omitted. There is selectiveness about images portrayed, particularly on television and in the press. For example, while images of the execution of Saddam Hussein were available on the internet, only an edited version was shown on terrestrial television. What is absent from the media is as significant as what is conveyed. This selectiveness by news broadcasters has led to criticism that news reporting sanitises war, not merely for the sake of government but also for the family and friends of those involved. Criticism about the representation of the 1991 Iraq war claimed that it was portrayed as a remote, bloodless, push-button war, where images of the consequences of violence and civilian injuries were rarely shown.

An important distinction occurs when reporting what is considered to be legitimate or illegitimate violence. Media portrayal of 'legitimate' violence (often government sponsored violence such as war) is less likely to represent the victims of violence than media representations of illegitimate violence such as 'terrorism'. Thus the selected representations convey ideologies and values that support the definitions of both legitimate and illegitimate violence.

■ Investigating media

Closely analyse a news report on violence from a combat zone. Make notes on how the violence is represented through media language and narrative. Look across print media, television and web-based resources.

- How is the violence represented through media language and narrative?
- Is it portrayed as legitimate or illegitimate violence?
- Who is producing the violence?
- Who is the target audience?

■ Thinking about media

- By who, how and why do some forms of violence come to be seen as legitimate and others illegitimate?
- Whose version of reality do these representations convey?
- Where and how can these representations be challenged?

The significance of 9/11 on media representation

Representations of violence in both fictional and news media texts have shifted since the events of 9/11 (11 September 2001). The scale of the violence portrayed on both live television and via the internet has shifted media representations of perpetrators and victims of violence, placing greater emphasis, at least initially, on the threat from terrorism rather than crime, as evidenced in the popularity of the US series *24* (Channel 4, 2001–). News reporting of 9/11 selectively focused on the

Fig. 1.9 *Images from 9/11 (www.september11news.com/attackImages.htm)*

powerless victims of the Twin Towers in particular, which emphasised the illegitimacy of the violence. This particular focus, however, meant that references to the flights that crashed into the Pentagon and an area in Pennsylvania were often marginalised from news stories.

The footage of the second plane crashing into the Twin Towers was seen live by millions of people around the world, as was the subsequent crumbling of the towers. These images of the Twin Towers have become the most documented and most watched event in TV history. New technology led to a range of amateur footage from camcorders and mobile phones being shown on TV and the internet. The amateur nature of the footage gave it validity and credibility as the shaky hand-held images taken by the public affirmed the 'reality' of the disaster.

The realism of the event was however seen through the prism of all the disaster movies that audiences had previously watched. Initially it was felt that, having now seen the reality of disasters that are averted by an action hero who 'saves the day'; audiences would no longer be able to derive pleasure from action and disaster movies in the future. As a result Schwarzenegger's *Collateral Damage* (2002), an action movie in which the narrative focuses on a fire-fighter who seeks revenge for his wife and son who were killed in a terrorist attack, was withdrawn from release immediately after 9/11, but was later released.

Thinking about media

After 9/11 representations of New York itself were significantly altered. TV programmes such as *Friends* (1994–2004) and films such as *Spiderman* (2002) removed images of the Twin Towers from the iconic New York skyline. Further, New York could no longer realistically be portrayed as confident, upbeat and all white, for example, the lack of realism in *Friends* was suddenly brought into relief and the series ended in 2004.

Films subsequently represented New York in a more complex and less carefree way. For example, Spike Lee's film *25th Hour* (2002) criticises the main protagonist and his friend's wealthy New York lifestyle, showing it to be corrupt. In *The Day after Tomorrow* (2004), New York is under threat and survival is dependent on a stoical co-operation across all classes and races.

As early as 1992, Giddens had argued that individuals increasingly experienced the world in terms of hazards, fears and risks. After 9/11 media journalists and politicians represented the Western world as involved in a 'war against terrorism'. This representation has been used as a justification for invasions into Afghanistan and Iraq, as well as increased security measures while flying or in terms of border controls, visas and passports etc.

A constructionist critical perspective would understand the 'war on terror' to be a product of media representations, constructed through the specific media language and **political discourse** circulated in the media. Such a perspective suggests a heavy involvement and culpability of the media in politics. Alternatively a reflective version of representation would focus on the selectivity of the representations of 9/11, the 'war on terror' and wars in Afghanistan and Iraq.

The 'war on terror' and the events of 9/11 have been interpreted in a range of ways according to the political, religious and national associations of the media representing the story. Different versions of reality have circulated in the media about 9/11 and the subsequent 'war on terror' through new media such as satellite channels like Al Jazeera and websites like the Baghdad Blogger and LiveLeak. This has strengthened arguments that see new media as offering new outlets for divergent views in contemporary society.

> ■ **Key terms**
>
> **Political discourse:** refers to the scope of discussion and debate that goes on within political circles. Thus it includes topics discussed in parliament and by politicians and political journalists.

■ Thinking about media

What do you think is the media's role in political actions? Does it merely selectively report them or is it involved in bringing them about?

■ Investigating media

Compare the BBC News, LiveLeak and the Stop the War Coalition websites.

■ How differently do they represent the 'war on terror' or 9/11?

■ What audiences do you think they are geared towards?

■ Do you think the representations on LiveLeak and the Stop the War Coalition websites would have appeared in traditional media outlets such as radio, newspapers and terrestrial television?

ⓘ Who controls the media: audiences or producers?

While we understand that media representations are constructions of reality, it is important to think about *who* constructed these representations. Are they constructed by the institutions that produce media or by the audiences that consume media? Who has the power to determine the nature of the media texts and therefore the influential representations they convey?

There are two different critical perspectives that look at the relative power of media producers and audiences, and therefore who controls the media. These are:

■ market-liberalism perspective

■ political-economy perspective.

A market-liberalism perspective

This is a politically conservative perspective that stresses the power of audience over media producers in the marketplace. It suggests that audience preference decides what media texts are produced. An audience's preferences are expressed through the market by:

■ purchases of media texts, such as CDs, magazines and computer games
■ paying to access media texts such as films
■ taking out subscriptions that provide access to media texts such as Sky
■ recording 'hits' on internet sites
■ audience research.

This perspective suggests that a significant amount of power rests with the audience who get the media that they want. Market liberalists argue that this is vastly preferable to government controlled media which decides what 'is good for people'.

As most producers sell their media products to make a profit, it is argued they are particularly sensitive to the audiences. For example, after the death of Princess Diana in 1997, newspapers chose not to publish pictures of the gravely injured princess as they thought readers would be offended. The cost of misjudging audience or readers' preferences can be huge, as the *Sun* newspaper discovered in 1989, when the newspaper referred to many of the 89 Liverpool football fans who were crushed to death in the Hillsborough stadium tragedy as 'hooligans' and implied that their behaviour contributed to their deaths. Nearly two decades later, the *Sun*'s sales have not recovered in Liverpool. It is estimated that millions of pounds of profit have been lost by the *Sun's* owners News Corporation.

↘ Pre-testing and audience research

In order to ascertain audience preferences, media institutions are involved in a wide range of audience research and pre-testing. Commercial radio stations such as Power FM (Capital Radio's south of England station, aimed at the youth market) undertake regular phone polls to find out what music audiences want to listen to. They construct their play-list accordingly. Alternatively Classic FM invites the audience to vote annually for their favourite tracks. The chart of the top 300 tracks then contributes significantly to their play-lists on a number of programmes.

A number of computer games, films and some TV programmes are pre-tested on a representational group of the perceived audience. Feedback leads to alterations, changes and adjustments to these media. For example, following pre-testing it was decided that the Glenn Close character in *Fatal Attraction* (1987) should be murdered at the end of the film rather than commit suicide. Pre-testing on the romantic comedy *My Best Friend's Wedding* (1997) led to a softening of the Julia Roberts character. Most popular television programmes have an initial trial with an audience via a one-off pilot episode from which is it determined if the show is likely to be successful or not.

Investigating media

For commercial radio, the audience figures produced by RAJAR (the Radio Joint Audience Research Council) influence the price of the advertising slots.

■ Visit the RAJAR website and find out how the figures are gathered.
■ Do you think they are an accurate reflection of audience desires and wants?
■ When will it be most expensive to advertise on commercial radio?
■ On the basis of the RAJAR statistics investigate the image portrayed and the advertising rates for two commercial radio stations you are able to listen to in your locality.
■ Do you think there are any groups whose needs, wants or tastes are ignored by these radio stations due to the radio's focus on ratings and advertising revenue?

A political-economy perspective

A political-economy perspective stresses the power of the media producers over media texts and consequently media's influence over a particular audience. This perspective argues that markets appear to offer freedom – especially when compared to the state-owned and controlled media that operates under some authoritarian regimes. However there are many problems with media organised and run by the free market system – there is inequality in whose interests the media operates. Those with more money or those who are seen as appealing to advertisers will have a range of media products oriented to their needs while there are limits on the production of media texts for other groups.

Producers tend to avoid risk, shunning innovation and originality. Gitlin (2003), after interviewing a number of American television producers, concluded that the pursuit of audience figures had a negative effect on the quality of television. Hollywood cinema has a tendency to use tried and tested genres, styles, star actors, directors and screenwriters in order to avoid risk. Producers may also avoid any representations that might be seen as challenging the values and ideologies of the audience.

Advertising and sponsorship

Some media theorists, such as Curran (1986) argue that the advertising industry has a major influence on the structure and output of the British print media. Advertising and sponsorship contributes a significant proportion of the revenue for many media products. For magazines the revenue from advertising is 50 to 80 per cent and it is the main source of revenue for commercial radio and television companies and many websites. It is argued that media producers focus on providing the media for the sectors of the population that the advertising industry wants to address. As media is often produced to appeal to advertisers, it will always promote consumerism and is unlikely to discuss issues that might antagonise advertisers. For example, few girls' magazines will carry detailed discussions of the problems of child labour in clothes manufacturing as they get advertising revenue from cheap clothing companies.

A political-economy perspective suggests that rather than media producers responding to audience needs and wants, they are packaging audiences to sell them to advertisers. Founders of popular websites have been able to do this very efficiently with technology that is able to record exactly how many 'hits' or visitors they have in a day. It was the potential advertising revenue that motivated ITV's purchase of Friends Reunited and News Corporation's purchase of MySpace.

■ Link

A good example of the way in which an audience is packaged and sold to advertisers can be seen on the International Movie Database website, www.imdb.com. There is heavy advertising and a link to Amazon, online sellers of DVDs, music and books.

■ Investigating media

■ Do a content analysis of a popular 'glossy' magazine. Count the number of pages given over to key contents, advertising, editorial, fashion, news items, etc.

■ Look at the magazine's website and investigate how the magazine promotes itself to potential advertisers.

■ Who do you think has most power or influence over the content of the magazine: the readers, the producers or the advertisers?

Finally the political-economy perspective sees the power of media organisations as open to abuse; some media producers are seen as promoting particular political positions in their texts, for example, in America, Fox News is seen to support the Republican Party and the Bush administration. It could be suggested that media producers silence or restrict certain political debates, issues or viewpoints being expressed to help support certain political agendas.

Case study: Silvio Berlusconi

It has been suggested that Italian media mogul Silvio Berlusconi, who has been elected to serve a second term as prime minister, has exerted a powerful influence over the Italian media to his own advantage. Millions, however, have protested in the streets against his policies and made fun of him, which suggests power acquired through ownership of media production companies is perhaps more limited than it might at first seem.

Thinking about media

- Would you object to politicians owning significant areas of the media in Britain?
- Do you think that owners of large media organisations influence politics?

Different types of media organisation

There are a wide range of different media organisations.

- *Monopoly* – a single media organisation that dominates production and distribution in a particular industry either locally or nationally, such as Microsoft's dominance of the computer operating systems market.
- *Oligopoly* – a small number of organisations that dominate an industry either locally or nationally, such as Emap and IPC's dominance of the UK magazine industry.
- *Conglomerates* – a collection of companies owned by a single institution. Diversification provides protection to the whole company so that if one part of the business is in difficulties, the other parts can prevent it failing. Examples include News Corporation, Time Warner and Disney.
- *Multinationals* – organisations that have institutions in more than one country.

Time Warner, Disney and News Corporation are all multinational media conglomerates based in the USA, each with revenue of approximately 30 billion dollars a year. They each own a range of inter-related media organisations that complement each other through synergy. Time Warner's varied business interests include television (they were the distributors of popular series *Friends*), magazines, film studios and cinema chains. They can make, distribute, promote and exhibit a film without relying upon or involving other organisations.

News Corporation own 135 newspapers worldwide (including the *New York Post*, *The Times* and the *Sun*), 25 magazines, 22 US television stations (covering 40 per cent of US households), satellite TV stations (including BSkyB and Fox Studios), Fox Television and News and book publishers HarperCollins. The synergies between these companies is beneficial, for example, a film made by Fox Studios is likely to be favourably reviewed on BSkyB and in *The Times*, while the *Sun* often carries heavy advertising and promotion for sporting events only available on pay per view via BSkyB.

■ *Independent producers* – self-funded, smaller organisations.

Advances in technology have made cheaper and smaller media production equipment available and facilitated the rise of a number of small independent production companies. They produce, for example, adverts, videos, websites, DVDs and music. Some of these companies produce predominantly commercial products such as corporate videos, while others aim to sell into mainstream media distributors. For example, Shed Productions have sold a range of programmes to ITV since their success with *Bad Girls* (1999), including *Rock Rivals* (2008).The high cost of film production means that there are fewer independent film producers. One famous independent production company is Spike Lee's '40 Acres and A Mule' Filmworks, which produced the award winning film *Do the Right Thing* in 1989.

Case study: *Fahrenheit 9/11*

Disney is best known for its cartoons and theme parks, but it also owns 10 TV channels and 2 radio stations in the US, 25 per cent of GMTV (providers of morning television on ITV in the UK), Miramax and distributors Buena Vista. There are however tensions between some of these organisations' interests.

In 2004, a dispute erupted around the distribution of the controversial film director Michael Moore's film *Fahrenheit 9/11*. This film accused President Bush of using 9/11 to promote support for a second Iraq war. The film was made through Miramax but took a long time to be released, as the Disney Corporation was concerned that it would antagonise President Bush's brother Jeb, then governor of Florida, and thereby jeopardise Disney's theme park's tax breaks.

Michael Moore provided a public screening of the film at the Cannes film festival, where it won the prestigious Best Film award. On its subsequent release by Miramax it became the first ever documentary to gross over $100m. Pirated and illegally downloaded copies reached a much wider audience. Its popularity was no doubt increased by both the controversy and the award.

Links

Read more about the controversy around the release of *Fahrenheit 9/11* on the internet. You can look at the Internet Movie Database entry on the film on the website www.imdb.com.

Key terms

Globalisation: refers to the way in which, in contemporary society, distant countries are inter-related and connected together by trade, communication and cultural experiences.

Globalisation

Globalisation is an important factor in the age of communication when the global sales of film, TV and media products, along with the internet, bring people in developing countries into direct contact with Western media products. One of the things that Disney, News Corporation and Time Warner have in common is their global reach; they distribute their media texts across all the continents of the globe. This distribution is facilitated by satellite and the internet enabling communications to travel from one side of the globe to the other, instantaneously. It enables events that are taking place in distant countries to be presented to us on our TVs and the internet 'live', evidenced in the coverage of 9/11.

According to Giddens (2003) we live in a 'runaway world' where cultures, economies and politics appear to merge across national boundaries. Significantly, TV consumption merges, so that TV programmes such as *Will and Grace, Frasier, Sex and the City, Friends, Simpsons, Grey's Anatomy, The Sopranos, Neighbours*, and channels MTV and CNN, are watched all over the world.

Case study: *The Simpsons*

Some media texts are orientated towards a global market, such as News Corporation's cartoon series *The Simpsons* (1989–). The distinctive yellow cartoon characters have little definable ethnic identity; instead they can be accompanied by dialogue in the language of the country in which they are broadcast. Cartoons do not share the same technical difficulties in matching dubbing that other film or television media texts do.

A political-economy perspective argues that the homogenisation of culture and communication leads to shared values and ideologies. The USA dominates world media with 85 per cent of the global film market and 68 per cent of the television market. A cultural-imperialism perspective argues therefore that American values and ideologies are imposed upon the rest of the world, through media texts.

There are a number of factors that contribute to the USA's dominance of the global media markets, such as:

- large home market
- dominance of the English language
- technical advantages.

Production costs of media texts are recouped by the USA home market enabling producers to sell their products abroad cheaply. The USA was the first producer of films with sound in the 1920s and colour television in the 1950s, giving them a technical advantage over other countries in these areas.

Case study: CNN

The Cable News Network (CNN) was founded by Ted Turner in 1980 as the first 24-hour rolling news programme. It now has over 150 correspondents and 42 news bureaux around the world. Although it was originally predominantly seen in Western hotel rooms, by the mid-1990s CNN provided news to 236 million households around the world, via cable and satellite TV.

The internationalisation of news involves audiences in a range of countries receiving news from other countries through both CNN and other 24-hour news channels and national news broadcasters broadcasting international news stories obtained from international news agencies. CNN has been seen as being under the control of its USA headquarters in Atlanta and is criticised as being too pro the American government. It has also been seen as influencing the UN and the views of political 'movers and shakers', bringing their attention to a range of humanitarian issues via their news-gathering bureaux around the world.

Further evidence that **cultural imperialism** is not straightforward comes from the success of the Indian film and television industries that have taken advantage of the south-east Asian Diaspora (defined in Chapter 2 in the section on post-colonialism). People who are culturally affiliated to south Asia live all over the world, and Europe, the Middle East and America provide a significant audience for India's biggest media conglomerate, Zee TV. As a result Zee TV is now available on four continents.

■ Media in action

Putnam (1997) suggests that the US government prioritised media for support as an important export industry that promotes both US values and US goods.

In 2007, Apple computers were not just advertised in trailers preceding films but also through product placement in films such as *The Bourne Ultimatum*, *Disturbia*, *Night at the Museum*, *Ocean's Thirteen*, *Wild Hogs*, *Transformers* and numerous TV series such as *24*.

A cultural-imperialism perspective is open to challenge. Many media texts such as *Marie Claire* magazine or the children's TV programme *Sesame Street* have carefully tailored regional variations that respond to local values and ideologies. Similarly, many media texts' formats are sold to the US from Europe, such as *The Office*, *Big Brother* and *Who Wants to Be a Millionaire?*

■ Key terms

Cultural imperialism: a process by which one country dominates other countries' media consumption and consequently dominates their values and ideologies.

■ Investigating media

An examination of audience figures suggests that many local media products are often more popular than imported globalised media. Look on the British Film Industry and the Broadcasters' Audience Research Board (BARB) websites for the recent audience figures for film and television viewing in the UK (for the web addresses, see the e-resources or do a search on the web).

- Do these statistics support the cultural-imperialism perspective?

A more complex challenge to the cultural-imperialism perspective comes from the work of anthropologist Danny Miller (1995). He looked at how the popular American melodrama *The Young and the Restless* (CBS 1973–) was viewed in Trinidad. Miller argues that viewers use the text to explore some of the social and moral contradictions of their own society. For others the text was empowering as it enabled individuals in the audience to cultivate a different persona or public self by using the images on display in the text. Some copied the style of dress in the text; others used the text's style ideas to make their own distinctive clothes and styles.

Concerns about globalisation and cultural imperialism rest upon critical perspectives, which assume that the producer holds all the 'power'. However the audience do have the power to:

- select the media texts they wish to watch
- influence the media producer to produce texts that appeal to local audiences by incorporating the local culture
- interpret the media texts according to their own lives and to create a range of meanings.

■ Case study: MTV

When MTV began in 1981 there had been a serious slump in the music industry. Record companies welcomed the opportunity to promote their music through music videos and provided much of the programming for free. MTV soon overtook radio as the US music industry's key link to youth culture.

Once MTV convinced cable channels that including a 24-hour music channel would improve their subscriptions, it was then able to deliver a teens to thirties target audience to advertisers. When it expanded into Europe in the early 1990s it provided the majority of its programming from local content. In this way MTV did not impose US cultural imperialism onto a European audience.

Similarly when MTV entered South East Asia, broadcasting via Sky's Star Satellite, MTV offered programmes in local languages with features such as Hindi music in India. Seventy to eighty per cent of content comes from local artists broadcasting from its regional base in Singapore. Thus, local audiences could be seen as exerting power over the media texts produced by MTV.

■ Investigating media

- If you are able to, watch MTV for one evening and make a note of which of the material you think would appeal to an international audience and which material is particular to a UK audience.
- What does this suggest about the inter-relationship of the local and global in media production?
- To what extent do you think that MTV's engagement with local music culture has been motivated by the need to respond to audience and/or advertisers' requirements?

▢ ◪ New media/digital revolution

In the last 20 years a number of technological developments have taken place that have facilitated changes in the ways in which media is both produced and consumed. For example, home computers and the internet have enabled news to be produced and distributed in new ways. Digital technology has also enabled a growth in the number of television channels, as well as a convergence between television and the internet.

New media and technology and the **digital revolution** includes the following:

- video and DVD
- portable camcorders
- home computer and games consoles
- cable, satellite and digital TV
- mobile phones and their convergence with other media photography and video
- the world wide web
- e-mail
- MP3
- podcasts
- webcams
- blogs
- social networking spaces such as MySpace or Facebook.

■ Key terms

Digital revolution: refers to the revolution in the production and distribution of media texts, which now rely on the digital codes used by computers and the internet.

■ Media in action

New media tends to be represented in **dystopian** or **utopian** terms. Habermas (1991) argues that media texts should provide a space for citizens to debate and criticise government actions and form public opinion. He has a **dystopian** view of new media, arguing that most media outlets, even new media, produce similar sorts of representations that focus primarily on celebrity and trivia.

Alternatively, Del Sola Poole (1977) takes a more **utopian** perspective on new media. He suggests that new media will facilitate a positive media world where there will be a much wider range of media texts produced that meet the needs and desires of many more groups in society. Importantly, new media provides individual citizens with the capacity to produce and publicise media texts themselves, utilising new technologies, which facilitates the growth of different media voices and representations.

■ Key terms

Dystopian: a perspective where everything is as bad as it can possibly be.

Utopian: the belonging to or characteristic of an ideal perfect state or place.

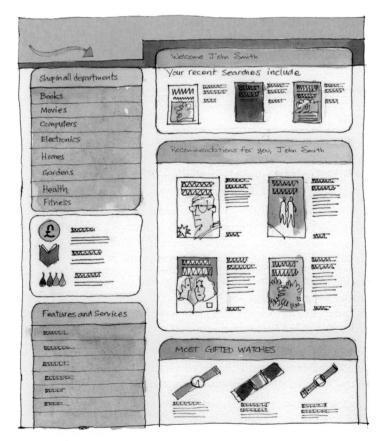

Fig. 1.10 *An artist's impression of an online store – an indication of things to come with Web 3.0 as new media becomes a marketing tool*

Initially web-based media tended to involve the consumption of material produced by media organisations, such as webpages of information. The slow dial-up connections commonly used limited its scale and scope. Early in the new millennium, however, a second generation of web-based material became available, known as Web 2.0, facilitated by speedier and more mobile broadband and wireless connections. Web 2.0's emphasis was on:

■ *interactivity*

■ *user participation*

■ *dynamic content* – that is content that is not fixed but shifting, changing and constantly reconstructed

■ *freedom* – for audiences and individuals to produce, consume and engage with a wide range of new media texts.

On Web 2.0 media audiences, through social networking sites like MySpace and Friends Reunited, were producing their own content.

In the last two years there has been discussion and speculation about what will follow Web 2.0, by implication Web 3.0. Some suggest, for example, that the next developments in web-based media will operate via a web of relationships, similar to social networking sites, rather than via webpages with individual content. They see a greater emphasis on distribution via viruses, whereby information, interaction and contact are spread invisibly. Alternatively others emphasise the potential for developments that produce a more personalised use of websites, focused on individual tastes and needs (Fig 1.10); in the same way that amazon.com personalises its response to individual customers, greeting them by name and making recommendations. Finally some suggest that a key element of Web 3.0 will be the inter-connectivity between different media platforms, such as the ability to watch TV over the internet and pick up e-mail messages on your mobile phone.

■ Case study: Al Jazeera

Since 9/11 one of the most significant alternative sources of television news is Al Jazeera. Based in Doha, Qatar, the channel was launched in 1996, when the BBC's Arab Service was shut down after its documentary criticising human rights abuses in Saudi Arabia.

The political upheaval in the Arab world in recent years – with wars in Afghanistan and the Gulf – have enabled it to become the channel to which many Arab-speaking people turn to find out about major events. In 2007, Al Jazeera launched its English Channel, the only 24-hour news channel with its headquarters in the Middle East.

It has targeted worldwide audiences and attracted a number of high profile journalists (such as Martin Bashir and Sir David Frost) with its independent focus. It has, for example, a published code of ethics, the first of which is to:

… adhere to the journalistic values of honesty, courage, fairness, balance, independence, credibility and diversity, giving no prior commercial considerations over professional ones.

Source: *Al Jazeera Code of Ethics*

Fig. 1.11 *An artist's impression of an independent news website*

There has been controversy over some of the material Al Jazeera has shown, including footage of the beheading of hostages from Iraq or broadcasting messages from Osama Bin Laden and Al-Qaeda. The channel can be described as politically more independent than many other world news channels and its reporting has challenged the actions and versions of reality presented by both Arab and Western governments and leaders. Al Jazeera has been criticised by all sides in the Middle East conflicts and its reporters have been thrown out of nearly all countries in the Middle East. This is evidence of its independent stance.

It can be argued that Al Jazeera's independence is related to its funding. In 1996, the Emir of Qatar provided $150 million on a five-year loan to help sustain the channel – many corporations were unwilling to advertise on the channel. However at the peak of the Afghan war it was able to demand £25,000 a minute for its advertising and has in recent years obtained advertising from international brands such as Sony, Hyundai and Chanel perfume.

■ **Thinking about media**

Do you think that obtaining advertising from leading brands such as Chanel and Sony will change the nature of the Al Jazeera channel?

Music production and distribution

MTV and the many music channels developed since the 1980s rely upon the development and adoption of cable, satellite and digital television. Other forms of new technology have also facilitated important changes to the music industry and youth-oriented media, such as walkmans, MP3 players and the iPod, enabling listeners to create their own soundtrack to their environment. Music has become the primary leisure resource of contemporary culture and is therefore an area of strong criticism and debate in relation to relative audience and producer power.

In the post-Second World War era Adorno and Horkheimer (1986) and the Frankfurt School (1986) identified popular music as part of a 'culture industry'. They argued that in the interests of profit, the music industry produced banal, interchangeable music for a passive, childlike and manipulated audience. During the 1960s, 1970s, 1980s and 1990s scorn was poured on groups such as the Beatles, the Bay City Rollers, Wham! and Boyzone. The fans' enthusiasm was explained in terms of an illness they had been stricken by, such as 'Beatlemania' or 'Rollermania'. It is important to note that such criticisms imply passivity and are often directed at less powerful groups in society, such as young girls.

Media theorists such as Fiske (1988) have challenged such perceptions, pointing to how active and discerning fans are not merely consuming popular music but using the music to create their own cultural artefacts and identity. Thus, in many schools and colleges musical taste is an identifiable feature of particular social groups. Music, bands and associated clothing styles clearly distinguish different sub-cultural groups in social spaces.

Within a group of music fans, information and facts about the bands are used as a language to express belonging. Phrases and words of songs and the exchange of information about the group contribute to the fans everyday chattering and conversations. Interviews with some groups of fans have suggested that selecting music that is disapproved of is an important element of the appeal of certain musical groups. As in times past, the music represents an assertion of identity against other peer groups or a different generation.

Furthermore, Fiske (1988) points out that the products used to promote the music and groups, including posters, magazine spreads, souvenirs from concerts, may be used by a fan in a creative way when they construct a collage of images in their room or decorate their college files. Thus to some media theorists fans are 'completists', who through their actions and interactions complete the construction of meaning that a text carries.

Thinking about media

Consider music that you enjoy. Do you think you actively use the music as part of your social interaction with friends and as part of your identity or do you see yourself as having been manipulated by media producers to like this music?

■ Case study: indie music

Arguably new technology such as the Internet has empowered audiences, enabling them to create their own selections of music, copying and downloading tracks that they enjoy. Importantly, audiences can choose from a much wider range of music available to them via sites such as iTunes and Rhapsody. Indie music, which defines itself as focusing upon self-expression rather than commercial interests, has been able to market itself through the Internet. For example, the band Wilko, which formed in 1994, fell out with its production company Warner-Reprise in 2002. Unwilling to change their sound to become more commercially viable, Wilko bought back their recording tapes, then streamed and sold them via the Internet.

POP PRINCESS LAUNCHES HER OWN VERSION OF MYSPACE

It's KySpace

By DAN WOOTTON

Pop princess Kylie Minogue is taking on MySpace – by becoming the first chart star to launch her own social networking website.

The pioneering singer, 39, wants her millions of fans across the world to chat to each other using their own profiles.

Users of KylieKonnect.com will even be able to contact the star via her profile – as well as read her blog, see sexy pictures of her, and watch an exclusive behind-the-scenes video.

They can also hear tunes not available elsewhere and download her hits.

The launch of the website, expected this week, will follow today's online release of the star's latest single 2 Hearts.

It is part of Kylie's comeback after her breast cancer and painful split from long-term boyfriend Olivier Martinez.

A source close to the project told the News of the World: "This is a very big move for Kylie, as no other pop star has ever tried anything like this before. It will make her an instant internet entrepreneur – and shows the way the music industry is heading.

Kylie and her record label Parlophone have been working secretly on the site for months.

They hope it will rival hugely popular networking brands like MySpace and Facebook.

The source said: "Kylie's fans are very loyal to her, so it is hoped a large number of them will decide to join her network.

"That could quickly make Kylie a big player in this business. But there's also the risk that her fans will only want to stick with their existing sites.

"It is a bold step for her to take. But it shows she is serious about becoming more than just a pop star and taking control of the business side."

A message on the page yesterday said: "Kylie Konnect allows you to blog and upload pictures from your mobile phone – so you can go to a concert and upload pictures of Kylie live on stage to let your friends know what they are missing."

The star – who also has a conventional website for fans – is also busy with the launch of her new album X, released at the end of the month. Her new single will be on CD in a week's time.

The source said: "Kylie will be 40 in a few months but she has no plans to quit music. This is all about trying different things.

"She's very proud of being the first singer to create a social networking brand."

dan.wootton@notw.co.uk

See more sizzling pics of Kylie at notw.co.uk

Fig. 1.12 *The development of – initially – websites and now social networking spaces by pop stars enables fans to actively participate with other members of the fan community* (**News of the World**, *4 November 2007*)

The ease of recordings and mixing via personal computers has enabled a far wider range of bands to enter the music scene, selling their DVDs when they play on the streets and in public spaces and promoting themselves and their gigs through social networking sites such as MySpace. Playing in a band has a long tradition in youth culture but the ability to record and circulate the music via MySpace and a range of other websites has blurred the boundaries between the producer and the audience.

Case study: reality TV and music

It could be argued that reality TV shows such as *Pop Idol* (ITV 2001–) and *X Factor* (ITV 2004–) seem to shift the power balance towards the audience. These programmes work by eliciting votes from the audience to select the winner, who then receives a recording contract. Paul Potts, the opera-singing winner of the *Britain's got Talent* first series in 2007, went on to sell 2 million copies of his first album and reach number one in the album charts in 15 countries. His success was attributed to his winning performance being played around the world via YouTube.

Interestingly, the way in which each show is constructed using media language, the way it is edited, the commentary, lighting and narrative, has put into question the power that the audience actually has and the extent to which these techniques influence voter choices.

Thinking about media

■ Do you think that the input of audiences voting for music stars on reality TV is really an indication of greater audience power?

■ Have new media empowered audiences and, if so, in what way?

Although voting can be done from any phone, these shows rely upon the wide ownership of mobile phones by audience members and are funded by premium phone lines. On 17 December 2005 there were 12 million calls to register votes for *X Factor* and *Strictly Come Dancing*. At one point 6 million voters rang to register their votes for *X Factor*.

In 2007 there were criticisms that reality TV and more importantly the musical taste of Simon Cowell dominated the Christmas pop charts. This domination is, it has been argued, at the expense of more unpredictable and innovative songs that reached No.1 in the past such as *Mr Blobby* in 1993 and the evangelical Christian song *Saviour's Day* in 1990.

X Factor winner on brink of Great American Dream

▶ First British woman at top spot for 20 years
▶ Oprah backing helped Leona Lewis to success

Adam Sherwin Media Correspondent

Leona Lewis performing at the Italian Song Festival in Sanremo, Italy. Oprah Winfrey called her the "real-deal girl", and she has won over American audiences with her single Bleeding Love

The television talent show winner Leona Lewis is poised to become the first British woman to top the US pop chart for more than 20 years.

Not since Kim Wilde, who scored a transatlantic hit with her version of *You Keep Me Hangin' On*, has a British woman provided the song that all America is humming.

By reaching No 1, Lewis, a former receptionist from Hackney, will become only the third British solo female to top the charts with her first single released in the US, following Petula Clark in 1965 and Sheena Easton in 1981.

Industry sources say that *Bleeding Love* has halted the charge of Madonna and bumped the R&B singer Usher off the top of the *Billboard* Hot 100 after a surge in download sales. An endorsement by Oprah Winfrey on nationwide television sent Lewis, 22, soaring to the top. The Hot 100 will be unveiled in New York today.

Topping the US charts is no guarantee of longevity, however. Wilde did not trouble the US compilers after her 1987 success and pursued a career in gardening.

American radio and the MTV network have become hostile to British rock and pop, preferring "nu-metal", rap and glamorous homegrown R&B stars such as Beyoncé.

Most of Lewis's

Top Brits

Kim Wilde
You Keep Me
Hangin' On
(1987)
Sheena Easton
(below) Morning
Train (1981)
Lulu
To Sir With Love
(1967)
Petula Clark
Downtown (1965)

new download buying American fans do not know that she shot to fame as the winner of *The X Factor* on ITV1 in 2006, or even that she is British. *Bleeding Love* was the biggest-selling British single last year.

Simon Cowell, Lewis's manager, took her to the US and negotiated a £5 million album contract with the music mogul Clive Davis, who signed Whitney Houston. She was sent to record with top US producers and a slick video designed for MTV was filmed for *Bleeding Love*.

Lewis soon began appearing in US entertainment "ones to watch" lists. Her breakthrough came this month with television appearances on *The Tonight Show with Jay Leno* and Winfrey's nationwide chatshow.

After earning a standing ovation with her Oprah performance, the host told Lewis: "You're the real deal girl. Talk about a star is born." Download and mobile phone track sales soared.

A strong line-up of British female singers is now hoping to emulate Lewis. There is a buzz over the Welsh singer Duffy, and Adele and Kate Nash are also hoping to make inroads. Winehouse has sold 1.5 million copies of her *Back to Black* album in the US, but has not topped the singles chart despite her Grammy awards.

Fig. 1.13 X Factor *2006 winner Leona Lewis achieved success in the American charts in March 2008, something that is perhaps more attributable to Simon Cowell's promotional techniques rather than audience power (**The Times**, 27 March 2008)*

Alternative media forms

In recent years not all media texts have been produced by large-scale media conglomerates. It can be argued that new media technologies facilitate small-scale media productions, which in turn provide for alternative views that challenge the dominant ideologies and values of society.

The Royal Commission on the Press (1977) defined alternative media as:

- dealing with the opinion of small minorities
- expressing attitudes hostile to widely held beliefs
- espousing views or dealing with subjects not given regular coverage by publications generally available at newsagents.

Investigating media

- Explore the existence of any underground radio stations near you. What views, ideologies and cultural norms do these stations challenge?
- Visit the website of Britain's leading Black newspaper – New Nation (www.newnation.co.uk).
- Read the section entitled 'About us' and what the paper tells potential advertisers about the publication and related publications.
- Would this publication be defined as alternative media according to the Royal Commission on the Press (1977)?

Some critical perspectives suggest that alternative media are run in a more egalitarian and democratic way; for example, the feminist magazine *Spare Rib*, first published in the 1970s, was collectively managed. The focus for alternative media in the 1970s was print, as the costs of production were lower than for film or television and distribution was cheaper.

New technology has facilitated the development of alternative radio stations and a range of alternative websites. These new media texts often challenge the consumerist norms of a capitalist society and may create ideological disturbance and disruption in relation to values and ideas about areas such as gender and sexuality, religion, environmental issues and animal rights. This is evidenced in the numerous websites that have emerged since the second Iraq war. These websites provide what can be referred to as 'citizen-journalism' – allowing ordinary people to give their own alternative versions of dominant news stories. Soldiers involved in the conflict have given their version of events; in so doing they politicise the repression of events and information produced in mainstream news, drawing attention to its selectivity. However, many question the validity of web-journalism and information as they are not necessarily restrained by professional or institutional codes and constraints.

An important restraint on many alternative media is their economically weak position as they are often unable to tap into the advertising revenue available to other more mainstream media. As new media technologies have reduced the cost of media production they can be seen as facilitating alternative media. Although alternative media websites do offer audiences the power to choose their media consumption from a wider range of media texts, they often rely upon mainstream media coverage to promote their websites or publications. Indeed many alternative websites are liable to be found via the Google search engine. This suggests that the inter-relationship between mainstream and alternative media texts may be closer than it appears.

Case study: McLibel and McSpotlight

The McDonald's company spends over $2 billion a year on advertising and as one of the largest global fast food chains it has received much criticism, for example, in Morgan Spurlock's documentary film *Supersize Me* (2004). In the 1990s, McDonald's issued writs on five members of the anarchist group London Greenpeace, for allegedly producing a leaflet criticising McDonald's. Three of the group apologised but the remaining two, Helen Steel and Dave Morris, defended themselves in a seven-year court case.

Initially, supporters were updated and canvassed via an alternative printed publication *McLibel Update*; however in 1996, taking advantage of new technology, the McSpotlight website was set up (www.mcspotlight.org). This accessed a wider audience at a significantly lower cost and provided the audience with an 'online interactive library of information'. This is a role it has continued to provide since the trial ended. A range of volunteers and contributors in over 15 countries produce a range of environmental information and continue to campaign against McDonald's and other anti-environmental corporations. In June 2000, the website claimed 1.5 million hits a month.

The distinctive feature of this website was the fact that it was frequently referred to and accessed via the mainstream media.

Fig. 1.14 *The McSpotlight website, a contemporary example of alternative media; however, one of the distinctive things about this site was the frequency with which it was accessed via and referred to in the mainstream media (www.mcspotlight.org.uk).*

Investigating media

- Look at the following websites:
  - Adbusters (www.adbusters.org)
  - LiveLeak (www.liveleak.com)
  - McSpotlight (www.mcspotlight.org)
- In what ways do these websites provide an alternative media space for those wanting to challenge dominant values and ideologies in contemporary culture?
- Do these sites go any way towards fulfilling Sola Poole's (1977) utopian idea of new technology?

MySpace revolution

■ Case study: interactive online dramas

Social networking sites such as MySpace and Facebook are examples of an area in which the audience have become the producers. A site such as YouTube enables video extracts to be uploaded by amateurs, based on material produced themselves or edited from other sources.

In 2006, the online drama of young girl entitled *lonelygirl15* became the most subscribed channel of all time on YouTube, even when it was disclosed that it was produced by a team of adult writers and not a troubled 15-year-old. It inspired the social networking site Bebo to set up its own on-line drama: *KateModern*, based on a 19-year-old university student in London. *KateModern* is described as an interactive online drama, which allows the audience to interact with and influence the story line, giving the audience immense power over the drama.

Alternatively *KateModern* can be seen as an efficient way of delivering a young audience, traditionally seen as hard to reach, to advertisers. Proctor and Gamble (whose products include Gillette, Tampax and Pantene), MSN, Orange Mobile, Paramount and Disney/Buena Vista paid £¼ million each for six months of product placement in *KateModern*. At the end of 2007, *KateModern* began featuring members of the band The Days, in episodes leading up to the launch of their debut album Evil Girls. Simultaneously, Bebo enabled fans to purchase the band's music from another part of their site.

■ Investigating media

Visit the two websites of the interactive online dramas *KateModern* (www.beebo.com/katemodern) and *lonelygirl15* (www.lg15.com/lonelygirl15).

■ Do you think they give more power to the audience?

■ How intrusive and how influential do you think the product placement on *KateModern* is?

💡 Current debates

Concerns about both the power of the media and who has power over the media in contemporary society have led to discussions about the effects of the media. As a result demands have been made to regulate the media and introduce censorship.

Regulations and censorship issues come together in many of the critical perspectives developing around new media. Indeed every new medium introduced in the 20th century led to public concerns and **moral panics** over their 'effects' and calls for regulation, as the following examples demonstrate:

■ *1900s* – concern over the sexual content of silent films

■ *1930s* – anxiety about the radio and the influence of crooners on housewives

■ *1950s* – anxiety about television's influence on the family

■ *1980s* – a moral panic over violent video nasties

■ Key terms

Moral panic: media-generated public outcry against a group, community or practice considered threatening and/or dangerous.

- *1990s* – anxieties over violence in computer games
- *1990s and 2000s* – concerns about the internet being used by paedophiles to contact children.

Springhall (1998) suggests that people are fearful of new technologies, such as computer games, because they challenge existing norms of powerful groups and governmental processes, especially because they are often embraced by the youth. In time, new technologies become incorporated into the norms of powerful groups and government processes. By the end of 2007, the Prime Minister's Office at No. 10 Downing Street had its own website and the Queen had placed her Christmas broadcast on YouTube.

Furthermore concerns about the effects of media, moral panics and **censorship** often focus on violent and sexual imagery, which are often of interest to younger audiences, fuelling concerns about the power and influence of the media.

Media effects

Throughout the 20th century and into the new millennium media studies has oscillated between a concern about the effect of media on individuals and the study of what individuals do with media. Research to identify a link between media content and the behaviour of viewers has been conducted since the 1920s, when radio came to the fore as a mass medium in the United States. With the ensuing rise of cinema and television, academics, advertisers and policy makers alike were keen to identify how the media influenced those who consumed it.

Media effects theories suggest that exposure to specific media content changes behaviour. Concerns about media effects rest upon a communications-studies perspective that suggests that media producers encode messages that audiences decode.

While it is clear that some media texts, such as advertising, do try to convey a clear message, there are also many other texts where the producer's motivation is primarily to make a profit. Profitability does not exclude a text containing a clear message; for example, the 2007 Hollywood film *Blood Diamond* is a popular action movie with a clear message against the illegal trade in diamonds from African war zones.

Sometimes it is assumed that many media texts carry hidden messages. Some of the high profile reporting of the killing of the toddler Jamie Bulger in 1993 by two young boys attributed the boys' behaviour to watching the horror film *Child's Play 3* (1991). This case and much of the research around media effects have a problem establishing evidence proving a clear causal link between media and behaviour. However, public outcry led to the amendment of the Video Recordings Act of 1984, which had required video-like films to receive age classifications. The amendment in the Criminal Justice and Public Order Act passed in 1994 resulted in harsher age constraints being placed on videos and later DVDs for home consumption than for cinema viewing. A film that has a 15 rating in a cinema frequently becomes an 18 when released on video and DVD.

It is often assumed that the effects of media content are negative; however media can also have a positive impact. The positive educative effect of media consumption lies behind many children's television programmes. *Sesame Street* was developed in the USA in the 1960s to address concerns about pre-school children's education and verbal and cognitive abilities. More recently a number of educational and social campaigns have seen media texts as an effective way of conveying their message, for example,

Key terms

Censorship: the restriction and control of media content by powerful groups such as governments and media producers.

Channel 4's youth-soap-opera *Hollyoaks* (1995–) has attempted to affect behaviour in relation to sexually transmitted diseases and drugs.

Social-learning perspective

The social-learning perspective suggests that viewers learn from media consumption. Bandura conducted a number of experiments in 1961, which have frequently but problematically been quoted in relation to media effects. Young children who watched a film of people behaving aggressively apparently replicated the behaviour afterwards in a research laboratory, hitting a blow-up 'bobo' doll.

There are, however, real questions about whether behaviour in a research situation really replicates everyday life. In particular, children may have identified the blow-up 'bobo' doll's purpose as being a game of hitting and the doll bounces back. The research may therefore provide no indication of how they would behave with other adults or children.

The cultivation perspective

The cultivation perspective suggests that it is not the content of an individual media text that affects people, but the cumulative effect of watching a range of media texts that has an effect. This is also known as the saturation perspective. It has, for example, been suggested that individuals become desensitised towards violence in the media over time. However, again this theory is hard to prove, especially as it relies on long-term exposure to media content. It is hard to differentiate between the influence of media texts and other environmental and cultural influences. Indeed, as early as the 1970s Gerbner pointed to the impossibility of proving the saturation perspective. Furthermore, an individual may become desensitised towards media violence but remain appalled by violence in their everyday lives. Alternatively, people with a tendency towards violent behaviour may choose to consume violent media texts as a form of release or catharsis.

Anderson and Dill (2000) undertook a study on the effect of violent video games on game players. They suggested that realistically violent video game play was related to aggressive behaviour and delinquency. The unique characteristics of the violent video games they focused upon included:

- the interactive style of play
- the active participation by players
- the addictive nature of the games.

Gentile and Anderson (2006) later argued that video games affected aggression in children because video games are engaging and reward repeated violent actions.

Further challenges to effects perspectives

In addition to concerns about research-related problems and actually proving if media has an effect, a number of other problems with these perspectives have been raised.

- These perspectives suggest that the creators of media texts manipulate audiences who are assumed to be passive and undiscerning.
- Effects perspectives tend to focus on 'vulnerable' groups and treat them as inadequate and unable to differentiate between lived experience and media.
- It is the least powerful in society who are seen as influenced by media content, thus effects perspectives become thinly masked criticisms of the media taste of these less powerful groups.

Link

You have already encountered discussion of audiences' different readings of media texts on pp41–70 of the AS book. Revisit this material to help you take a more critical perspective on some of the debates about media effects.

Thinking about media

Consider some of the areas of media that have been heavily criticised in recent years, such as hip-hop music, horror movies, violent video games, Marilyn Manson's music, etc.

■ In general, which groups in society consume these texts?

■ Do you think they are affected by them?

■ How could you go about proving whether the general public was affected by these texts or not?

■ **Media in action**

The challenge to the effects perspectives does not necessarily mean that there are no effects from consuming media texts or that they have no influence on individuals. A Foucauldian perspective based on the ideal of **discourse** argues that media shapes our perceptions and our knowledge of the world. This perspective underlies the constructionist approach to representation (see page 2).

Finally, although many critical perspectives see media as having some effects, debates continue to question:

■ the extent to which media content has an effect

■ whether individual texts directly influence people or whether it is the culmination of media viewing that has an effect

■ what kind of effect media content has – does it affect values and ideologies, or behaviour?

■ if media affects values and ideologies, then which values and ideologies raise concerns and why?

 Key terms

Discourse: a way of talking about or discussing a subject, which establishes 'common sense' or knowledge about that subject.

 **AQA** Examiner's tip

If you are analysing media texts where a media effects perspective may be drawn upon, use this material critically, and show the examiner that you are aware of the limitations and problems with establishing media effects.

Moral panics

The concept of moral panic was developed as a result of Stanley Cohen's studies of youth groups in the 1960s. Cohen (1972) argues that a moral panic occurs when society sees itself threatened by the values and activities of a group who are stigmatised as deviant and seen as threatening to mainstream society's values, ideologies and/or way of life.

The process by which a moral panic develops involves three stages:

■ the occurrence of a deviant act or social phenomenon

■ the act or problem being widely reported on in the media – initially reported in a range of news outlets, then discussed in internet chat rooms and quickly incorporated into fictional narratives, soap operas or detective series on television, in films and video games

■ a call for greater governmental control either from legislation, policy initiatives or the more vigilant operation of already existing social controls.

The process of a moral panic developing is not a linear one and the social control does not necessarily end the process. Changes in legislation may sometimes define new actions as illegal or deviant and the process may begin again. For example, concern about youth behaviour led to the introduction of ASBOs (Anti-Social Behaviour Orders) and now breaking the terms of an ASBO is a new deviant act. Thus an ASBO limits when and where someone can go; going to that place results in them committing a criminal act.

Although Cohen's original work was on the 'Mods and Rockers' of the 1960s and 'youth' continues to evoke moral panics, in the last 20 years there have also been moral panics about:

- HIV/AIDS
- ecstasy and designer drugs
- social security scroungers
- teenage pregnancy
- binge drinking and teenage girls' drinking
- junk food, poor diet and obesity, especially in relation to children
- asylum seekers
- religious fundamentalism
- dangerous dogs
- terrorism
- internet pornography
- gun crime.

■ Case study: Sara Payne

In July 2000 eight-year-old Sara Payne was abducted and murdered near her grandparents' home in West Sussex.

Widespread coverage of the search for Sara, the police investigation and the trial was followed across all news media. As a result of the story's 'popularity' the roadside near the place where her body was found became, for several months, a shrine visited by the general public.

When it was discovered that the man arrested and later convicted for killing Sara had a previous conviction for abduction and indecent assault, a media and public outcry against paedophiles erupted. The popular Sunday tabloid the *News of the World* launched a campaign for 'Sara's Law' to allow members of the general public with children to know if anyone living near them was on the Sex Offenders Register. They also published images and lists of suspected paedophiles, although these lists were not always accurate.

The *News of the World* campaign was not successful in changing the law but two years later when two 10-year-old girls, Holly Wells and Jessica Chapman, were murdered by someone who worked at their school as a caretaker, the procedures for Advanced Criminal Records Checks on anyone working in education were strengthened.

Throughout the 1990s and early 2000s, a number of television crime series explored the issue of paedophilia, such as *Prime Suspect* (1995). These programmes fed into the moral panic around paedophilia. When Chris Morris produced an episode of the comedy sketch show *Brass Eye* in 2001 which attacked this moral panic, he and Channel 4 received heavy criticism.

Thompson (1998) argues that in recent years there have been an increasing number of moral panics that have become all-pervasive. For example, the moral panic on paedophilia now affects the institution of family and all of those looking after children, who feel their behaviour is brought into question. Thus, moral panics do not only affect those who are stigmatised as deviant but also restrain other members of society keen to disassociate themselves from the deviant group.

Censorship and regulation of media

Media is regulated as a result of concerns about the potential power of the media to influence its audience, as well as the way in which media effects theories have, to a significant degree, become accepted by many people and politicians in the UK. The media is regulated **positively** by obligations being placed on media institutions, for example, radio stations must regularly broadcast news. Alternatively **negative** regulation prevents or censors certain media content.

Some content is regulated by the general laws of the country, which also apply to the media, for example:

■ the Race Relations Act (1976) makes it illegal to broadcast or publish material that could be deemed offensive to ethnic or racial groups
■ the Official Secrets Act (1989) prevents those in the military, government or police from speaking to the press without permission
■ libel laws state that if a media institution publishes anything that is considered to be harmful and untrue, the victim can sue for libel and make a claim for financial compensation of their damage.

There are three inter-related areas of media regulation.

■ *Economic regulation* – where economically powerful groups, advertisers and sponsors exert pressure to limit the content of media texts.
■ *Cultural regulation* – where the cultural attitudes and values of the audience limit the content of media texts.
■ *Legal regulation* – where acts of Parliament or governmental organisations or government approved industry institutions regulate media content, such as the Video Recordings Act (1984) or the British Board of Film Censors.

A political-economy perspective is most concerned about economic regulation, while a market-liberal perspective emphasises cultural regulation. Arguably institutions and organisations set up by the government or industries aim to oversee the balance of power between the producer and the audience for the benefit of the community and the protection of vulnerable individuals.

Self-regulation

Many media industries try to avoid government regulation and **censorship** by regulating themselves. For example, you have probably heard of the '9 o'clock watershed', before which time in the evening terrestrial television broadcasters avoid broadcasting certain swear words and sensitive material. Another example of an industry setting up a form of self-regulation is the Press Complaints Commission, set up in the 1990s to oversee the regulation of newspaper content in Britain. It has produced a code of conduct to which newspapers should adhere.

Similarly, the British Board of Film (BBFC) was set up in 1913 by the film industry to provide guidance on certification for films prior to their release. The BBFC is however only an advisory body; final decisions on film exhibition rest with local authorities, which can lead to inconsistencies between different areas.

■ Key terms

Censorship: the restriction and control of media content by powerful groups – whether governments or media producers.

The growth of new technology and its use for distribution and copying of visual media has undermined the role of the BBFC. As early as 1994, while the BBFC were debating what should be cut from the film *Natural Born Killers* to enable it to be granted an 18 certificate, pirated copies of the film were for sale at car boot sales and on street markets.

💡 *Government regulation of media*

In 2003, the Communications Act resulted in the setting up the Office of Communication, known as Ofcom. This new office brought together the work previously done by the:

- Independent Television Commission
- Broadcasting Complaints Commission
- Radio Authority.

Ofcom regulates the content of radio, television and wireless telecommunications and regulates the operation of these industries. As television has gone from a scarce, to a mass, to a saturation medium, it has become impossible for Ofcom to review all material before it is shown to the general public.

- In 1951 there were only three-quarters of a million TV licences.
- In 1953, when Queen Elizabeth II was crowned, the number of TV licences overtook the number of radio licences.
- In 1958 there were 9 million TV licences.
- In December 1980 there were approximately 300 hours of TV programming available pcr week.
- In 2000 there were 40,000 hours of television available per week.

Unlike the BBFC, Ofcom only looks at broadcast material in response to complaints made by the general public or pressure groups. The setting up of Ofcom was a move away from censorship and towards informed choice for the viewer, allowing even pornography channels on satellite TV on the proviso that they were subscription only and not freely available to children. The huge quantity of material on television, radio and wireless telecommunications makes it impractical to attempt to actively censor it therefore Ofcom issues guidelines to assist media producers to regulate their own media texts.

The Ofcom advisory code suggests that the following must be considered:

- degree of offence likely to be caused
- the likely size and composition of audience
- likelihood of people being unintentionally exposed to material
- maintaining independence of editorial control
- responsibility with regard to religious programming.

The Ofcom guidelines rely upon cultural regulation to a significant extent; what is unacceptable at one point in history may be quite acceptable at another time. For example, the use of swear words was seen in the 1960s as totally unacceptable on television, but they are now acceptable if used after the 9 o'clock watershed and if there is a pre-programme warning that the programme contains bad language. In looking at which texts are likely to cause offence it can be useful to consider the core concepts.

- *Media language* – media that uses more creative and original media language is often allowed to push the boundaries with regard to content, for example, art films can be much more sexually explicit than mainstream blockbusters.

■ Investigating media

Visit the BBFC (www.bbfc.co.uk) and the Press Complaints Commission (www.pcc.org.uk) websites.

- How do they define their roles?
- What do you think are their key concerns?

- *Institution* – due to the BBC's national status, its website and its television channels cannot show the same material, for example, a boundary-breaking show such as *South Park*, as other institutions.
- *Genre* – comedy is allowed to refer to a number of topics that would not be acceptable elsewhere, for example, in relation to sex, bodily functions and body parts.
- *Representation* – negative representation and treatment of some groups is tolerated, for example, criticism of working class people or homosexual men, whereas negative representation in terms of race or gender may produce more cultural regulation.
- *Audience* – an adult audience or an audience at a cinema can watch more sexually explicit or violent material than on television at home.
- *Ideologies and values* – some values and ideologies are censored in mainstream media, for example, support for people who are considered terrorists, such as the IRA in the 1980s and Al-Qaeda in the new millennium.
- *Narrative* – censorship often considers the narrative of the text, for example, are violence or sexual misdemeanours punished?

■ Media in action

Regulatory institutions administer the censorship of some areas of new media such as DVDs, computer games, satellite TV and mobile phones, but they do not regulate the internet. The global nature of the world wide web and the huge quantity of material it produces makes it very difficult to censor its content. For some people this is one of the benefits of this new area of media and why it is able to facilitate a wide range of voices and opinions. Other critical perspectives are concerned with the content of the material on the internet and its effects, particularly on the youth.

■ Link

Explore current criticisms of media content and the harm it can do by visiting the website of MediaWise (www.presswise.org.uk). MediaWise (formerly PressWise) is an independent charity, set up in 1993 by 'victims of media abuse'.

■ Investigating media

- Visit the Ofcom website (www.ofcom.org.uk) and explore what the procedure is to make a complaint.
- Who do you think is likely to make a complaint and why?
- Have a look at a couple of examples of recent Ofcom rulings. Do you agree with them?

Protection of the minority perspective

This perspective argues for control of media content to protect the rights of individuals, minority groups and those who may be harmed by the media. It assumes that the media has an effect either on the behaviour or values and ideologies of the general public. For example, people supporting this perspective may argue against 'Page 3 girls' in the *Sun* and internet pornography.

Freedom of speech perspective

This argues that freedom of expression is paramount and that criticising the government and those who are powerful in the media is important to ensure that democracy works. This view stresses that even if, at times, harm is done by material in the media this is better than allowing governments to censor media content.

■ Case study: Gina Ford and Mumsnet

Mumsnet.com is a parenting website that was set up by eight mothers. It receives 650,000 hits a month and as many as 15,000 postings a day and has become a popular space to discuss views on parenting. In 2006, Gina Ford, a childcare expert and author of *The Contented Little Baby Book* (2002), began a libel action against the website. She argued that not only were there a number of criticisms of her methods on the website but also strong personal attacks on her.

Although those running websites in the UK are not expected to monitor every post on the website, they are expected to remove offensive material when it is pointed out to them. Gina Ford and her solicitors argued that the Mumsnet.com developers had not done so; at one point in the protracted legal dispute the Mumsnet. com website requested there was no mention of Gina Ford's methods on the site at all. The case was settled out of court, with a five-figure sum being paid to Gina Ford.

The Mumsnet.com case raises a number of issues. Many who contributed to Mumsnet.com felt that their freedom of speech was being curtailed. Others argued that an internet chat room is more like a private conversation and should not be censored. For Gina Ford however the potential number of people who could read the offensive comments on the internet meant it was not a private conversation but public expression.

Case study: economic regulation and censorship

In the USA Wal-Mart dominates CD sales, having 20 per cent of the market in 2003. This gives the retailer significant influence over the recording industry and consumer choices.

A system has been developed in the USA whereby CDs with an adult content or whose lyrics or CD covers could be seen as offensive carry parental advisory labels. Wal-Mart however refuses to stock CDs with a parental advisory sticker or CDs dealing with topics such abortion, rape, homosexuality or Satanism.

Wal-Mart's policy is based upon their Christian 'family-values' policy. They do, however, sell guns and ammunition. In September 1996, when Sheryl Crow released a CD entitled *Love is a Good Thing*, Wal-Mart objected to the following lyrics:

'Watch out sister,
Watch out brother,
Watch our children as they kill each other,
with a gun they bought at the Wal-Mart discount stores.'

Crow, with the backing of her record company (A&M Records), refused to change the lyrics and accused Wal-Mart of banning her album because it directly criticised its sale of guns. This was an allegation the store denied, although admitting that it took objection to Wal-Mart being 'insulted'.

For many this is a case study of the potential economic power of some of those involved directly or indirectly in the media industries who are able to censor criticism against them.

💡 Chapter summary

There are a number of areas of the media that appear to represent reality – they are however all constructed representations.

Whether the representations are of violence, news, celebrities or reality TV you need to take a critical perspective of the text and consider:

- how have these representations been constructed (focus on their use of media language and narrative in particular)?
- what values and ideologies do these representations convey?

- why are these representations constructed in this way?
- how powerful or influential are these representations in constructing our understanding of the world?

Representation influences our perception and knowledge of the world around us.

Representation can be seen through a reflective or constructionist perspective but it is always selective.

Both media producers and media audiences exert power over the content of media texts.

From a market-liberal perspective more power lies with the audience; for a political-economy perspective more power lies with the producer.

Media effects and censorship are areas of debate that require a critical engagement, especially in the changing landscape of new media.

There is considerable debate about where the balance of power lies between producers and audiences and whether new media has shifted this balance of power. Both producers and audiences exert power over the nature of media texts that are produced.

In looking at media texts and considering the degree to which producers and audiences have exerted power you need to consider:

- what sort of a media organisation produced this text
- how the media text has been financed
- how the media text has been influenced by its need to make money
- where and how can the audience express their views on the text and how much influence do these views have?

There remains strong debate about the media-effects perspective and yet it is popular with the general public and politicians and often lies behind demands for censorship.

The media is often seen as contributing to the creation of moral panics.

In practical terms, censorship is a growing problem with the advent of new technology.

In looking at contemporary debates about media effects, moral panics and censorship you need to consider:

- what are the potential harmful effects of media content?
- can they realistically be prevented?
- are potential harmful effects so significant that they justify censorship?

Media theories

AQA Examiner's tip

Chapters 3 (pages 74–95) and 4 (pages 96–138) have as their first assessment objective that you must achieve the following.

■ Demonstrate knowledge and understanding of media concepts, contexts and critical debates.

■ Use media theories to deepen your knowledge of media concepts and develop your knowledge of the critical debates that are taking place in media studies at present.

Key terms

Denotation: refers to the simplest, most obvious level of meaning of a sign, be it a word, image, object or sound.

Connotation: refers to the second order of meaning in which a wider range of associations may arise.

Myths: frequently told stories that a culture repeats in order to convey the dominant values and ideologies of that culture.

This chapter focuses on the media theories that underlie many critical perspectives; some of these offer over-arching approaches for studying media. Many of the ideas you will be introduced to in this chapter are concerned with power, but they also question and explore the reasons why the media is the way it is. Although you may find these theories challenging, understanding them and being able to apply them when discussing media texts is essential to gaining higher grades in A2 Media Studies.

■ Structural theory

Semiotics, structuralism and post-structuralism are theories that explore the way in which audiences gain meaning from media texts.

Semiotics

Semiotics is the study of codes or languages and the signs from which they are made, such as words in a spoken or written language. There is a range of other languages or codes that we have learnt to read. For example, nodding or shaking your head means yes or no in body language.

Semiotics has been extended into many different areas, for example the car someone drives or the clothes they wear convey a certain message and give information to the 'viewer'. A Porsche's driver can be interpreted as being wealthier than the driver of a Nissan Micra. On a different note, dogs decode their owner's putting on of Wellington boots as a sign that they are going for a walk.

During AS Media Studies you began to understand how audiences read media language, such as colour, camera work, clothing, editing and 'mise-en-scène', in media texts such as films. Saussure (1983) suggested that there are three levels on which we read media texts:

■ *syntactic level* – identifies the basic denotations in the text, its dominant elements, for example the colour or overall effect

■ *representational level* – looks at the representations conveyed in the text

■ *symbolic level* – involves the hidden cultural or symbolic meanings that the text conveys.

There are two steps to reading signs:

■ **denotations** – occur immediately to the audience

■ **connotations** – rely on the representational and symbolic levels of meaning that can be associated with or suggested by a sign. These meanings often depend on the culture and background of the 'reader'.

Barthes (1967) developed Saussure's ideas to analyse media texts in relation to culture. He suggested that our understanding of many media texts rests not merely upon what the texts portray but on the texts' relationship to frequently told stories or **myths** in our culture.

Many media texts convey or tap into popular myths. For example, the romantic comedy genre of films often draws on the Cinderella myth. In

How do I find a holiday in France or Spain with real

freedom?

We know a way

Nothing beats the freedom and convenience of taking your car on holiday and having your own place in France or Spain – at least for a week for two! You'll be free from airport delays; free to pack all you need to enjoy your holiday to the full; and free to explore the surrounding area at your own pace.

Choose from hundreds of great value cottage, villa and casa holidays, each one hand-picked by us – leaving your free to do as much or as little as you like. Book by the end of January and *save 15% even during school holidays.*

book early
Save 15%
on every holiday

Brittany Ferries
— Holidays —

Book online or call for a brochure
brittanyferries.com/holidays
0871 244 0834

Fig. 2.1 *The meaning of this advert relies upon a series of myths: holidays as freedom; childhood as both fun and freedom; the rural as space for escape and freedom; and finally Europe and especially France as romantic, picturesque, wine-growing* (**Independent magazine** *14 July 2007*)

this frequently repeated narrative a girl (who is often poor, oppressed or bored) is rescued from her miserable life (or from poverty) by the love of a rich, handsome man. This myth can be identified frequently in romantic comedy films such as *Pretty Woman* (1990), *Maid in Manhattan* (2002) and *Bridget Jones's Diary* (2003).

For Barthes (1967), the final layer of signification in media texts relates to cultural meaning. In terms of the Cinderella myth the cultural meanings or rather the ideologies and values conveyed are that men are active and women are passive, that men are economically powerful providers and a women's key role is to be sexually alluring.

Fiske (1982) warns that there is a tendency to read connotations as if they were self-evident truths – as if they were denotations. However, connotations are codes that are particular to specific cultures. As a result audiences in different cultures may interpret media texts differently. Some media texts attempt to limit the interpretations of media texts, for example, in newspapers the meanings of photographs are anchored by the captions.

Investigating media

Look up the stories of each of the three romantic comedies mentioned above on the internet, using the Internet Movie Database website (www.imdb.com).

Try to think of three recent films that also use the 'Cinderella' myth.

Case study: front cover of Disney's *Princess* magazine

The Disney Corporation's magazine *Princess* can be seen as one of many spin-off products from fairytale cartoons such as *Pocahontas* (1995), *Beauty and the Beast* (1991) and *The Slipper and the Rose: the Story of Cinderella* (1976). The text in each of these films is open to a number of semiotic interpretations.

Look at a copy of *Princess* magazine. An analysis of, for example, the front cover of the March 2008 edition offers some obvious interpretations such as the use of colours to give an overall impression of a female fairytale world. For example, the use of pink indicates femininity and the colour gold indicates royalty and wealth. The roses placed on each of the girls' dresses depict love and romance, while the sparkling stars and diamonds indicate wealth and engagement rings. The banner at the bottom of the page, which says 'Stories, Colouring, Make-its', anchors the meaning of the cover images and informs the reader of what follows in the magazine.

The *Princess* magazine articulates the Cinderella myth, and is based on the assumption that every little girl wants to be a princess. The princesses' exaggerated hour-glass figures, their full, open, pouting lips and sexually-alluring gaze emphasise the ideology embedded in the text – that the path to wealth and success for girls and women is based upon their sexual allure.

Understanding signs

- There are many different types of signs, but each has two parts: the **signifier** and the **signified**.
- An iconic sign has a signifier that bears a close relationship to the object being signified. For example, a photograph of a person has a close relationship to the person whom it signifies.
- An indexical sign assumes a relationship between the signifier and the signified, so that when we see one, we expect the other. For example, smoke signifies fire.
- Symbolic signs have no obvious relationship between the signifier and the signified. Examples are the use of red for hot on a tap, blue for a boy or the symbol of a dove signifying peace.

Symbolic signs make up most of the spoken language and much of media language. The relationship between the signifier and the signified is arbitrary. It relies upon culture and it can change. For example, the meaning of some words has changed over time – 'fit' used to refer to someone's athletic or sporting prowess or the state of their health, now 'fit' is used to refer to someone's sexual appeal.

The construction of any media text involves choosing particular signs from a wide range of possible signs. For example, the choice of red or yellow for the colour of flowers or a woman's dress will change the meaning the audience gains from the text. Selecting a high camera angle will make someone appear vulnerable, while a low camera angle will make them appear powerful. Signs are chosen in media texts to influence meaning.

Signs are not value-free; they come with culturally specific meanings and interpretations and often shape our sense of the world. For example, try to make a list of all the words that describe a sexually promiscuous man and a sexually promiscuous woman. Your list may quickly grow much longer for women than men, and the list for women may well be more

Key terms

Signifier: the visible part of a sign, such as an image, letter, colour or diagram.

Signified: the idea, meaning or concept that is represented by the signifier.

Media in action

Compare the pairs of newspaper headlines below and think about how the choice of words conveys different meanings to the reader.

Terrorists shot by police
Freedom fighters shot by police

Heroic British team loses to Spain
Shambolic British team loses to Spain

The victim's grieving father pleads for action
The victim's irate father demands action

negative. These words and their contribution to language can be seen to legitimise certain values and ideologies of sexuality in a specific culture.

In A2 Media Studies, it is key to look at both *how* a chosen sign influences meaning and also *why* a particular sign has been chosen. It is easy to assume that people producing media texts make the choice of which sign to use because it seemed natural or looked right. However, theories about the politics of media suggest that what appears to be natural is in fact a reflection of the deeply held power and status divisions found in society, in relation to class, gender, sexuality and race.

Structuralism

Structuralism utilises a semiotic perspective in which societies, cultural practices and artefacts, such as media texts, can be analysed as languages or signifying systems. Theoretical approaches based on structuralism however look for patterns across texts rather than focus on the individuality of a particular text. For example, Barthes (1974) argued that there are narrative codes that are identifiable across a range of media texts:

- action codes
- enigmatic codes
- symbolic codes.

Action codes

This is where a series of actions facilitates a viewer to follow the details of a plot sequence, enabling the viewer to become absorbed in the narrative. For example in action films explosions, fights and car chases are actions that draw the audience into the narrative.

🔍 Enigmatic codes

Using enigmatic codes involves structuring the plot sequence around a series of questions (major or minor) that maintain the audience's interest and fascination in the text. For example, in many television-based detective programmes, the audience is absorbed in trying to work out who is the killer, while in a soap opera questions about what will happen next ensure that the viewer watches the next episode.

🔍 Symbolic codes

The use of symbolic codes involves identifying a text's major structuring themes. Symbolic codes are often expressed in binary opposites (man and woman, active and passive, public and private or criminal and police) or in **psycho-analytic themes** (male emasculation anxiety or a father versus son competition).

Case study: *The Bill*

The ITV police drama *The Bill* (ITV, 1984–) is an example of a media text where action, enigmatic and symbolic codes are identifiable. Action sequences such as car chases and crimes being committed move the narrative forward. In each episode a series of questions or enigmatic codes hold the audience's attention, relating to both the social interaction between members of Sun Hill Police Station and the solving of crimes (who committed the crime and how, when and who will catch the criminals). Finally the text is also structured in relation to a range of binary opposites, for example, good versus bad, police versus criminals and legality versus illegality.

Genre and **auteur theory** are two other areas dealt with by structuralism. Structuralist approaches to genre emphasise the patterns that can be identified within genres. For example, films in a Westerns genre can be interpreted as being structured around a series of binary opposites, such as cowboys versus Indians, society versus outlaws or civilisation versus barbarism. Patterns within genres are dealt with in detail in Chapter 4, page 117.

Structuralism has also influenced auteur theory, which looks for patterns in the films of particular directors who are seen as the 'authors' of their films. For example, Grist (2000) argued that the films of director Martin Scorsese always explore themes of masculinity and repression.

Post-structuralism

Post-structuralism challenges many of the assumptions of structuralism, most importantly the idea that a text has one single, identifiable meaning. It plays down the role of the 'author' (writer or director) of texts and emphasises instead the range of different meanings and interpretations that different audiences can create.

Post-structuralism challenges the notion that it is possible to identify clear structures in texts and emphasises the arbitrary relationship between signifiers and the signified. Post-structuralism suggests that many media texts contain floating signifiers that can be interpreted differently by audience members. There are a number of overlaps between post-structuralism and post-modernism that are covered in more detail on pages 85–88.

Case study: ghdhair.com

Between late 2007 and early 2008 ghd hair products launched an advertising campaign to promote sales of their hair styling products such as straighteners, hair mousse and shampoo. These adverts could be interpreted on a semiotic level – both the colours chosen (black and gold) and the uncluttered feel of the advert signified sophistication. The caption 'Thy will be done' (a quote from the Christian religion's *Lord's Prayer*) and the use of a cross symbol for the letter 'T' at the beginning of 'This Valentine's' created a link to the by-line 'ghd a new religion for hair'. However, many of the meanings in the advert were obscure and left open to the reader's interpretation. Not all readers would have picked up the Christian references. Furthermore, what was actually being advertised was not immediately obvious; the text stated that it was a styling set but what the set contained was unclear.

Political theory

In A2 Media Studies you are required to demonstrate your knowledge and understanding of a range of critical debates and apply them to the analysis of media texts. Critical debates in media studies have often been developed and influenced by political ideas, therefore an understanding of some political theory and how different political theories frame analysis of media texts is an important element of developing your critical awareness of media debates.

Marxism and hegemony

In Chapter 1, the political-economy approach to media production was covered (pages 22–23). This approach, developed by the Frankfurt School

Key terms

Auteur theory: suggests that the director is the author of the film and that films reflect his or her particular visual style, themes, values and ideologies.

and writers such as Adorno and Horkheimer (1944), is heavily influenced by Marxism.

■ Media in action

Marxism is based on the writings of a 19th-century philosopher and social activist Karl Marx. His writings were a response to the extremes of poverty and exploitation he witnessed in the years after the British Industrial Revolution. His most famous book *Das Kapital* (1867) argued that in a capitalist society the most important and fundamentally antagonistic divisions are along class lines and that there are two fundamental classes:

- the proletariat or workers who have to sell their labour to survive
- the bourgeoisie who own a range of different types of capital (wealth, factories, shares or property).

There are divisions and tension between these two classes and in contemporary society people following a Marxist worldview suggest that the bourgeoisie includes a middle class who, although they do not own capital, identify and serve the interests of those who do. Marx argued that under capitalism, the bourgeoisie dominates and exploits the proletariat in pursuit of profit. Marx and Marxists are concerned with how and why the mass of the population accept a system they see as unfair and exploitative. Marx suggested that ideology, values and beliefs are important in persuading the proletariat to accept the power of the bourgeoisie.

In Chapter 1, issues about the power of media producers and industries and how representations can construct an audience's view of the world were discussed (pages 20–23). Marx's ideas have been applied to media in contemporary society to suggest that the view of the world constructed in most mainstream media contributes to persuading the proletariat to accept capitalism as natural and inevitable, whilst simultaneously distracting them from complaining about exploitation.

These ideas were further expanded by the Italian writer Antonio Gramsci who in the 1920s and 1930s first introduced the concept of **hegemony.** He used this concept to explain how popular culture contributed to the manufacturing of consent for bourgeoisie power within capitalist societies (translated and published in the UK, 1971). For example, it can be suggested that repeated media representations of middle-class people in positions of power, control and leadership, such as reading the news or as experts, suggest that class division in society are 'common sense' and natural. Marxism focuses on power relationships based on class; however it should be noted that the concept of hegemony can also be applied to the power relations found in gender, sexuality and race.

■ Key terms

Hegemony: the process by which a power relationship is accepted, consented to and seen as natural or as 'common sense'.

■ Investigating media

In an evening's television programming, make a note of whether characters in dramas, the announcers, newsreaders or hosts on chat or game shows have a middle-class or a working-class accent.

- How often are those with a middle-class accent in positions of power and authority?
- Do you think this contributes to our perception of the world and naturalises class divisions?

Case study: lifestyle television

Lifestyle programmes are now very popular on British television and cover a wide range of areas of domestic and personal life. Subjects covered include cooking (*Nigella Express*, BBC2, 2007), childrearing (*Supernanny*, Channel 4, 2004 and *Honey We're Killing the Kids*, Channel 4, 2005), dog training (*Dog Borstal*, BBC3, 2006) and clothing (*What Not to Wear*, BBC1, 2002 and *Trinny and Susannah Undress*, Channel 4, 2007).

It can be argued that these programmes involve the retraining of members of the working or lower-middle class into the values, ideals and tastes of the bourgeoisie. It is not coincidental that many of the experts in these programmes, such as Nigella Lawson, and Trinny and Susannah are clearly defined by accent, home, background and demeanour as members of the upper-middle class. McRobbie (2004) argued that the denouncement of the taste and behaviour of the participants, often central to these programmes, is a form of symbolic violence. For example, in early episodes of *What Not to Wear*, Trinny and Susannah destroyed participants' clothes by cutting or tearing them up. They also humiliated participants by criticising their clothing style in front of family and friends. Participants were frequently reduced to tears.

Chomsky and Herman (1988) argue that the media manipulates populations to prevent them from rebelling against the powerful or dominant classes. This is done through 'manufacturing consent' by filtering available information through the media and therefore controlling the audience's ideas and thoughts. Chomsky and Herman do not suggest that this filtering is done deliberately or conspiratorially, but is done through a media institution's own censorship of what is included in media texts. This filtering is often based on the media institution's need for profit and to appeal to consumers.

Thinking about media

Chomsky has been particularly critical of the role of the media in producing propaganda that supports the American involvement in a range of 20th and 21st century wars, including the Vietnam and Iraq wars. It is important to think about the degree to which such theories are challenged by the rise of new media and the scope of expression and objectivity that new and alternative media provides (see Chapter 1, pages 23–26).

Investigating media

- Compare a range of news programmes and/or newspapers on one day.
- Do you think that they support Chomsky's views that news is often propaganda?

Criticism of Marxist theories

One of the criticisms of some applications of Marxist theory, in particular the political-economy approach (see Chapter 1, pages 22–23), is that it assumes the audience is passive and easily manipulated by media producers. However, a cursory exploration of the number of advertising campaigns that are unsuccessful and the number of media products rejected by audiences implies that perhaps audiences are not as easily manipulated as might be thought. For example, the *Adventures of Pluto Nash* (2002), a science-fiction comedy staring Eddie Murphy, was a huge flop despite the best efforts of the media producers.

Some theorists have developed Marxist theory to present a more complex picture of media power. Stuart Hall's (1981) interpretation of

Gramsci's concept of hegemony emphasises that consent for bourgeoisie is fragile, fleeting and has to be constantly worked at and re-established. He suggests that popular culture is a site for the contestation over ideologies, values and hegemony, and does not merely manufacture consent. A close examination of many popular media texts suggests that the texts are **polysemic**. This means that, rather than having one clear message that supports the dominant values and ideology, text meanings are contradictory. However, recent work by Hall and others (1998) emphasises that it is important to be aware of the way in which debates and contestation are constructed within media texts.

> ■ **Key terms**
>
> **Polysemic:** open to a range of different readings and interpretations.

🔃 Liberal pluralism

Liberal pluralism challenges Marxist approaches as it sees society as being made up of competing interest groups, rather than seeing society as dominated by bourgeoisie. Liberal pluralism does not understand media as operating to maintain the hegemony of the bourgeoisie, but rather the media is perceived to be subject to the wishes of its consumers. This approach is supported by a market-liberalism approach covered in Chapter 1 (pages 20–21).

Liberal pluralists argue that instead of media conveying hegemonic values or ideologies a range of views and opinions are passed through the media, for example, television shows broadcast competing party political issues.

Disney cartoons 'contain secret messages on the environment'

Mark Henderson Science Editor

Walt Disney films such as Bambi, The Jungle Book *and* Pocahontas *have played an important role in educating the public about the environment, a new book by a University of Cambridge academic has claimed.*

The stories of animated Disney characters, from Snow White *in 1937 to the clownfish* Nemo *in 2003, have built "a critical awareness of contested environmental issues", according to David Whitley, a lecturer in English.*

How animation brought green issues to life

Snow White and the Seven Dwarfs (1937) The jealous Queen arranges for the death of Snow White who escapes to the forest and befriends dwarfs and woodland creatures.
The message: "The forest's pastoral setting gives viewers a sense of the integrity and separateness of nature from the world of humans, which is shown as oppressively unbalanced. Snow White is also a role model, showing how humans can protect nature and even bring order to it."

Bambi (1942) The plot follows Bambi through his friendships with Thumper the rabbit and Flower the skunk, the death of his mother at the hands of hunters and his ascent to prince of the forest.
The message: "A classic example of the use of animated detail to represent the idyllic realm of nature rendered vulnerable by human incursions. The film is credited with having influenced a generation of conservationists."

Cinderella (1950) Under the thumb of her cruel stepmother and step-sisters, Cinderella's only friends are animals. After attending the royal ball, the mice help the Prince to find her.
The message: "Cinderella's relationship with an extensive subculture of friendly animals demonstrates that she is wholesome and good. The animals help to subvert the authority of a repressive, self-regarding human culture cut off from nature and represented by the ugly sisters."

The Jungle Book (1967) Ten years after he was found by Bagheera the panther, it is decided that Mowgli, a feral child, should return to the world of human beings to escape Shere Khan, the tiger.
The message: "Mowgli demonstrates not just a desire to protect the animal kingdom but to become part of it. The film introduced young viewers to some of the competing theories about the consumption of natural resources."

The Little Mermaid (1989) Ariel, the mermaid princess, longs to be part of the human world. She falls in love with Prince Eric and temporarily becomes a human being.
The message: "This suggests a fundamental division between humans and the natural world that can, at least partially, be overcome. The film persuades viewers that the human and natural worlds are comparable and equivalent."

Pocahontas (1995) Pocahontas, a Native American, falls in love with John Smith, an English settler. She shows him that her people have an intimate and spiritual relationship with nature.
The message: "Pocahontas's decision to stay among her own tribe teaches that the natural world is not there to be harnessed by the civilising effects of humans. The historically inaccurate reconciliation with the colonists implies that our rift with nature can be healed."

Tarzan (1999) Tarzan is raised by gorillas. A group of humans arrive, including Jane, who falls in love with Tarzan after he rescues her. Tarzan saves the gorillas from Clayton, a hunter who wants to capture them. *The message:* "The human impact on the environment is seen at its destructive worst in the form of Clayton's efforts to exploit the natural world for commercial gain."

Finding Nemo (2003) Nemo, a clownfish, is embarrassed by his overprotective father, Marlin. He is captured and taken to Sydney. *The message:* "The theme of letting go of one's protective anxieties accepts the dangerous aspect of nature, but we are encouraged to tolerate freedom with all the precariousness that entails."

> **Walt Disney films have played an important role in educating the public about the environment.**

Fig. 2.3 *Whiteley's work suggests that even a large multinational conglomerate, such as Disney, can produce texts articulating values and ideologies that are not dominated by the bourgeoisie – in this case an environmentalist perspective* (**The Times**, *25 March 2008*)

The liberal-pluralist perspective suggests that media audiences select and reject from a range of opinions, values and ideologies offered to them by the media. A liberal-pluralist approach, therefore, offers a more active perception of the audience than a Marxist approach does.

Liberal pluralism also suggests that the media can operate as a crucial element of a democracy. This is done through the reporting of events on TV news and in newspapers, thus keeping the electorate informed about the actions of the government and the legal system. There are however economic and institutional considerations that limit the inclusiveness of views across the media, especially when commercial concerns are paramount, and consequently there are many people who question liberal pluralism.

Case study: YouTube

YouTube was launched in February 2005 as a video-sharing website where users can upload, view and share video clips. By 2008, it became so popular that some employers were banning employees from using it as critics were expressing concern about the level to which it drains the internet's capacity.

YouTube provides a space for a wide range of opinions to be expressed, not just those of the major political parties, but also, for example, the Green Party. It is an example of Del Sola Poole's (1977) argument that new media allows a 'flowering of hundreds of different voices' (see pages 27–29 in Chapter 1).

The ease and relative cheapness of uploading a video can be seen as enabling for previously marginalised political groups. For example, over 4 million people viewed Barack Obama's website on YouTube. This is seen as having a major contribution to his success in the race for Democratic Party's presidential nomination in America in 2008.

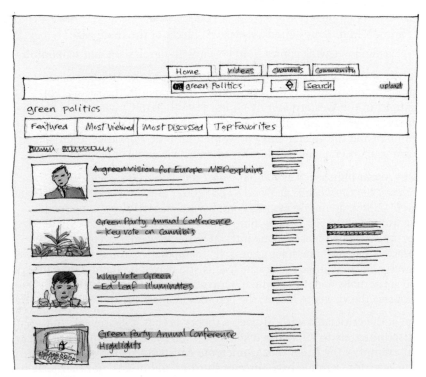

Fig. 2.5 *Websites where users post their own material provide space for a range of political views (this artist's impression shows the results of a search for green politics)*

Investigating media

Watch the first 10 minutes of two TV programmes, such as *Question Time* (BBC), *Newsnight* (BBC) or *The Politics Show* (BBC), that are intended to portray a range of competing opinions and debate a contemporary political issue.

■ Consider which viewpoints are being debated and which viewpoints have been excluded from the debate, and therefore what views, values and ideologies have been excluded from the debate?

■ It is likely that the three main political parties may have their say, but what about the Green Party, the British National Party or the Taliban?

■ Is there an over-representation of any particular social class, age group, race, gender, sexuality or religion?

Feminism and queer theory also raise questions about the political significance of the media, but focus specifically on the role of representation. These theories have developed, in part, from the belief that the British media tends to under-represent some political and social groups as well as their views and values. When a particular group is not visible in media culture it implies, as Graham Murdoch (1999) argues, that that group is not included in the dominant perception of society. Absence from media representation implies a sense of 'otherness', of not belonging and marginalisation. Individuals from an under-represented group may internalise this and consequently feel alienated from society. Representation is therefore a political issue. You have already encountered some debates about representation in Chapter 1, pages 1–4. In this chapter you will look at the political debates about the representation of gender, sexuality and race in contemporary media culture. In Chapter 4, pages 100–104, you will return to representation when you look at how to approach topics critically.

Feminism and post-feminism

One of the first groups to draw attention to the politics of representation in the media were the feminists of the late 1960s and 1970s, who pointed out the limited range of representations of women in the media. Feminists argue that social divisions in society benefit men in terms of work and educational opportunities, wages and access to political and economic power. They see media representations as often naturalising the power imbalance between men and women by emphasising that a women's role is a domestic one, as mothers, carers and housewives.

Many feminists argue that there is also an emphasis on sexuality and physical appearance in the representation of women. Laura Mulvey's (1975) influential work 'Visual Pleasure and Narrative Cinema' argued that mainstream Hollywood film was the product of a male-dominated and controlled industry and that in such texts:

■ men controlled the action and were responsible for moving the narrative along
■ women were represented as passive objects of the male gaze
■ pleasure in viewing comes from voyeurism, **narcissism** and **scopophilia**.

Mulvey studied films of the 1940–60s, but even in the 1970s she had a problematically uniform representation of women in the media. For example, in the Western *Johnny Guitar* (1954), Joan Crawford had already portrayed a strong, gun-slinging bar owner. Arguably with the rise of feminism and the greater entry of women into the workforce, there has in recent years been a greater plurality of representations of women in films.

Many recent films, such as *Kill Bill: Vol. 1* and *Vol. 2* (2002 and 2004), *Pirates of the Caribbean: At World's End* (2007), *Atonement* (2007) or *Casino Royale* (2006), do not necessarily comply with all of Mulvey's arguments. The women portrayed in these films are not passive objects of the male gaze; they are active heroines who are integral to the forward movement of the narrative, and are sometimes aggressive, manipulative, ruthless or violent. However, in these films the female lead is still played by glamorous actresses, who are sexually appealing to men. Often the camera movement seems to encourage the viewer to look at the heroines in a voyeuristic way.

One of the criticisms with Mulvey's theory is that it is applied indiscriminately to all media texts. There are many areas of the media that exemplify the belief that women are constructed as objects for the male gaze, for example page three of the *Sun* and men's magazines such as *Nuts*, *Zoo*, *Playboy* or *Mayfair*.

■ **Key terms**

Narcissism: the identification with or erotic appeal of an idealised image of oneself.

Scopophilia: the finding of pleasure in looking at other people as objects.

■ **Thinking about media**

Think about the last three films you have seen. Do you think that Mulvey's theories are useful for analysing the representation of the women in them?

AQA Examiner's tip

When answering exam questions, try to avoid simplistic use of theories. Remember that a theory is a starting point that indicates a particular way of looking at a media text. Theories need to be used carefully and critically in relation to the actual texts that you are looking at.

It is sometimes problematic to apply Mulvey's theory across all media texts. Television, for example, is constructed for the glance not the gaze with a greater emphasis on sound, as viewers are often doing other things at the same time as watching television. Consequently *Coronation Street* (ITV, 1960–) with its focus on narrative and humour uses many older character actors and actresses and perhaps does not seem, in the main, to present images of women merely for the male gaze. Furthermore women's issues are often the main focus of the plot and they are often responsible for narrative progress. Alternatively, the soap opera *Hollyoaks* (Channel 4, 1995–), orientated at a youth audience, has received a significant level of criticism for its portrayal of women, which emphasises the importance of sexual attractiveness.

The limitations of Mulvey's theory have been pointed out by Gammon and Marshment (1988) who suggest that in recent years a number of texts have represented men as objects for the female gaze. They go on to suggest that women viewers are not merely passive but active and discerning and engage critically with media texts by selecting texts that have meaning for them. Furthermore, women often identify with aberrant or villainous characters or place their own interpretations on the representations in media texts. Thus, Gammon and Marshment stress the importance of the audience's role in the construction of meaning in media texts and emphasise the range of interpretations that any text offers. In recent years there have also been a range of media representations of men for women to view scopophilically.

Fig. 2.6 *Look at these two adverts produced 50 years apart and consider whether you find Mulvey's (1975) theories to be helpful for their analysis* (**Picture Post**, *2 July 1955;* **Love It**, *25/31 March 2008*)

Fig. 2.7 *Stars such as Jonny Wilkinson often appear to be represented in media texts as objects of the 'female gaze'; womanrepublic.co.uk/entertainment provides a range of images and information about pin-ups such as Brad Pitt, Jonny Wilkinson and Justin Timberlake. How are men portrayed differently in such websites and magazines from the representation of women in* **Nuts** *and* **Zoo***?*

■ **Key terms**

Gender trouble: refers to any behaviour and representation that disrupts culturally accepted notions of gender.

 Thinking about media

Can you think of other groups who may be under- or misrepresented in the media because they are unlikely to play a controlling or dominant role in media industries, for example young people, disabled people and single mothers.

Post-feminism

With the introduction of equal pay for equal work, equal rights legislation, as well as the increased numbers of women in both higher education and the workforce, it has been argued that women have new opportunities, options and choices, making feminism no longer necessary.

In a post-feminist era it is argued that many media texts take a playful and irreverent attitude to the traditional gender divisions of the past. For example, the 'girl power' of the Spice Girls in 1996, with their hit song *Wannabe*, suggests that women could have it all in a new consumerist world. The enduring appeal of this ideal is evidenced in the popularity of the Spice Girls' 2007/8 tour along with their appearance in a range of television adverts.

 Investigating media

■ Do you agree with the argument that feminism is no longer necessary?

■ Use the internet to research women's pay and the number of women in positions of power in Parliament, the judiciary and in top-paid jobs.

■ What role do you think the media now plays in making certain roles, jobs and attributes seem 'natural' for women?

A contemporary approach to gender representation has been introduced by Judith Butler (1999) who suggests that gender is not the result of nature but is socially constructed. That is to say, male and female behaviour and roles are not the result of biology but are constructed and reinforced by society through media and culture. This theory understands that media and culture offer men and women a range of 'scripts' for gender roles, which audiences both interpret and perform in their everyday lives.

Butler argues that there are, however, a number of exaggerated, disruptive 'tongue-in-cheek' representations of masculinity and femininity, which draw attention to the idea that gender is socially constructed and cause what she refers to as '**gender trouble**'. For example, singers such as Joss Stone and Amy Winehouse have built their success on subverting expected notions of femininity; Joss Stone by being so overtly sexual at a young age and Amy Winehouse by living up to her 'bad girl' image with excessive consumption of drugs and alcohol. Similarly, the appeal of the hit TV series *Desperate Housewives* (Channel 4, 2004–) can be argued to be based on excessive portrayals of suburban femininity, which suggest that there is nothing natural or ideal about the role of the American housewife.

🔎 Queer theory

Butler's theories of gender trouble have also been linked to queer theory, which explores and challenges the way in which heterosexuality is constructed as normal and the media has limited the representations of gay men and women. It has been suggested that, for example, Hollywood films construct and portray images of 'normal', happy heterosexual couples, while homosexual couples are often represented in terms of sin or sickness.

Queer theory challenges the traditionally held assumptions that there is a binary divide between being gay and heterosexual, and suggests that sexual identity is more fluid. An example of the fluidity of gender can be seen in the character of 'Captain Jack Sparrow', played by Johnny Depp in *Pirates of the Caribbean: At World's End* (2007). In this film, the character uses an ironic and 'over-the-top' performance of a pirate, which includes wearing an over-elaborate costume and eye make-up, using feminine and camp gestures and avoiding anything that could be interpreted as machismo.

Queer theory also suggests that there are different ways of interpreting contemporary media texts, by looking at the fluidity of gender representation. This theoretical perspective has offered alternative ways of interpreting texts that were broadcast before homosexuality was decriminalised in 1967. For example, queer theory offers alternative interpretations of Batman and Robin's relationship in the TV series of the early 1960s, now being re-broadcast on digital TV.

Interpreting media texts using queer theory can also be applied to contemporary texts where heterosexuality is dominant. The US sitcom *Frasier* (Channel 4, 1993–) portrays two brothers Frasier and Niles, whose feminine tastes, preference for opera, fine wine, designer clothes and interior decoration have facilitated audiences to interpret them as being gay and discussing this at length on a range of internet sites.

Similarly, the relationship between the two brothers in the television drama *Kingdom* (ITV, 2006–) can be given a queer theory interpretation, The main star of the series Stephen Fry is openly gay in his off-screen life, while his screen character Peter Kingdom is an unmarried Norfolk lawyer, middle-aged, caring, kind but a bit eccentric with a strong relationship with his aunt. Emotionally in the first series he yearns for his brother whom he assumes to be dead. This more physically attractive brother reappears temporarily in the second series; his disappearance again leaves Peter Kingdom distraught and yearning, as if for a lover. This yearning in the text seems to suggest the impossibility of a satisfactory relationship for Peter Kingdom within the heterosexual culture in which he lives.

Arguably there have been a number of changes in attitudes to homosexuality in recent years that give some credibility to queer theory's suggestion that there is a more open and fluid approach to sexuality. For example, the decriminalisation of homosexuality in 1967, the introduction of civil partnerships in the new millennium and the popularity of Russell T. Davies's drama *Queer as Folk* (Channel 4, 1999). This drama focused on the lives of Stuart, Nathan and Vince and the gay culture of Manchester's Canal Street. What was radical about *Queer as Folk* was that it represented gay culture, rather than an individual character operating as a trendy appendage to straight characters, as in previous media texts such as *This Life* (BBC, 1996–7).

Fig. 2.8 *Amy Winehouse mixes an excess of traditional 1950s–60s femininity in a knowing way by wearing retro dress that emphasises the female shape and long hair with a range of tattoos that would once have been associated with machismo*

Thinking about media

- Do you agree with the idea that there is a greater fluidity in gender representation in contemporary media texts?

- Do you think that this is particular to specific genres or to media that is orientated towards particular audience groups?

Case study: *Brokeback Mountain*

Many people saw the success of the Hollywood film *Brokeback Mountain* (2006) as an indication of changing and more progressive attitudes towards homosexuality. The film portrays the homosexual relationship between two 1950s cowboys, which began when they worked as shepherds on Brokeback Mountain and continued in secret, on fishing trips. It came to an end when one of the characters is lynched and murdered because of his sexuality.

For some, the film challenges two quintessential traditional images of American masculinity – the 'cowboy' and the 'fishing trip'. However, the emphasis placed on close male relationships within the Western genre has meant that many have seen these relationships as having a homosexual element to them.

Furthermore, it can be suggested that the homosexual relationship portrayed in *Brokeback Mountain* is presented as tragic, leading to unhappiness and loneliness – a long way from the idealised representation of heterosexual relationships in many mainstream Hollywood films. The film, being set in the 1950s, can also be interpreted as suggesting that issues of homophobia belong in the past and in so doing sideline their existence in contemporary society.

'Camp', which is linked to Queer theory, involves an exaggerated performance of femininity, usually by men. A camp performance often involves an emphasis on style, image, irreverence, breaking taboos and poking fun at authority and is often used in comedy, game and chat shows such as those presented by Paul O'Grady and Graham Norton. A camp style draws attention to how masculinity is constructed and in so doing challenges the traditional notions of masculinity.

■ Case study: *Will and Grace*

Will and Grace (NBC, 1998–2006) is a popular mainstream sitcom seen by some as an indication of changing attitudes to homosexuality, as it contains a number of overtly gay cultural references. However a less progressive interpretation of the text might argue that although Jack the supporting character is portrayed as camp, the main character Will (whose name in the title gives him a centrality in the text) spends much of the time playing 'straight', having dinner parties or flat-hunting with female lead Grace.

Indeed Will's long-standing relationship is with Grace, and his boyfriends only provide fleeting relationships. Furthermore the problem or 'comic trap', in which the characters find themselves and which structures the text, enabling the series to continue through several series, is that Will is gay, and if he were straight Will and Grace could become a couple.

As Will and Grace have had a relationship in the past and are best friends, the future and whether Will will become straight remains a tantalisingly open narrative; undermining the degree to which this text is really queer.

Finally, although never made illegal, lesbianism has been suppressed in British culture in the 19th and 20th centuries. Consequently, it is important to point out that media representation of lesbians, except in male-aimed pornography, are far less frequent. Recently there have been one or two notable exceptions, for example *Sugar Rush* (Channel 4, 2005–6), *The L Word* (Living, 2004) and *Tipping the Velvet* (BBC 2, 2002).

◙ Post-colonialism

The issue of 'race' is another area in the politics of media representation in which media theory has developed in recent years. It is important when looking at theories of race to be aware that there are a wide range of representations of non-white identity groups that have changed over time.

In the 19th and early 20th centuries, Britain and other European powers such as France and Portugal held large colonial empires in Africa, Asia and South America. These colonial empires were often built upon the profits of slavery and the exploitation of natural resources such as gold, diamonds or oil. It is important to note that both the populations of colonised countries and of colonising countries, some of who experienced voluntary or forced migration, have been influenced by colonialism. The colonial empires justified the production of films such as *Saunders of the River* (1935), which portrayed ideologies naturalising colonisation. Similarly advertisements in 19th- and early-20th-century Britain for a range of products, including tea, chocolate and soap, carried racist imagery.

This imagery should not be seen as merely the product of the 19th century; the film *The Four Feathers* (1939) articulated ideologies that suggested the key role of the British army was to bring a civilising influence to India and Egypt, while *Zulu* (1964) represented the Zulu tribe in Africa as violent savages.

As, theoretically, no colonial empires remain in existence, the present era is known as a '**post-colonial**' era. However, it can be argued that the term 'post-colonialism' is problematic as it suggests that the influence of colonialism is a thing of the past, whereas in economic and diplomatic terms this is often not the case. For example, many British owned and managed companies, such as BP (British Petroleum) and British Airways, retain strong links with and have powerful presences in the countries that were once colonies of the British Empire.

Post-colonial theory challenges some of the ideas of globalisation covered in Chapter 1 (pages 24–26), for example the interconnectivity of countries across the world and questions of cultural imperialism. However, in looking at contemporary media, focusing on the legacy of colonialism and the slave trade is essential. Post-colonialism does not emphasise a new, technologically inter-related media world, but the importance of the cultural, economic, political and military dominance of the past. An important element of this dominance is the absence of non-white images in the media, which visually suggests the dominance of the white culture.

Post-colonialists argue that in looking at images, media analysis should consider what is not there as much as what is. For example, with the notable exception of Naomi Campbell, fashion models are predominantly white.

In many areas of media Western media organisations remain dominant. For example although the BBC renamed its 'Empire Service' the 'World Service', the London and American-based news agencies, such as Reuters and CNN, retain a high degree of dominance.

Edward Said (1995), introducing the concept of **Orientalism**, suggested that Western culture is constructed against an assumed 'other' and that a sense of the Oriental 'other' is embedded in European culture. He argued that for the West, the Orient holds both a fascination and a fear. He also argued that this sense of the Orient is central to the development of European culture, which has constructed a sense of itself in relation to and against their images of the Orient. For example, the villain Fu Manchu, as both a fascinating and frightening villain, appeared in *The Mystery of Dr Fu Manchu* (1923) and *The Face of Fu Manchu* (1965).

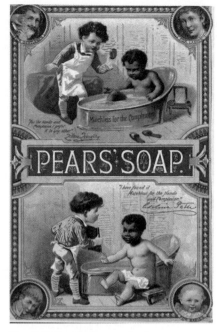

Fig. 2.9 *The ideology and values conveyed in this image suggest that black skin is undesirable and white skin is desirable. Images like this helped to reinforce a sense of superiority of colonising populations and marginality of the colonised African countries*

Key terms

Post-colonialism: a theory that suggests issues of race and the legacy of colonialism have a strong influence on media and media representations.

Orientalism: a perspective that suggests the East and the Orient are represented as provoking both fear and fascination within Western culture.

Thinking about media

- Do you think the British media reflects the multi-cultural nature of British society?
- Are there particular racial groups that appear to be excluded from the media?
- Are these absences uniform across all media platforms?

Supermodel Jourdan Dunn, face of Gap, veteran of US *Vogue*, and most talked-about model of spring/summer 2008 Fashion Week (in which she walked in an incredible 75 shows including Louis Vuitton and Valentino) has something she'd like to put straight. 'Everybody says I was spotted shopping in Primark. I wasn't *shopping*. I was with my friend: she wanted to go in, I wanted to go home – and we were just mucking about in the sunglasses section.'

It's an important distinction when, like Jourdan, you're 17. The tale of the Greenford schoolgirl, discovered by top agency Storm Management in a Hammersmith store in 2006, who goes on to become one of the biggest new models in just two years is too pat for her. When approached by the scout, Dunn knew the Storm name from magazines and *America's Next Top Model* ('I thought: Kate Moss!'); she instantly rang her receptionist mum, Dee, whom she and her two younger brothers live with in west London – 'She was screaming, I was screaming.' But she wasn't shopping in Primark. She was *mucking about*. She's still unjaded enough to care about truth rather than received wisdom.

Dunn is a fashion star, but first and foremost she's a teenager, and a very smart one. She's articulate and observant not only about her own history but about the fashion industry. At London Fashion Week in February, her comments about race made the news. 'London's not a white city,' she told the press. 'So why should our catwalks be so white?'

Race replaced weight as the story of Fashion Week and anonymous 'fashion insiders' opined that the industry had to bow to customer demands: customers who apparently demand white, thin, blonde models. 'The way people said I was stupid made me feel horrible,' says Dunn, 'saying that fashion's just a business so they need to use models who sell things.' Seeing Naomi Campbell and Tyra Banks when she was growing up made her believe maybe she could be a model. It's hard to think of other names who could have inspired a teenage black girl. 'I don't see a change. It needs to be said because I think about these things and other girls do too.'

Dunn agrees with Campbell's mooted plan to establish a modelling agency that will promote different races. 'I'm really ambitious. When I go back into education, I'm going to do business studies. Naomi's idea is good; I'd do an agency for black girls – and Asian and Spanish, because there aren't enough of them on the runway either.'

Dunn proved her point when, the week after

her comments in London, she became the first black model on Prada's catwalk in Milan since 1997 – when Campbell walked for the label.

It's going to be hard for Dunn to avoid the subject of race now, but it won't be the only reason she's famous. 'Not many British girls make a mark on the fashion world,' says Sarah Doukas, Storm's MD. 'When she went to Paris Fashion Week after the Prada show she got standing ovations from the big fashion houses. Jourdan's also rather wonderful – she's strong-minded and funny. She has us in stitches.'

Dunn finds it hard to be away from home – 'I miss out on getting on my brothers' nerves, so when I get back I have to get on their nerves on purpose to catch up' – but she's very happy working as a model (though she misses her drama studies and talks about opening a performing arts school one day). 'My mum

used to come on castings with me – I was scared because there were all these models with their nice shoes and handbags. But now if I don't get the job it doesn't bother me. You can't take it too seriously.'

At the *Observer* shoot, unlike many models, she takes the time to sift through the clothes rail because she's genuinely interested. She sits patiently through hair and make-up. 'I like seeing how I can look in a photo,' she says over the blast of the hairdryer. 'I like having spikes coming out of my head or being in something I'd never wear. It's fun looking at myself in a different way.'

Supermodel, international catwalk star, accidental spokesperson on race, teenager mucking about in Primark... Hopefully everyone will find a different way to look at Jourdan Dunn. **Interview Alice Fisher**

Fig. 2.10a *At London Fashion Week in February 2008 model Jourdan Dunn made the news when she asked reporters, 'London's not a white city. So why should our catwalks be so white?'* (**Observer Magazine**, *6 April 2008*)

Case study: film and the Orient

During the later part of the 20th century there were a number of examples of action films where a fear and fascination of the Orient is constructed. For example, the role played by North Korea as a threatening 'other' in the James Bond film: *Die Another Day* (2002) corresponding to an increasing concern about North Korea's nuclear capacity.

In the new millennium, there has been an increase in the popularity of films set in China, Hong Kong and Japan, such as *The Painted Veil* (2006) and *Lust, Caution* (2007), possibly a reflection of the increasing importance of China and the East for trade, and as a holiday destination, especially with the Olympics being held in Beijing in 2008. In *The Painted Veil*, a 1920s British doctor, motivated by vengeance, takes his unfaithful wife to live in a small Chinese village. Here he fights an outbreak of cholera, hindered by disputing Chinese political factions. Chinese culture is portrayed as both fascinating and threatening for the doctor and his wife – the doctor's wife is intimidated and physically threatened by the local Chinese; whilst China is presented as a place of sexual freedom for Westerners, both alluring and fascinating. Cholera operates as a metaphor for a deeper sickness that only a British doctor can combat, even though the attempt kills him.

Lust, Caution (2007) is an espionage thriller set in Shanghai during the Second World War, where a group of naïve students opposed to the emerging communist rule become embroiled in a plot to assassinate a local political leader. The dangerous emotional intrigue and sexually explicit scenes in the text serve again to provide a representation of the Orient pivoted upon an axis of fear and fascination.

Fig. 2.10b *The opening page of the Jourdan Dunn spread* (**Observer Magazine**, *6 April 2008). The subhead reads 'She's the London teenager whose looks – and outspoken comments – stole the spring shows. Here, Jourdan Dunn talks Prada, Primark and black role models'*

Many people, whose families suffered forced or economically driven migration and who have experienced racism in their country of residence have developed a sense of 'otherness' and **Diaspora identity**. It can be argued that this sense of alienation or otherness is emphasised by a lack in contemporary media of any cultural representations of their lives or experiences.

Diaspora identity is not always negative, as can be seen by looking at the Asian music scene in Britain. For example, the group Swami, whose distinctively British–Asian music is an increasingly popular fusion of Western and Eastern music styles, such as hip-hop, RnB and a futuristic sound, to produce something that asserts a positive Diaspora identity.

One of the first film directors to assert a positive British–Asian identity in the media was Gurinder Chadha. Her films, such as *Bhaji on the Beach* (1993) and *Bend it Like Beckham* (2002), were seen as groundbreaking as they represented Asian culture in popular film, in a non-stereotypical way. More recently Chadha's film *Bride and Prejudice* (2004) reworked the narrative of Jane Austen's 19th-century novel *Pride and Prejudice* into a modern-day romance that fused Asian and British movie styles and themes. The film is set around an Indian wedding, in India. The film's stylistic mixing of a literary classic with a **Bollywood** musical gives it a distinctively post-colonial feel.

Key terms

Diaspora identity: the result of forced or voluntary migration where people experience both a sense of belonging to a cultural group that is 'other' to the dominant culture of their country of residence.

Bollywood: refers to the large Indian film industry whose output often exceeds that of the US film industry.

Investigating media

Use a search engine such as Google to look up Gurinder Chadha and her films.

■ How do her life and the themes of her films suggest a post-colonial identity?

It can be argued that Chadha's films' representation of a Diaspora Asian identity in contemporary British culture are exceptional in contemporary media representation; many more of the wide range of racially-specific representations that have evolved and been circulated in media texts are founded upon negative historical myths from the colonial past. Thus Alvarado (1987) has suggested that there are four types of representations for members of the black community:

■ *the humorous* – comedians such as Lenny Henry
■ *the exotic* – models such as Naomi Campbell
■ *the pitied* – representation of needy black communities through charity advertising such as Live Aid or in films such as *Blood Diamond* (2006)
■ *the dangerous* – portrayed in news and documentary reports of black inner-city gangs or gun crime.

The following positive and negative black media stereotypes are often seen in contemporary British media:

the humorous and/or exotic, such as entertainers:

■ *musicians* – jazz (Gary Crosby), hip-hop (Sway), soul (the film Ray, 2005)
■ *sportsmen and women* – Thierry Henry, Kelly Holmes
■ *comedians* – Eddie Murphy, Chris Rock;

the pitied and/or dangerous, represented as 'social problems' in the British media:

■ *criminals* – drug dealers or gangsters, for example *American Gangster* (2007)
■ *socially dysfunctional* – single-parent families, unemployed and academically under-achieving youths in documentaries and newspapers;

the exotic and dangerous, such as the sexually promiscuous:

■ *the prostitute or sexually promiscuous woman* – in films *Sapphire* (1959), *Mona Lisa* (1985), *She's Got to Have It* (1986) and more recently in a range of hip-hop videos
■ *the stud and the pimp* – the film *The Nutty Professor* (1996).

It is important to consider the narrative function that black and Asian characters have in media texts. Historically black and Asian people are often overly represented in negative roles, such as the villain, or take subservient or 'helper' roles rather than being constructed as the hero. Further, these representations, particularly in soap operas and dramas, have often relied on a series of myths that relate to a colonial past and post-war immigration, such as the Asian shopkeeper or arranged marriages. Examples include Dev Alahan in the long-running soap opera *Coronation Street* (ITV, 1960–) and Zainab Masood in *EastEnders* (BBC One, 1985–), as well as the film *East is East* (1999).

Representations and stereotypes of race and gender are often constructed in terms of binary oppositions, suggesting that individuals can be divided into two diametrically opposed groups, for example black and white, British and immigrants or Christians and Asians. Such representations exaggerate differences and minimise the similarities between people in different groups, which can legitimise often negative attitudes and values that emphasise the boundaries and differences between groups.

It can be argued that there has been an increase in the diversity and frequency of representing different races in recent years. This could be explained by rise of black British independent community media production, for example newspapers aimed at the British black population such as *The Voice* or magazines for black women such as *Ebony* and *Asian Woman*.

Fig. 2.11 *Since 1990, when* **Pride Magazine** *became the first monthly magazine for black women, sales have grown to 40,000 with a readership of five times this number. In 2004 an annual supplement called* **Pride Parent** *was added to 'target parents with children of ethnic background'. Similarly* **Asian Woman**, *which was launched in 1999 now has monthly sales of over 90,000 and a readership figure of 10 times this, with 23 per cent of readers coming from outside the Asian community (www.asianwomanmag.com)*

These shifts in representation exist alongside many traditionally 'white' texts such as *Friends*, the significant under-representation of black groups on websites such as YouTube and the emergence of some problematic new representations of non-white racial groups, such as the 'terrorist' and the 'asylum-seeker'.

The 'terrorist' is defined by a number of key characteristics:

- religious or national extremism
- illogical and irrational behaviour
- disregard for human life
- sexism
- frequent use of violence and cruelty
- often characterised as ethnically Middle Eastern or Arab.

Examples of how terrorists are represented are seen in, for example, the American television series, *24* (Channel 4, 2001–), which focuses, in each different series, on a different racially distinct group of terrorists threatening America's survival. Another example is in the film *Casino Royale* (2006), which opens with James Bond pursuing African terrorists and portrays racially coded terrorists as a dangerous threat.

The image of the asylum-seeker or immigrant as a lazy, threatening individual, who survives illegally in Britain by living off the British social system, has been prevalent in British tabloids since the late 1990s. The tone and language of the reporting has led to a moral panic with demands that government action be taken. In October 2003, the Press Complaints Commission warned newspaper editors that there was a 'danger that inaccurate, misleading or distorted reporting may generate an atmosphere of fear and hostility that is not borne out by the facts'.

The media representations made little distinction between illegal immigrant, asylum-seeker, legal immigrant and non-white British citizen. The MediaWise Trust, an independent charity set up by victims of media abuse, carried out research into the representations of asylum and refugee issues, and produced guidelines for journalists in an attempt to try and prevent harmful and often racist reporting. Despite these guidelines a number of television police and crime dramas, such as *Prime Suspect* (ITV, 2003) and *Trial and Retribution XII – Paradise Lost* (ITV, 2007), have focused their narratives around illegal immigrants, further fuelling the moral panic.

There remains much critical debate about representation and a need to question whether the British media recognises the country's multi-cultural make-up and if media representations are really changing or remain influenced by the colonial past.

In this section, you have explored how political theory has informed a number of debates about power, ideology and values and representation. How audiences interpret media texts is, however, open to debate, as are the power and significance of representations.

🔍 📰 Audience theory

Some debates around audience power and whether it is the media producers or the audience that have the power to determine the sort of media texts that are produced were explored in Chapter 1 (see pages 20–23). Questions about how the media shapes an audience's perception of the world were also looked at in Chapter 1 (pages 20–23). Audience theories suggest that representations are open to different interpretations and that their meanings are not fixed. This approach focuses not on what the media does to the audience, but rather what the audience does *with* the media.

Investigating media

- Using the internet, look up the MediaWise Trust guidelines on diversity (www.presswise.org.uk).

- Do you think that these guidelines are followed in examples of press reporting that you have observed?

Audience theories have become a particularly important area in the development of media theory with the development of new technologies such as the internet, iPods, satellite television, DVDs and user-demand TV (TiVo and Sky). These technologies increase the potential for greater audience control and have allowed the boundaries between audiences and producers of media to become more fluid.

Before considering some of these theories it is important to be aware of the various media texts and how they are consumed in different ways in different situations. Some media texts are made for a mass audience, meaning they are made for as wide a range and high a number of people as possible, such as soap operas. Alternatively some texts, such as the magazine *Practical Caravan*, is produced for a much smaller, more specialised or niche audience of caravanners.

Consumption of media

Although most media texts are produced with specific audiences in mind, there are also different ways of consuming media texts.

- *Primary media* – such as films shown in cinemas, demand close and concentrated attention from the audience.
- *Secondary media* – such as radio or some television programming, provide a background for an audience who are often doing something else at the same time and are distracted. For example, this audience glances at the TV screen while making dinner, or listens to the radio while driving to work or dressing in the morning.
- *Tertiary media* – these are media texts that are consumed by audiences who are almost unaware of their own engagement with the media, such as advertising or radio stations broadcasting in shops.

The Frankfurt School and the work of Adorno and Horkheimer (1940s–60s), described in Chapter 1 pages 8–10, expressed concern that cultural industries, including the media, influenced the political views of its audiences. Their criticisms stemmed from the concern that audiences passively consumed popular media texts embedded with particular values and ideologies. They argued, for example, that certain media texts influenced ordinary people to support Fascism in Nazi Germany in the 1930s and American capitalism in the post-war era. This argument can be seen as consistent with a communications model, suggesting that media producers encode messages into texts and that audiences decode and absorb these messages into their daily lives.

However Gerbner (1956) suggested messages do not just flow from the text to the audience, but instead there is another step in the process as audiences discuss the ideas they acquire from media with each other. They may debate and challenge the values and ideologies that the media conveys, which consequently reduces the power of the text.

Although it is clear that some media texts, such as advertising, do try to convey a particular message, there is much debate about whether others, such as soap operas or quiz programmes, intentionally do. It can be argued that in order to appeal to a wide range of people many texts are deliberately constructed to be read in a number of different ways – to be polysemic. For example, the popular *Shrek* films (2001, 2004, 2007) are designed to appeal to child, adult and teenage audiences. Thus the ironic humour, which relies upon an awareness of a number of other popular media texts, is often missed by the younger audience members but maintains the older audiences' engagement.

It can also be argued that audiences have the power to choose the media they consume to suit their needs. The 'uses and gratifications theory' developed by Blumler and Katz (1974) suggests that an audience uses media socially and for psychological gratification. In the sitcom *The Royle Family* (BBC, 1998–2002), for example, almost all the action and dialogue takes place whilst the family sits around the television. Discussion, debate, criticism and speculation about the contents of programmes provide the basis for the family's interaction, suggesting that television may make an important contribution to family cohesion and companionship. Other examples of the uses audiences make of media include:

- sharing and discussing experiences with others
- obtaining information about the world
- helping to gain identity.

Examples of the gratifications audiences may gain from the media include:

- finding a distraction or diversion
- seeing authority figures inflated or exalted
- seeing others make mistakes or making fools of themselves
- reinforcing a belief that justice will ultimately triumph.

Uses and gratifications theory also offers explanations of an audience's motivations for consuming media texts. McQuail (1997) summarises these as:

- information
- learning
- personal identity
- social interaction
- entertainment.

Alternatively, it can be argued that people may regularly watch TV programmes such as soap operas, read a daily newspaper or a weekly magazine for the following reasons:

- to provide a sense of routine to their lives
- as a reward for work
- as a way of escaping loneliness
- as an escapist fantasy
- to provide a focus to think about or discuss social and moral issues.

Buckingham's work in the late 1980s, for example, pointed to the significance of watching *EastEnders* (BBC One, 1985–) in playground interaction and discussion. A further development to the idea that the media is used to combat loneliness is Shaun Moores's (1998) argument that media texts often allow the audiences to perceive themselves as part of an **imagined community**. This imagined community may be fans of particular pop group, players of an online fantasy game or viewers of a popular TV programme. The audience feel that they have something in common with other imagined members of the audience.

Key terms

Imagined community: a term developed by Benedict Anderson (1980) to refer to communities that predominantly exist in people's minds and give them a sense of identity.

Case study: TOGs

Britain's most popular radio programme, Radio 2's Terry Wogan show, reinforces the audience's sense of belonging to a community by giving the listeners a name. They are referred to as TOGs – Terry's Old Geezers (or Gals). Their letters, requests, the show's website and their involvement in the BBC's annual Children in Need appeal all give the audience a sense of being part of an imagined community.

Investigating media

Drawing upon the approaches outlined in uses and gratifications theory (1974), it has been suggested that viewers use quiz programmes in four ways:

- *self-rating* – to see how good they are compared to others
- *social interaction* – enjoying watching and discussing the programme with others
- *excitement* – to see who wins and what they win
- *education* – as a source of knowledge.

Watch an episode or extract of a recent quiz programme with your family and/or a group of friends and observe their interaction with the text.

What uses and gratifications do you think it is offering for this particular audience?

Investigating media

Look for examples of how the media you consume constructs an imaginary community of its audience through, for example:

- using a particular name for the audience
- using specific language or terms that become familiar to loyal fans and gives them a sense of identity
- references to previous incidents or episodes in the history of the programme
- providing spaces that the audience can communicate with each other, for example an Internet chat room.

Media in action

In the 1980s and 1990s a number of media theorists built upon the uses and gratifications approach to explore the reception of the media by audiences. David Morley's work in the 1980s discussed the gender politics around who, in the home environment, controls the television remote control and therefore who decides what television channel is watched. He suggested that men and women had different styles of television viewing, for example, women often watch television while completing domestic tasks such as ironing. Do you think he would observe different things if he carried out his research in contemporary culture?

Critics of uses and gratifications theory point out that an audience has a limited range of media texts from which they gratify their needs. The theory does not explain why different members of an audience interpret a text differently. It has further been suggested that this active view of the audience undermines the power of the media to manipulate audience's needs, such as in advertising.

Ang's (1985) work looked at the popularity of the 1980s American TV drama *Dallas* (BBC, 1978–91) and explored the range of gratifications that it offered Dutch audiences. These gratifications included identification and fantasy. For example, some of the audience identified with the problems Sue Ellen had in her marriage, while others enjoyed the fantasy of imagining themselves in the wealthy lifestyle portrayed in the programme.

More recently Hill's (2005) work on the reality television genre has explored the way in which one of the gratifications offered by reality television are discussions around the degree to which such programmes are constructed or staged. Like all other media theories there are debates about all this research; some suggest that it lays too much emphasis on the interpretative role of the researcher.

Beyond the text

Morley (1990) argues that it is important to understand media, not just as programming and text, but as objects that in themselves carry meaning and value. These values and meanings do not necessarily rely on the use of that particular media text, for example, some media such as widescreen TVs and Apple iPods operate as status symbols.

Media technology entering the domestic space of the home during the 20th century has been steadily incorporated into everyday life. The radio in the 1920s and 1930s steadily moved from being 'unruly guest' to part of the family. Spigel (1999) argues that in the 1950s television also moved from being seen as an intruder into domestic life to being incorporated into the home. Occasionally TVs were disguised as a piece of furniture to ease this transition. In the late 20th century a similar process of adjustment and incorporation was recognised, as many people began to own a personal computer (PC). Although there are debates about the role or influence of TV, PCs and the internet on the 'family', they are seen by many as an integral part of the family household (Gunter and Svennevig, 1987).

Silverstone (1994) argues that the television provides a sort of security and reassurance for many adults and young people by giving them the comfort once provided to them as young children by teddy bears or blankets. This argument can equally be applied to the internet. He argues that: 'the continuities of sound and image, of voices and music, can easily be appropriated as comfort and security, simply because they are there' (1994). As TV, radio and PCs are constantly present in the home, they can provide reassurance to their audience of a link with the outside world. It is for this reason that many people turn the TV, radio or computer on even when they are not watching, listening to or using it, especially when at home alone.

Another theory that explores the role of the audience beyond the text is Couldry's (2004) concept of the 'mobile audience'. Couldry argues that audiences saturated by contemporary media engage in media tourism. Audience do not only listen to and watch media texts in their own homes but also visit places related to media production, such as television and film studios or, for example, going to the Yorkshire Dales to see where *Heartbeat* (ITV, 1992–) and *Emmerdale* (ITV, 1972–) are made.

Audiences can now spend much more time in the consumption of media texts, but not always in clearly defined spaces at particular times. Audiences watching TV programmes such as *Big Brother* (Channel 4, 2000–) can also supplement their viewing by participating in related online chat rooms, reading about the contestants in tabloid newspapers or celebrity magazines, engaging in online voting or even editing their favourite parts of the programme and uploading them onto YouTube. Furthermore, many people are also willing both to travel and spend large amounts of time to become part of a TV or radio studio audience or take part in auditions for reality TV shows such as *Big Brother* or *The X Factor* (ITV, 2006–).

According to Abercrombie and Longhurst (2005), audience involvement beyond the text is part of a wider shift in the audience's experience, allowing the boundaries between the audience and the producer of media texts to become more fluid. Many areas of new media, such as chat rooms and social networking sites like Facebook and MySpace rely on audiences literally to construct them. Other areas of the media rely upon a high degree of audience input and participation, such as voters on a reality TV show. The rise of phone-ins on radio, as well as reality and confessional TV, such as *The Jeremy Kyle Show* (ITV, 2005–), rely upon ordinary people becoming participants. Abercrombie and Longhurst suggest that as a result many people live their lives as if they were players in a TV show; constructing narratives of their relationships and family lives as if they were explaining them on television or the radio.

Audience versus media producers' power

To some media analysts these changes have resulted in a shift of power away from media producers in favour of the audience. There are, however, a number of factors that limit the audience's or participant's power. Often the audience can only participate within carefully constructed and framed spaces, for example, the website Facebook has tight stylistic norms, as do other sites that invite audience comments and contributions, such as Wikipedia, Amazon and the International Movie Database. Similarly, the use of media language in reality and confessional TV programmes limits the audience's or participant's control of the text, for example:

- the programme's hosts' or experts' views are dominant – they speak first, often stand in a dominant position in relation to the participants and decide which participant will be allowed to speak and when

- the programme's hosts or experts may have a privileged relationship with the camera and the use of a voice-over or narrator emphasises the particular views of the media producers

- editing reality and confessional shows ensures that the producers retains control of what is finally aired

- the producers of the shows have constructed the scenarios and narratives, such as selecting the tasks completed on *Big Brother* or deciding who will appear first on *The Jeremy Kyle Show*.

For media producers, increasing audience participation is good for business. The related media spaces and opportunities make money and build up audience loyalty. There is, however, debate as to whether these tertiary media texts actually empower audiences or not.

The active audience

Underlying many of the critical debates surrounding audiences are differing viewpoints about whether the audience is active or passive. Media effects theory (explored in Chapter 1, pages 30–33) and some Marxist theory assumes that the audience members are passive recipients of the values and ideologies expressed in the media.

Alternatively, uses and gratifications theory and reception studies tend to assume that the audience members are active and discerning, making active choices about what media they consume and giving the texts meaning in relation to their own experience and everyday lives.

The concept of the active audience takes this further, suggesting that rather than meaning being contained in a text as a consequence of the media producers, audiences actively construct interpretations and meanings from the texts they encounter. The active audience brings their own experiences, values, ideologies and identity to each encounter with a media text. Hence they all interpret texts differently. Morley's (1980) study of the local and national news programme *Nationwide* (BBC, 1969–83) emphasised that the text was interpreted differently by different social groups.

Case study: the OJ Simpson case

In 1995, the USA experienced a media phenomenon when the black ex-footballer and film actor OJ Simpson was put on trial for the brutal murder of his ex-wife and her friend. It was one of the first examples of blanket media coverage of the court case, with the trial broadcast daily on a new daytime television channel, Court TV. At the beginning of the trial the vast majority of black Americans thought that OJ Simpson was innocent and the vast majority of the white population thought he was guilty. The active audiences consumed many months of television coverage and at the end of the trial (when OJ Simpson was found not guilty) almost no one had changed their views of his guilt or innocence. They all interpreted the evidence shown on television from their own experience as a black or white American.

With many contemporary media texts it is harder to identify specific social groups who will interpret the media text in a particular way. Thus the notion of the active audience has been extended to suggest that there are, arguably, as many interpretations of a text as there are members of the audience. This perhaps explains why there can be huge debate about the meanings and interpretations of media texts, between friends discussing them and critics analysing them.

⁊ Postmodernism

Postmodernism is a theory that works on a structural and a political level. It is a useful perspective to apply to the texts and topics in Unit 3 and to your research and production in Unit 4. In particular post-modernism may assist in analysing the fragmentary and contradictory nature of many of the contemporary media texts you encounter in relation to the cultural context of the text's production, the visual style of the text and the inter-relationship between media texts.

There is considerable debate over both the definition of postmodernism and when and where it occurs. One way of understanding post-modernism is as the social, political and cultural values that were prevalent at the end of the 20th and early 21st centuries.

The following are some of the identifiable elements of a postmodern context:

- the decline of party politics and trade unionism
- the collapse of communism and a belief in the ability of governments to centrally plan societies
- insecurity and uncertainty
- media-saturated society with instantaneous communication
- an emphasis on difference rather than uniformity
- increasing emphasis on the importance of style and the visual.

These elements can be seen as the context within which contemporary media texts are produced. This culture may be reflected in or constituted by media texts. In a postmodern culture there is a greater sense of 'anything goes', with audiences constructing their own meanings from a range of cultural and media artefacts. Furthermore, it has been suggested that it is increasingly more difficult to produce original media texts; hence a focus on reproducing previous works, such as *Alfie* (2004), a remake of the 1966 British film of the same name, and *Charlie's Angels* (2000), based on the 1976 American TV series.

Lyotard (1984) has suggested that in a post-modern period, over-arching theories or explanations of the world or **metanarratives**, such as Marxism, capitalism, religion and science have been debunked, leading to greater instability in society. It is questionable as to whether this is really the case. It can be argued that there is a greater range of religions and interpretations of previously established religions, so that individuals can take a pick and mix approach to find a religion that suits them. It is possible that people have turned to religious groups, which offer clear guidelines on how to live and consequently offer certainty, as a way of coping with living in an unstable society.

■ Key terms

Metanarratives: over-arching explanations of society sometimes referred to as grand narratives.

In a media-saturated world, individuals can 'channel hop' between TV programmes or click between internet sites, while listening to a range of music from an iPod. As a result different media and film products are being produced, which merge and blend across previously clear boundaries of taste, style and genre.

Identifiable characteristics of post-modern media texts include:

- **intertextuality**
- *bricolage*
- merging of genres, styles and media
- an emphasis on image and style rather than narrative and meaning
- elements that draw attention to the construction of the media text
- playful and ironic elements
- a mixing of elements of 'high' or élite culture within popular culture
- fragmentation
- diversity of representations and viewpoints
- **pastiche** and parody.

Over the last 10 years there have been a growing number of media texts that display some, or all, of these characteristics. The films of director Baz Luhrmann, such as *Romeo + Juliet* (1996) and *Moulin Rouge* (2001), mix narratives from 'high' culture – a Shakespeare play and the opera *La Bohème* – with a pop-video playful and fragmented visual style.

Case study: *The Sopranos*

The American TV series, *The Sopranos* (HBO, 1999–2007), incorporated numerous inter-textual references to previous gangster movies and other popular culture texts, whilst mixing the generic elements of gangster movies and soap operas. It incorporated a number of film-like dream sequences giving it a fragmented feel. Interestingly, in 2007 one of Hilary Clinton's presidential election adverts made numerous inter-textual references to *The Sopranos*. It featured many of the actors from the series who appeared alongside the Clintons in a scene that replicated the final scene of the series, where Tony Soprano's family share a meal in a café. This playful mixing of the genres of political broadcast and popular TV is also popular on YouTube.

There are a range of areas in the media where a post-modern style is easily recognised, as in the following examples.

- DVD boxed sets, which package DVDs on the making of films along with the actual film, drawing attention to how the film was constructed.
- In the cross-over between films and advertising, not only in terms of product placement in films, but also adverts that feature film stars, are shot on lavish film sets and incorporate the visual style of various films.

One of the most influential theorists for understanding the relationship between media and the contemporary post-modern world is Baudrillard (1983). He argued that we live in an era of **hyper-reality**, whereby the daily world and the world of media are merging and media texts seem more real than the reality they seek to convey. In this world media merely

Key terms

Intertextuality: when a media text uses elements or references from other media texts.

Bricolage: the process of creating a media text out of a series of artefacts, styles and signs from other media texts or cultural artefacts.

Pastiche: a creation of a media text out of elements of, or with reference to, other media texts in a mocking or caricatured way.

Hyper-reality: refers to the fact that the distinction between the real world and the media world is disappearing.

AQA Examiner's tip

In an exam, try to illustrate examples of postmodernism in your media studies texts, rather than simply defining the term itself.

represents other media; it is a **simulacrum**. For example, *Headcases* (ITV, 2008), a computer-generated satirical programme, is first and foremost presented as an updated version of the satirical puppet show *Spitting Image* (ITV, 1984–96). *Headcases*, in the main, focuses on celebrities; the butt of its satire being the media representations of celebrities such as Jordon and Peter Andre and their repeated appearances on digital television channels.

Another way in which simulacrums work is through the representation of places. Places can be represented in relation to other media texts rather than any real experience that the audience might have of a place. For example, London can be represented by red buses, taxis, Big Ben and Beatles music; New York by yellow taxi cabs, the Statue of Liberty, Central Park, Bloomingdales and the theme from *Friends* (Channel 4, 1994–2004). Tourists visiting these places will look for the imagery they have seen in media and films and interpret them according to the media representations they have experienced.

■ **Media in action**

In contemporary media one popular example of a post-modern merging of genre, mediums and forms is the inter-relationship between film and video games. Some films are based on video games rather than 'real' life. For example, *Pokémon* (1997), owned by video game giant Nintendo, has become one of the most lucrative game-based media franchises. Five *Pokémon* films (1998–2002) have been produced, followed by a further six films that were released straight onto video and DVD, as well as a number of TV series. Although the films have been criticised as poor quality children's entertainment and a cynical bid to make money, they have been successfully accompanied by the sale of cards, books, toys and other media.

The most well-known example of video-game-based simulacrums are the films based upon the Lara Croft character, namely *Lara Croft: Tomb Raider* (2001), followed by *Lara Croft Tomb Raider: the Cradle of Life* (2003), with a third movie in the planning.

Cyberspace and virtual reality

For many media consumers video games have provided their first encounters with computer generated imaginary worlds. These games enable a **virtual reality** to be created whereby participants can view and move around in an imaginary 3D world. Virtual reality can be used for work and training, for example flight simulators are used to train airline pilots, but in the main it has become a place to play games and act out fantasies, leading to much critical debate.

Criticisms directed at virtual reality see it in dystopian terms, suggesting, for example, that virtual reality:

■ destroys a sense of reality

■ inhibits normal brain development

■ stifles the development of relationships.

Lying behind many of these concerns are anxieties about children and moral panics over new media. There are concerns about the hyper-reality that these texts create. One element of the post-modern media-saturated culture is **cyberspace**. For example, sending an email, purchasing goods online and sending information takes place in a cyber culture. The *Matrix* films (1999 and 2003) took this to another level representing a whole imaginary cyberculture world.

Cyberspace has opened up the scope for audiences to interact much more actively within virtual reality. This is seen particularly where the world of video games is replaced by shared virtual reality on the internet. For example, on the Activeworlds website participants can build worlds, visit shops and interact with shopkeepers, meet new friends and construct identities for themselves. Indeed Haraway (1991) has argued that the ability to construct identities unrestrained by the restrictions of our physical bodies is one of the most liberating elements of cyberspace. However, other critics are particularly concerned about the likelihood of predatory individuals using virtual reality to gain access to vulnerable participants, especially young children and are concerned about youngsters' unsupervised entry into imaginary worlds offered via the internet.

Key terms

Cyberspace: the virtual world of computers and telecommunications, which connects millions of individuals without reference to geographical places.

Investigating media

Undertake internet research on virtual reality games by, for example, visiting the Activeworlds and Outerworlds websites (www.activeworlds.com and www.outerworlds.com), and try and assess the following.

- In what ways is participating in a virtual reality game different from watching a film?
- In what ways is the audience able to be more interactive?
- Do these games represent a hyper-reality and/or a simulacrum?

Chapter summary

This chapter described a range of media theories, which provide alternate explanations of why media texts are constructed the way they are.

- Semiotics, structuralism and post-structuralism are each theories that explain how audiences extrapolate meaning from the text.

- Marxism and liberal pluralism explore the role of the media in supporting or challenging powerful groups and maintaining hegemony.

- Feminism, Queer theory and post-colonialism are theories that discuss the political significance of media texts and representations and how they are embedded with values and ideologies.

- Audience theories explore the ways in which audiences use media texts.

- Post-modernism is an interpretation of the contemporary culture and how it is reflected in media texts.

Approaching texts critically

In Chapters 1 and 2 you were introduced to a range of critical approaches, theories, debates and issues in contemporary media studies. In this chapter you will begin to focus on how you can use all of these to analyse media texts, in particular how you can use them in Unit 3 of the A2 exam. In the examination, Unit 3 has two sections, and the first of these will ask you to compare and contrast two unseen media texts in response to three compulsory questions.

■ Investigating texts

At AS Level, when analysing media texts, you discussed *how* they were constructed; at A2 Level you need to go further and explain *why* media texts are constructed in particular ways. To do this you need to draw upon the key media concepts, theories, critical perspectives and media issues and debates discussed in Chapters 1 and 2. It is also important to think about the wider context in which media texts are produced. When investigating texts, the following areas need to be considered:

■ how to apply concepts and theories to interrogate a media text

■ what issues need to be addressed when investigating media texts

■ what wider contexts need to be explored in understanding media texts

■ how critical perspectives are used in critically analysing texts.

This will enable you to demonstrate that you have met the two assessment objectives of Chapter 3:

■ *AO1* – demonstrate knowledge and understanding of media concepts, contexts and critical debates

■ *AO2* – apply knowledge and understanding when analysing media products and processes to show how meanings and responses are created.

🔍 Applying concepts

Using the core concepts of media investigation learnt at AS Level is an important starting point in analysing any media text. However at A2 Level application of these core concepts needs to go further to include the debates and theories that help explain not just *how* media texts are constructed, but *why* they are constructed in particular ways. It is necessary to look at and understand the inter-relationships between the different core media concepts. These core concepts are:

■ representation

■ ideology and values

■ media language

■ genre and narrative

■ audience

■ institutions.

Representation

Representation refers to what is presented to an audience through a media text. A representation is not reality but is a likeness, an interpretation or even a symbol of the reality being portrayed. In investigating media texts, it is important to consider who holds the power and influence over the construction of media representations, as well as how these representations conform to or challenge other representations in the media. It is also important to consider what ideologies and values influence the construction of any representation.

Ideology and values

Ideology and values reflect the opinions, beliefs and ways of thinking that are characteristic of a particular person, group or nation. Their inclusion in media texts is not always deliberate, but consideration needs to be given to the influence that the ideologies and values of both the producers and the audience may have on a particular media text.

Media language

Media language refers to the wide range of codes used in the construction of a media text to give it meaning. It includes, for example, camera angles and editing, choice of colour and font, the soundtrack and accents spoken. A media producer's choice of specific media language is influenced by a range of factors, such as:

■ pressures to conform to or challenge the genre conventions or media platforms

■ financial or technical limitations

■ the need to meet the expectations of the target audience

■ tendencies to conform to or challenge representational practices

■ an inclination to copy, quote or relate to the styles of media language currently in fashion

■ a desire to express an individual style.

Genre and narrative

Genre is a form of classification that groups together particular media texts, for example, soap operas, hip-hop music, gangster films, social network websites. In interrogating media texts, it is important to ask why specific genres are produced at particular points in history, with reference to economic and institutional factors. It is also important to be aware of how an audience's expectations of a specific genre can influence the construction of that media text.

Narratives are the storylines that media texts use to convey events, meaning, images and representations. Narrative structure is influenced by genre, media platforms, audience expectations and institutional needs, such as keeping to schedule or appealing to certain advertisers.

Audience

'Audience' refers to the people who consume media texts. Remember, however, that consuming media texts is not necessarily a passive activity; it may involve constructing meaning or contributing to the media texts in a range of ways. An example might be posting information and content on websites. It is important to examine how the desire to appeal to specific audiences shapes media texts and consider how audience expectations influence the construction of a particular media text.

Institutions

Institutions are the private or public organisations or companies that produce and/or distribute media texts. Institutions have particular cultures, aims, practices, histories and financial constraints that shape their media output. Certain institutions have established an expertise and reputation for producing or distributing a particular genre of products or have established specific audience profiles.

 Investigating media

- Use the internet to search for the websites of a number of key television, radio, film, web-based and print media institutions, such as Channel 4, BBC, News Corporation or Disney.
- Make a note of each institution's aims, media output, history and guiding principles or practices.
- Consider how the institutions' aims, guiding principles and practices are translated into particular media texts. For example, the BBC's public service ethos of informing, educating and entertaining can be identified in its school programmes, its many lifestyle programmes and on the BBC website.

Addressing issues

Understanding the context in which media texts are produced includes keeping up to date with and understanding the current media debates and issues that are taking place in both the popular media and the academic study of media. Looking at the media supplement of the *Guardian* newspaper on Mondays or reading the online version from the *Guardian's* website are good ways of doing this. Try to build up a file of extracts or printouts, or make notes of any of the following areas:

- changes in media technology and the digital revolution
- debates about regulation and censorship of the media
- any moral panics about the media and within the media
- globalisation
- debates about the effects of media on its audience
- debates about news values (see pages 11–14 of Chapter 1) utilised in media
- changes in the ownership and control of any media institutions.

When presented with unseen media texts, consider any current debates and issues that may be raised by these texts. For example, there have been debates in the media recently about the use of size zero models and pressure on texts aimed at young girls to avoid an emphasis on ultra-thin images. In looking at representation in teenage girls' magazines, this debate should be borne in mind. As with critical perspectives, there are no right or wrong debates and issues, but when thinking about any issues that may be raised considering the current, relevant debates around the issue is a good starting point from which to analyse a media text.

Investigating media

Look at the following pairs of media texts:

Example 1

See Fig. 3.1 and Fig. 3.2.

Example 2

See Fig. 3.3 and Fig. 3.4.

Example 3

See Fig. 3.5 and Fig. 3.6.

■ Write down any points of interest that relate to the core concepts of investigating media.

■ Then write down:

  – any media debates or issues that are raised by the examples

  – any relevant contextual issues that may help in analysing the examples

  – how the application of a particular critical perspective will assist in analysing the examples.

Example 1

Outrage at Bimbo website for girls

▶ Children of 9 urged to embrace plastic surgery

▶ Parents attack perils of deadly role models

Steve Bird

A website that encourages girls as young as 9 to embrace plastic surgery and extreme dieting in the search for the perfect figure was condemned as lethal by parents' groups and healthcare experts yesterday.

The Miss Bimbo internet game has attracted prepubescent girls who are told to buy their virtual characters breast enlargement surgery and to keep them "waif thin" with diet pills.

Healthcare professionals, a parents' group and an organisation representing people suffering anorexia and bulimia criticised the website for sending a dangerous message to impressionable children.

In the month since it opened the site, which is aimed at girls aged from 9 to 16, has attracted 200,000

The internet game, aimed at girls aged 9 to16, gives users "bimbo dollars" to buy lingerie, diet pills and nightclub outfits. It has attracted 200,000 members in Britain

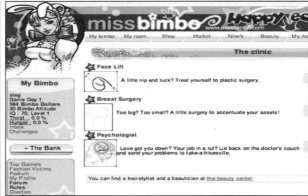

members. Players keep a constant watch on the weight, wardrobe, wealth and happiness of their character to create "the coolest, richest and most famous bimbo in the world". Competing against other children they earn "bimbo dollars" to buy plastic surgery, diet pills, facelifts, lingerie and fashionable nightclub outfits.

Dee Dawson, the medical director of Rhodes Farm Clinic, which treats girls aged from 8 to 18 who suffer eating disorders, said: "This is as lethal as pro-anorexia

websites. A lot of children will get caught up with the extremely damaging and appalling messages."

Susan Ringwood, the chief executive of Beat, an organisation that supports those suffering eating disorders, said that the website could make girls believe that weight and body size manipulation were acceptable.

This is as lethal as pro-anorexia sites
Dee Dawson

Fig. 3.1 *Newspaper article about Miss Bimbo website (**The Times**, 25 March 2008)*

Addiction to internet 'is an illness'

Heavy users suffer isolation, fatigue and withdrawal symptoms, says a psychiatrist

by David Smith

Technology Correspondent

Long hours spent online can cause a compulsive-impulsive disorder.

TENSE? ANGRY? Can't get online? Internet addiction is now a serious public health issue that should be officially recognised as a clinical disorder, according to a leading psychiatrist.

Excessive gaming, viewing online pornography, emailing and text messaging have been identified as causes of a compulsive-impulsive disorder by Dr Jerald Block, author of an editorial for the respected *American Journal of Psychiatry*. Block argues that the disorder is now so common that it merits inclusion in the *Diagnostic and Statistical Manual of Mental Disorders*, the profession's primary resource to categorise and diagnose mental illnesses. He says internet addiction has four main components:

- Excessive use, often associated with a loss of sense of time or a neglect of basic drives;
- Withdrawal, including feelings of anger, tension and/or depression when the computer is inaccessible;

- The need for better computers, more software, or more hours of use;
- Negative repercussions, including arguments, lying, poor achievement, social isolation and fatigue.

A primary case study is South Korea, which has the greatest usage of broadband in the world. Block points out that, after 10 people died from blood clots – from remaining seated for long periods – in internet cafes and another was murdered because of an online game, South Korea 'considers internet addiction one of its most serious public health issues'. The government estimates that around 210,000 South Korean children are affected and in need of treatment, of whom 80 per cent might need

drugs targeting the brain and nearly a quarter could need to go to hospital.

Block, a psychiatrist at the Oregon Health & Science University in Portland, writes that the extent of the disorder is more difficult to estimate in America because

people tend to surf at home instead of in internet cafes. But he believes there are similar cases, concluding: 'Unfortunately internet addiction is resistant to treatment, entails significant risks and has high relapse rates.'

ARE YOU A NET JUNKIE?

If you answer 'yes' to five or more of these questions, you may have an internet addiction.

- Do you feel preoccupied with the internet? (Think about your online activity or anticipate your next online session.)
- Do you need increasing amounts of time on the net in order to achieve satisfaction?
- Have you repeatedly made unsuccessful efforts to control, cut back or stop internet use?
- Do you feel restless, moody, depressed, or irritable when attempting to cut down or stop internet use?
- Do you stay online longer than originally intended?
- Have you jeopardised or risked the loss

of a significant relationship, job, educational or career opportunity because of the internet?

- Have you lied to family members, a therapist or others to conceal the extent of your involvement with the internet?
- Do you use it to escape from problems (eg, feelings of helplessness, guilt, anxiety, depression)?

Source: Centre for Internet Addiction Recovery (www.netaddiction.com)

Fig. 3.2 *Newspaper article about internet addiction* (**Observer**, *23 March 2008*)

The two newspaper articles used in **Example 1** (Figs 3.1 and 3.2) in the exercise above invite debate around media audiences. In relation to the articles' social context, they can be seen as reflecting the growth of new media and the moral panics surrounding its effects, for example the anxieties about early sexualisation in young girls, anorexia and diet found in the article on the Miss Bimbo website (Fig. 3.1). A range of media debates and issues are raised here, including dystopian or utopian perspectives on new media, the regulation of new media as well as raising debates around passive and active audiences. A Marxist or feminist critical perspective may be utilised to explore the values and ideologies of websites such as Miss Bimbo. The main aim of the website is to make money but it can also be seen as promoting the make-up, fashion and plastic surgery industries.

Example 2

Fig. **3.3** *Newspaper article about 'Black Britannia'* (**Daily Mirror**, *20 March 2008*)

MUST-SEE TV

PICK OF THE DAY

The No.1 Ladies's Detective Agency

BBC1, 9pm

It would be surprising if this feature-length adaption of Alexander McCall Smith's bestseller were not a triumph: it is produced by Sydney Pollack and directed by Anthony Minghella, who co-wrote it with Richard Curtis.

The acting is top-notch, too, with Grammy Award-winning singer Jill Scott (above) as Precious Ramotswe, the sweet but sharp-eyed sleuth who overcomes considerable odds (a violent ex-husband and a stillborn child) to set up her own private detective agency. Scott is beautifully supported by Anika Noni Rose (*Dreamgirls*), who plays eccentric secretary Grace Makutsi, and Lucian Msamati (*Spooks*) as JLB Maketoni, an honourable mechanic who falls in love with Precious, despite her annoying habit of driving with the handbrake on.

When Precious's agency opens, opposite the Last Chance Hair Salon in the Botswanan capital of Gaborone, business is non-existent. It's not long, though, before suspicious locals start knocking on her door, and soon she is staking out the house of a 'dubious daddy' and slinking around a dodgy nightclub in the hope of catching a cheating hubby mid-grope. There's some heavier casework, too, namely tracking down a missing boy who Precious suspects has been abducted by dealers selling children's body parts to witch doctors for medicine. Beautiful photography, costumes, sets and actors – everyone is good-looking – plus a colourful insight into life in Botswana and a gently witty script makes for first-class, feel-good Sunday-night viewing.

★★★★★

Fig. **3.4** *Newspaper TV preview about The No. 1 Ladies Detective Agency* (**Mail on Sunday**, *23 March 2008*)

The two newspaper extracts in **Example 2** (Figs 3.3 and 3.4) raise debates about representation. The relevant political and social contexts that frame these articles can be found in debates about what it means to be British in a multi-cultural society. These debates coexist with debates on racism, racial tension and racially motivated violence. A range of media debates and issues including celebrity, hegemony (see page 50) and the politics and power of representation can also be discussed in relation to the two newspaper articles. It is also relevant to draw upon a post-colonialism (see page 59) perspective and to discuss the role of the BBC as a public service institution.

The articles used in **Example 3** (Figs 3.5 and 3.6) suggest discussion of media institutions, both the media producing institutions, such as the BBC, and the institutions regulating the media, such as Ofcom. It is important when comparing these articles to consider the very different

Example 3

Viewers attack BBC for foul-mouthed comedy

Adam Sherwin – Media Correspondent

The *Catherine Tate Christmas Special* was the most offensive programme yet broadcast by the BBC on Christmas Day, according to complaints from outraged viewers.

Ofcom, the television watchdog, is to investigate complaints of excessive swearing by Tate's foul-mouthed Nan character. A sketch about a Northern Irish family prompted accusations of bigotry. The BBC defended the sketch show, which attracted 6.4 million viewers to BBC One at 10.30 on Christmas night, describing the award-winning Tate as a comedy "genius". But Ofcom said that it would ask if the programme had been appropriate for Christmas night, when many children would be watching.

The programme, which followed the more placid *To the Manor Born*, began with an avalanche of swearing from Nan Taylor. Kathy Burke, playing her daughter, embarked upon a swearing competition with Nan. A

representation of a Northern Ireland family receiving Christmas presents attracted complaints that Tate was exploiting lazy stereotypes. The grandmother opened her present to find a balaclava, which she put over her head. Her husband received a knuckleduster and the mother received an apron with a balaclava-clad terrorist and the words "Remember Everything, Forgive Nothing". A gay son was handed a chocolate penis.

One viewer wrote on the BBC online message board: "What had the contents of this to do with Christmas? Crude language just for the sake of it – and being repeated time and time again." Another commented: "Maybe the lowest point for BBC One on Christmas Day ... ever."

Ms Tate admitted that the language may have got out of hand. "I don't know how this Christmas special got so depraved because it isn't what I set out to do," she told *Radio Times*.

Fig. 3.5 *Newspaper article about swearing on the BBC* (**The Times**, *28 December 2007*)

Fallout as Ramsay drops 'C bomb'

Gordon Ramsay, who served up a second course of 80 F-words during an episode of his programme

Australia may review TV code after chef's outburst

Paul Larter Brisbane

A liberal peppering of profanities would hardly be out of place at lunch in the heart of a robust political culture. The Australian Parliament was reaching for the water jug, however, after Gordon Ramsay's latest televisual taste test.

The country's broadcasting code of conduct could be overhauled after a recent episode of *Ramsay's Kitchen Nightmares* featured the hot-blooded chef spitting out two C-words. Then,

for a second course, 80 F-words, in prime-time viewing.

Such outbursts have prompted just 60 complaints since the free-to-air Nine Network recently brought the programme forward an hour from its 9.30pm timeslot, but some of the most unhappy customers are in Parliament.

Cory Bernardi, of the Liberal Party, part of the opposition coalition, said the "dropping of the C bomb" during a recent episode was a word too far and his views have inspired a parliamentary inquiry.

The ruling Labor Party and minor parties have voted with the coalition to establish an investigation into the frequency and use of swearing on television, the effectiveness of classification standards and the complaints process. "I am a viewer and I have quite enjoyed the show but with the dropping of the C bomb and F-words on several occasions

I believe we are reaching the absolute limits of acceptability," he said.

The senator denied being a "wowser", Australian slang for a spoilsport, but he complained that the frequency and range of profanities on television was increasing and it was time to set stricter boundaries.

Ramsay's Kitchen Nightmares has become one of Australia's most watched programmes, topping the ratings in its timeslot nationally with an average audience of 1.4 million.

The Office of Film and Literature Classification, an independent statutory body, had recommended the series for mature audiences, who are given warning of moderate coarse language. Frequent swearing is permitted if it is important to the storyline and in context.

The channel argues that Ramsay's swearing was indicative

of the stressful environment in the kitchens of leading restaurants and that in another context such language might be bleeped out. "This is about people's freedom of speech. This is what people have chosen to watch," the network said.

Family advocacy groups say, however, that classification standards appear to be slipping and could contribute to a decline in social standards. "I think there are a lot of indications that broadcasters are pushing the boundaries," Angela Conway, of the Australian Family Association, said.

Of the 914 written complaints against television stations in 2006–07, 18 were upheld and only a few were for coarse language. Four related to an interview with a pop performer and one to an interview with an Australian Rules footballer after a grand final.

Fig. 3.6 *Newspaper article about Gordon's Ramsay's bad language* (**The Times**, *24 March 2008*)

culture and everyday speech is seen as more constrained and regulated than in Australia and this needs to be considered, as well as issues around media regulation and censorship, media effects, the politics of representation and globalisation. Semiotics, post-structuralism and post-modernism (see pages 45–70) may provide useful critical perspectives to discuss the significance of language raised by both these newspaper articles.

Exploring contexts

An important consideration for investigating media texts is how the social, political, historical and **economic context** of both a media text's production and its consumption influences why a media text is constructed in a certain way. The concerns, values, ideologies, attitudes and politics of the society in which a media text is produced and consumed all play a vital role in shaping a media text.

Examiner's tip

As a Media Studies student it is important to apply your knowledge of concepts, issues and debates, contexts and critical perspectives and their inter-relationship to the media texts that you are presented with in the exam.

■ **Key terms**

Economic context: refers to the financial opportunities and constraints that govern a media text's production and distribution.

■ Media in action

What is meant by social, political historical and economic context?

Social context refers to the society in which is a text is produced. That means the society's values, norms, ways of life and everyday practices – including clothes, eating, use of language and attitudes to gender and sexuality. Social context changes over time and is historically specific. If you watch an old black and white movie on television, for example, the language, behaviour and attitudes of the characters may seem very dated.

Historical context relates to major political events that may influence the media, for example economic crises, wars and changes of government (in Chapter 1, pages 18–20 we looked, for example, at the influence of 9/11 on the media).

Political regimes, laws of censorship and economic constraints and the need to make a profit from most media products all constrain the nature of media texts.

Social and political contexts

The social and political contexts influencing a media text are often very clear. For example, the film *Dirty Pretty Things* (2002) reflects the moral panic at the time over illegal immigration through its depiction of how illegal workers in London are exploited. Recent American films, *World Trade Center* (2006) and *Charlie Wilson's War* (2007), reflect the USA's attempt to come to terms with the events of 9/11. The values and ideologies conveyed in these media texts can be understood as reflecting or constructing the values and ideologies of the society in which they were produced and initially consumed. All the core concepts for investigating media are influenced by contextual factors. For example, an awareness of the context of post 9/11 and the opposition by many to the Iraq War will contribute significantly to an analysis of the films *World Trade Center* and *Charlie Wilson's War*.

Remember that it is important to be aware of both the context in which institutions produce and distribute media texts, as well as the context in which an audience consumes the media text. Thinking about the context of an audience is particularly important in a globalised media world where producers and consumers of media texts may be in very different countries, with very social and political contexts. Assumptions about audiences, their expectations, and how and where they will consume a media text, all also influence the construction of a media text. For example, a mainstream blockbuster film such as *Spiderman 3* (2007) assumes that its primary audience will be watching in the film on a large screen. The producers therefore make use of technology to create special effects and stunts, which will have their maximum effect on a large screen. In addition, as a mainstream Hollywood film, *Spiderman 3* was made with the expectation of world-wide sales, therefore producers may have been subject to constraints in the film's construction so as to ensure they appeal to as wide an audience as possible.

Cross-cultural factors and different society values, ideologies and attitudes explain why instead of exporting television programmes directly, television producers often sell or franchise the idea for a programme to other countries. The idea is then constructed to fit in with the values, ideologies and cultural milieu of the country in which it will be consumed. Examples of this include comedy programmes, such as *The Office* (2001 and 2005), reality TV shows such as *Big Brother* (1999–) and quiz programmes such as *Who Wants to be a Millionaire?* (1998–). For example, the producers of *Big Brother* in other European countries such as Holland and Italy geared the programme to be much more sexually explicit than it was in the UK.

> ### Key terms
>
> **Cross-cultural factors:** the differences in culture between nations and groups within nations. Culture includes values, attitudes and everyday practices and lifestyles.

> **Thinking about media**
>
> ▪ Select one British-made media text and consider how you think it would need to be adjusted, altered and developed to be sold to the USA, India or Japan.
>
> ▪ Look at a popular media text that is produced in another country (a US film, computer game or an Australian soap opera). In what ways do you think it would differ if it had been produced in the UK?

Historical context

Cultures, values and ideologies are not static; they change over time. For example, the last 30 years have seen changes in attitudes to issues such as race, ethnicity, the role of men and women and homosexuality. Recognising what a text's historical context is helps explain why particular representations occur. Understanding a media text's historical context is also an important key to interrogating media texts.

> ### Investigating media
>
> Watch TV programmes or films that are 20 or 30 years old (pre-1980) and think about the following questions.
>
> ▪ How are the media languages (spoken and moving image) used in these media texts different from those found in contemporary media texts?
>
> ▪ In what way do representations in terms of race, class, gender and sexuality differ from contemporary texts?
>
> ▪ Are there any groups that are not represented within the text?
>
> ▪ What values, attitudes and ideologies are articulated in the text that you would be surprised to experience in a contemporary media text?

Changes in relation to media technology also form part of a text's historical context. Consequently a film made in the 1950s may seem to use static camera work and slow editing, which is due to the fact that the cameras that directors were working with were far more cumbersome and unwieldy than those used today, and editing was undertaken by literally cutting and joining strips of film.

It is not merely differences in technology or values and ideologies that make historical context important when investigating media texts. An awareness of the political concerns and issues of the historical period in which a media text is produced also provides insight into a media text. For example, Ken Loach's award-winning film *The Wind that Shakes the Barley* (2006) is a period drama set in Ireland after the First World War. It follows the IRA guerrilla war against the British and the internal strife that followed the establishment of the Irish Free State in 1922. However, the film was released in 2006 during the Iraq War, so its exploration of the brutality utilised by an occupying force fighting a guerrilla war gave the film a contemporary contextual relevance. To many, the film was seen as a representation of Loach's criticism of Britain's involvement in the Iraq War.

Historical events, such as wars and changes of government, all provide important contextual factors that may affect the construction of a media text. It may be useful to give yourself an overview of the key historical events that have taken place in Britain and the US in the last 50 years so that you are able to understand the historical context of a media text. Use the BBC history website (www.bbc.co.uk/history) or Wikipedia (www.wikipedia.org) to broaden your contextual knowledge of events.

National and historical contexts can also influence the stylistic characteristics and use of media language in particular texts. Producers of media texts are influenced by the other media texts, which then form a national media culture for a particular period. Almost all media texts make inter-textual references to other texts; even a text that challenges the dominant conventions of the contemporary media milieu can only be really understood in relation to an understanding of this media milieu.

🔍 Case study: heritage films

Since the 1980s an important strand of British film and television production has been **heritage** films and history TV programmes. Examples include *Shakespeare in Love* (1998), *Elizabeth, the Golden Age* (2007) and *The Other Boleyn Girl* (2008) in film, and the popular Channel 4 series *Edwardian Country House* (2002). These texts are often based on novels, with a heavy focus on period authenticity and country house settings, linear narrative structure, conventional camera work and editing, and an emphasis on the lives of the wealthy.

Media analysts, such as Andrew Higson (2003), have seen heritage films as a response to the social, political and economic context of Britain at the end of the 20th and early 21st century. It is suggested that the media's focus with heritage is a response to Britain's loss of economic and political power and therefore highlights previous periods when the country was more influential.

Looking at the economic context surrounding the distribution and exhibition of heritage films suggests an alternative view. This view says that heritage films and programmes have been produced because they are a very commercially viable version of '**Britishness**' for the American market.

Investigating media

■ Visit the British Film Industry (BFI)'s online resources on the history of film and television (www.bfi.org.uk and www.screenonline.org.uk) and the National Media Museum's websites (www.nationalmediamuseum.org.uk) to learn more about the historical shifts in media technology and development of media culture in Britain. For the web addresses, see the e-resources or do a search on the web.

■ Construct a timeline or chart of the significant changes in the media in the 20th and 21st centuries.

Key terms

Heritage: refers to media texts that are set in or portray the past, in an often idealised or romanticised way.

Britishness: refers to the essence of what it is means to be British. This is more often a media representation than an agreed shared set of values.

Economic context

The expected world-wide media sales contribute to the economic context governing a film's production. Alternative media products that have limited national audiences are likely to be constrained to fit within a tighter financial context.

■ Thinking about media

Try and make a list of how old media texts are recycled and redistributed, for example, via the internet, as freebies in newspapers etc. What contextual factors bring this about?

The economic context of a media text includes the following:

■ the economic framework of production needs to consider how the production of the text is being funded, and whether there is limited or plentiful finance

■ the issues and economics of distribution and/or exhibition, including how the text will be paid for – via purchase price, advertising or subscription – and how this might influence it

■ globalisation and cross-cultural factors, such as the need to sell the text or idea of a text in more than one country.

Using a critical perspective

Using a critical perspective when analysing media texts means utilising the core concepts (see pages 41–43) of media analysis, as well as drawing on your understanding of the theories, current debates and issues found in media studies. Some of the theories discussed in the previous chapters may relate to specific concepts. For example, debates about globalisation and Marxism and political economy may inform discussion about institutions, whereas debates about audience power, active audiences and post-modernism inform discussions about the role of the audience.

Alternatively some theories provide an overarching critical perspective through which particular media texts can be analysed, for example:

■ semiotics and post-structuralism

■ Marxism or liberal pluralism

■ feminism and post-feminism

■ Queer theory

■ race and post-colonialism

■ post-modernism.

You can use these theories as a starting point for investigating texts and then draw on the relevant core concepts to deepen your investigation. In the past media academics utilised one of these overarching critical perspectives in their analysis of media texts. For example, Modeleski (1982)

Fig. 3.7 *Look at this film poster for the film* **The Manchurian Candidate** *(2004) and try to decide what theory or theories would be useful for analysis*

looked at the soap opera genre from a feminist perspective; Collins (1992) explored the television drama series *Twin Peaks* (Channel 4, 1990) from a post-modern perspective; while Dyer (1997) looked at film from the perspective of race.

It is more common in contemporary media studies to take a more eclectic view of critical perspectives and therefore select the perspectives that seem most appropriate for the concerns and themes of the individual media text.

Case study: *Heat* magazine

Heat is a gossip magazine that was established in 1999. The magazine now reaches sales of nearly 600,000 copies. It is owned by Emap, one of the largest publishers of magazines in the UK, as well as being a cross- media conglomerate with significant advertising and retail businesses. *Heat* is now available online, as well as on radio and mobile phone platforms.

Heat magazine can be analysed according to any of the critical perspectives mentioned on pages 43–44. Both the front cover of the printed magazine and the opening page of the website lend themselves to a close semiotic analysis, with specific reference to media language used, for example, the use of the colour red for the word 'heat' signifies the hotness of the gossip in the text. The range of bright colours and crowded layout of the page signify the text's popular and frivolous content.

Post-structuralist analysis would raise the question as to whether the meanings of the various signifiers (colours used, images, fonts etc.) were fixed or if they are interpreted differently by different audiences.

Marxist perspectives could be used to analyse the capitalist production process of the magazine and Emap as an institution. The role of advertising revenue and the degree to which the magazine contributes to the hegemonic consumerist values and ideologies could also be

Fig. 3.8 *There is a range of critical perspectives that can be used to analyse contemporary media texts (***Heat***, 3–9 May 2008)*

Fig. 3.9 *A range of feminist perspectives can be useful in analysing this feature (***Heat***, 26 April–2 May 2008)*

investigated using a Marxist perspective. Notice, for example, the emphasis on the image of the female stars and their designer clothes.

A feminist perspective can be employed to explore the representation of women in the magazine and whether they remain the object of the male gaze. Alternatively a post-feminist perspective would see these women represented as playing at being 'girlie' in a 'tongue-in-cheek' way or even as drawing attention to the way in which gender is merely a performance that individuals engage in (see Chapter 2, pages 54–56). Feminist perspectives can also explore the uses and gratifications of the predominantly female audience. It can be argued that the magazine provides information, social interaction and entertainment.

Queer theory could be used to explore the heterosexual representations, values and ideologies within the magazine and to discuss the appeal of Russell Brand's image as playing with gender norms. In addition, it can also be used to look at the interpretations placed on the mainly female audience's consumption of images of women.

Critical perspectives based upon race and post-colonialism illuminate the construction of 'whiteness' in the magazine, illustrated by the absence or marginalisation of non-white representation in these examples and the discourses that surround this representation. This may lead to a discussion of whether the magazine and its construction of beauty are indicative of the values and ideologies that predominate in a post-colonial, multi-cultural Britain. Given that the magazine focuses upon media and celebrity, the very limited non-white representation could be seen as a reflection of the limited spaces for non-white representation or the lower status given to non-white celebrities.

Finally a post-modernist perspective of *Heat* magazine could focus on the irreverence and playful media language style. An example is the letter about Trevor Eve and the image of a head posted onto the body of an old man under the title 'wrinkly torso of the week'. The inter-textual media focus of the celebrities in the text, the range of readings that active audiences could place on these ironic pastiches, is varied.

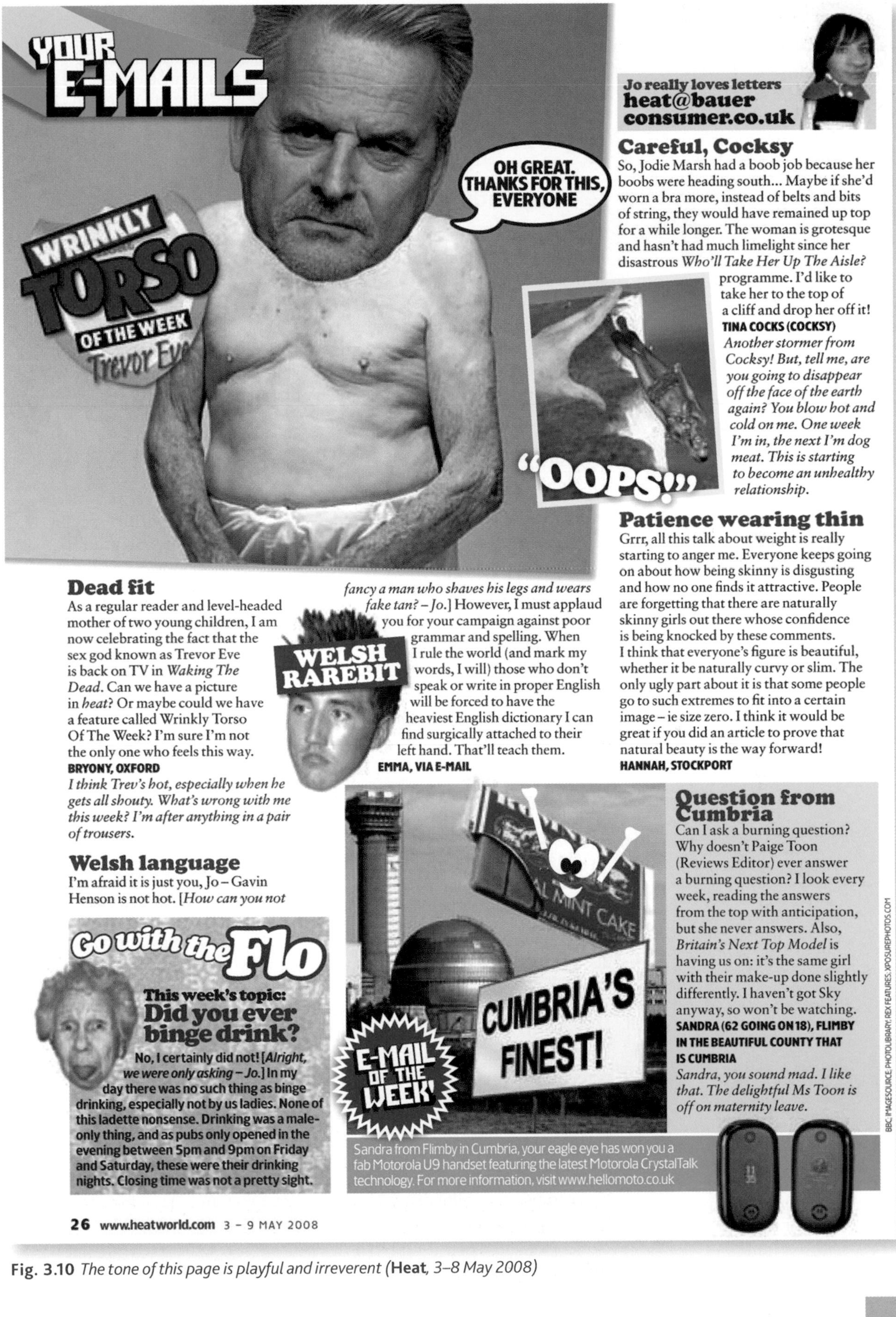

YOUR E-MAILS

OH GREAT. THANKS FOR THIS, EVERYONE

WRINKLY TORSO OF THE WEEK Trevor Eve

"OOPS!"

Jo really loves letters
heat@bauer consumer.co.uk

Careful, Cocksy

So, Jodie Marsh had a boob job because her boobs were heading south... Maybe if she'd worn a bra more, instead of belts and bits of string, they would have remained up top for a while longer. The woman is grotesque and hasn't had much limelight since her disastrous *Who'll Take Her Up The Aisle?* programme. I'd like to take her to the top of a cliff and drop her off it!
TINA COCKS (COCKSY)
Another stormer from Cocksy! But, tell me, are you going to disappear off the face of the earth again? You blow hot and cold on me. One week I'm in, the next I'm dog meat. This is starting to become an unhealthy relationship.

Patience wearing thin

Grrr, all this talk about weight is really starting to anger me. Everyone keeps going on about how being skinny is disgusting and how no one finds it attractive. People are forgetting that there are naturally skinny girls out there whose confidence is being knocked by these comments. I think that everyone's figure is beautiful, whether it be naturally curvy or slim. The only ugly part about it is that some people go to such extremes to fit into a certain image – ie size zero. I think it would be great if you did an article to prove that natural beauty is the way forward!
HANNAH, STOCKPORT

Dead fit

As a regular reader and level-headed mother of two young children, I am now celebrating the fact that the sex god known as Trevor Eve is back on TV in *Waking The Dead*. Can we have a picture in *heat*? Or maybe could we have a feature called Wrinkly Torso Of The Week? I'm sure I'm not the only one who feels this way.
BRYONY, OXFORD
I think Trev's hot, especially when he gets all shouty. What's wrong with me this week? I'm after anything in a pair of trousers.

Welsh language

I'm afraid it is just you, Jo – Gavin Henson is not hot. [*How can you not*

WELSH RAREBIT

fancy a man who shaves his legs and wears fake tan? – Jo.] However, I must applaud you for your campaign against poor grammar and spelling. When I rule the world (and mark my words, I will) those who don't speak or write in proper English will be forced to have the heaviest English dictionary I can find surgically attached to their left hand. That'll teach them.
EMMA, VIA E-MAIL

Question from Cumbria

Can I ask a burning question? Why doesn't Paige Toon (Reviews Editor) ever answer a burning question? I look every week, reading the answers from the top with anticipation, but she never answers. Also, *Britain's Next Top Model* is having us on: it's the same girl with their make-up done slightly differently. I haven't got Sky anyway, so won't be watching.
SANDRA (62 GOING ON 18), FLIMBY IN THE BEAUTIFUL COUNTY THAT IS CUMBRIA
Sandra, you sound mad. I like that. The delightful Ms Toon is off on maternity leave.

Go with the Flo

This week's topic: Did you ever binge drink?

No, I certainly did not! [*Alright, we were only asking – Jo.*] In my day there was no such thing as binge drinking, especially not by us ladies. None of this ladette nonsense. Drinking was a male-only thing, and as pubs only opened in the evening between 5pm and 9pm on Friday and Saturday, these were their drinking nights. Closing time was not a pretty sight.

CUMBRIA'S FINEST!

E-MAIL OF THE WEEK

Sandra from Flimby in Cumbria, your eagle eye has won you a fab Motorola U9 handset featuring the latest Motorola CrystalTalk technology. For more information, visit www.hellomoto.co.uk

BBC. IMAGESOURCE. PHOTOLIBRARY. REX FEATURES. XPOSUREPHOTOS.COM

Fig. 3.10 *The tone of this page is playful and irreverent (***Heat***, 3–8 May 2008)*

It is important to remember that the examiner is not asking you to list the learning theories, concepts and critical perspectives, without their application to media texts. The concepts, theories and critical perspectives must be used to interrogate the media texts that you will encounter in Section A of Unit 3, with an awareness of the current issues and critical perspectives to explain *why* the media text is the way it is.

Importantly you are likely to be comparing texts from two different media platforms and need to consider the relevance of different theories for each platform.

The three questions do not carry the same number of marks. The allocation of marks should guide the amount of time you spend on each question. You have a total of one hour to complete this section of the exam.

Investigating media

Look for examples of texts from different media platforms that can be analysed using different critical perspectives. Examples are a web-based text that is open to feminist or queer readings, a film or TV programme that can be analysed in relation to post-colonialism and the politics of race.

■ Responding to texts

This section focuses on how to respond to media texts in an exam situation. A2 Media Studies – Unit 3: Media Critical Perspectives is designed to test synoptic skills, what you have learnt during your media studies course and to see if you have begun to formulate your own views of the media and the role of media in today's society. In Section A of the exam you will be given two unseen media texts that will form the stimulus for your answers to three compulsory questions. The texts may be taken from any of the three media platforms:

■ print

■ e-media

■ audio or moving image texts.

Texts from each of these three mediums are produced within specific economic and institutional contexts; they have their own textual conventions and are consumed in different circumstances by different audiences; an awareness of these should frame your response to the texts.

The three compulsory questions will give you the opportunity to show the general media knowledge and understanding you have gained from your study of concepts, media forms and platforms, as well as the specific media knowledge and understanding of the two pre-set topics and the debates and theories relating to your case studies. This is particularly important if you are asked to compare and contrast texts from two different mediums.

You will have 15 minutes to watch or listen or read and study the unseen stimulus media. If there are audio or moving image texts you will be able to see them three times. It is advisable to just study the text on the first viewing or listening and to take notes during the next two viewings. If you are given printed copies of the text, begin with your overall image or impression and then look in more detail at each aspect of the text.

Your response to the text will be framed by the concepts, contexts, debates, issues and critical perspectives that you have studied during this course. However, it can be challenging to organise your learning into appropriate responses to the questions. The first question is likely to ask you to compare and contrast the two given texts – study both texts carefully to find any similarities and differences. One way of organising your thoughts is to consider each text in relation to:

■ production

■ text

■ audience.

You can use the following questions to give you an idea of how to respond to an unseen text.

Production

Production issues to be considered focus on the influence of media institutions and the wider context in which the text was produced.

Media institutions

- ■ Is the text produced by an alternative or mainstream institution?
- ■ Is there evidence that a conglomerate organisation is attempting to tie this media text in with other media texts they also produce or control – music, computer games, Internet sites etc.?
- ■ Has the text been produced by a national, multinational or global institution?

Wider context

- ■ How has the national context in which the text was produced shaped the text?
- ■ Are there any economic, ideological, political and/or cultural concerns that can be identified within the text?
- ■ When was the text produced and how might that influence the text's focus and themes?
- ■ How has the text been shaped by economic concerns, for example, raising advertising revenue, selling the media product, making a profit?

Text

When thinking about the text, draw upon the core concepts for analysing media looking in particular at how media language, narrative and representation are utilised to convey values and ideologies.

- ■ To what extent does this text challenge or conform to the conventions of its particular medium – print, e-media, audio or moving image-based text?
- ■ What genre(s) does the text belong to and to what extent does this text conform to or challenge the genre conventions? Is this linked to the context of production and/or consumption?
- ■ What narrative conventions or codes does this text utilise and why?
- ■ Who is represented in this text and how? What is the political significance of these representations?
- ■ Does the narrative structure convey values and ideologies? If so, to which groups in society do these values and ideologies belong?
- ■ Does this text serve to manufacture consent for powerful groups or to represent a plurality of voices and opinions?
- ■ Which groups in society have their values and ideologies portrayed in this text and why?
- ■ Is the text's main reference point other media texts or lived experience or everyday life?
- ■ To what extent does the text rely upon inter-textual references, irony and *bricolage*?

Audience

'Audience' focuses on who is consuming this media text, how they are consuming it and in what context they are consuming it.

- ■ Is this a primary, secondary or tertiary media?
- ■ How, in what context and by whom is this text consumed?
- ■ Is there a niche or general audience for this text?

■ Are there other audiences who will also consume it?

■ Does the audience continue to consume or gain pleasure from the text in other areas of the media?

■ Does this text raise issues in relation to media effects or moral panics?

■ To what extent does the audience consume this text actively?

■ Is this text open to a range of different readings, for example, readings from a queer theory perspective?

These questions are not exhaustive; they serve as a starting point to help you respond to texts in ways that do not just consider how media text is constructed but also why it is constructed in a particular way.

💡 Approaches to moving image texts

The economic context and institutional context of moving image texts are important factors to consider when analysing this type of media text. Especially in relation to the dominance of Hollywood, the significance of production and distribution institutions, stars and directors on the shaping of film texts must be seen in relation to the influence of the economics of production. Films rely on a wide range of revenue streams: ticket sales; DVDs; TV rights; tie-ins (for example, McDonald's Happy Meal promotions tied in with children's films) and the sales of related products such as toys, books, games, mugs etc. Meeting these needs often shapes the construction of film texts.

The economic contextual framework of television production is a highly competitive multi-channel, globalised television environment. The availability of thousands of hours of television programming has resulted in a severe squeeze on a producer's revenue from advertising, sponsorship and subscription or licence fees. In responding to TV texts, you need to be aware that tight budgets have led to the rise of reality TV, lifestyle TV, chat shows and a range of cheaply produced programmes. These programmes have been accused of 'dumbing down' programming standards. Criticisms of television in this economic context have often focused on its lack of innovation and a tendency to use tried and trusted formats.

The narrative of moving image texts is highly significant and the establishment of action or enigma narrative is the key in gaining audience interest. It is important to be aware of the specific media language utilised by moving image texts, for example, the importance of editing, the use of direct address in television or the importance of the setting and *mise-en-scène*. The presumed domestic setting of the television audience and consequent 'family' orientation of much programming influences the representational practices of many moving image texts. Television has a tendency to focus on families or domestic and everyday relationships and events, as well as using domestic settings. For example, many chat shows construct the set to look like a sitting room of a house with sofas and coffee tables.

An awareness of the different and changing audience consumption patterns of moving image texts should also frame a response to these texts. Whilst films watched in cinemas may be a primary media, television is increasingly becoming a secondary media, occasionally glanced at, often only on as a background to other activities. TV texts therefore use sound, especially music, to focus distracted audiences and often recap on narratives, for example, at the beginning of the show or after commercial breaks. Audiences are also often given 'tasters' of future elements of the programme to encourage them to watch more attentively.

Investigating media

Keep a diary of your television consumption in one day: how often are you busy with another activity while the TV is on? How do you think this is reflected in the very different construction of daytime and prime-time TV texts?

Watch the opening five minutes of a two daytime television programmes, for example, a chat show such as *The Jeremy Kyle Show* (ITV, 2005–current) and a lifestyle programme, such as *To Buy or Not to Buy* (BBC One, 2003–current). Make notes and compare the texts in relation to:

■ how they establish and try and draw their audience into the show's narratives

■ how they are constructed for casual or distracted viewing

■ their focus on family and domestic life

■ the costs of production and the institutions that produce them.

Approaches to print-based texts

Print-based media are in a time of change with traditional daily newspapers steadily losing their readership and the remaining readership being increasingly older. One of the reasons for declining sales of newspapers is the availability of alternative media sources of news, such as television, radio and the Internet. Consequently newspapers are becoming more focused on discussion, opinion, gossip and celebrity; a move that is often criticised. Furthermore print media is now inter-related to other media platforms and most newspapers and magazines have related websites.

Free newspapers, such as *Metro*, which is available in London, are becoming more popular as a way of counteracting the limited enthusiasm for newspaper purchase among the young. Magazines that focus on specific audiences or interest groups are also becoming more popular in the contemporary, fragmented, post-modern world. An important first step in approaching print media texts is to think about whom the intended audiences are and how this influences the text. The magazine industry is highly competitive and also in flux, for example, magazines such as *Nuts* and *Zoo* aimed at young men are now in decline, and an awareness of such changes provides an important context for analysis.

Print media focuses on written and visual media language; the tone and rhetoric of language, layout, images and fonts are all key areas to focus on when you approach print media. The layout, in particular, of a publication is key. Research has shown that people tend to flick through newspapers and magazines, reading only headlines and the first few sentences of each article; they look at images and spend approximately three seconds looking at a whole page advert. This knowledge shapes the construction of the text, especially in an economic context where the need for advertising revenue shapes print media production, both encouraging and limiting content.

Finally, it is important to be aware that unlike moving image media, print media publications take overt ideological positions, often supporting particular political parties or interest groups. Although the allegiances of different newspapers change over time, at present the *Mirror* supports a Labour viewpoint; *The Telegraph* and the *Daily Mail* support the views of the Conservative party; and the *Guardian*, *Observer* and *The Independent*'s views, broadly speaking, reflect the liberal tradition espoused by the Labour party and the Liberal Democrat party.

■ Case study: newspaper magazine supplements

The following points are examples of how a media text can be approached. Look carefully at the texts and make notes on some other areas that could also be discussed, for example, representations of race, women and gay men.

■ In comparing and contrasting these two texts there are a range of areas that could be discussed – the following provides some ways that the texts could initially be approached by utilising the specific medium's context, media language and audiences.

■ Both these publications are produced within the competitive and depleting newspaper market. Weekend newspapers charge a higher price and these two texts are examples of the range of supplements provided to the reader to justify this price increase. Importantly, these magazine supplements provide an ideal vehicle for colour adverts, which bring in much needed revenue for the newspapers. The layouts of such supplements are designed to encourage readers to look through the magazine closely, enabling readers to notice the adverts.

■ Both magazines' focus is on 'soft' news. The *Observer*'s section on 'Life and Style' looks at lifestyle issues, the *Mirror*'s 'We Love Telly' summarises current TV soap narratives and the *Observer*'s feature on Stephen Hawking, as well as the *Mirror*'s feature on Christopher Biggins, focus on celebrity. The *Mirror* supplement, as a magazine about the current week's television, uses post-modern inter-textual reference. This gives weight to the argument that newspapers no longer just provide news, but often operate as an escapist and fleeting pastime for readers.

Fig. 3.11 *'We Love Telly' supplement* (**Daily Mirror**, *1 March 2008*)

Fig. 3.12 *Title page* (**Observer** *magazine, 2 March 2008*)

■ The texts both assume the reader's intimacy with celebrities and offer to extend their knowledge, for example, the *Observer*'s feature on Steven Hawking offers an insight into his private life. Similarly, the *Mirror*'s discussion of Christopher Biggins confirms and legitimates readers knowledge of him with an inter-textual reference to his success in *I'm A Celebrity ... Get Me Out Of Here* (ITV, 2002–). The use of colloquial language under the headline 'Look Who's Back' claims an intimate relationship with the reader and is consistent with the informal language used in this text.

■ A comparison of the two celebrities – one a scientist, the other a television celebrity – give insight into the indented audience of each magazine. The *Observer*'s audience is in general more **left wing** and wealthier, compared to the *Mirror*'s. In line with this, this edition of the *Observer* magazine carries an article on the parents of a girl killed in the Arab–Israeli conflict. The political context of this story is softened by its focus on the family and the overall tone of the magazine.

■ The intended readership influences the layout, for example, a page in the *Observer* is more restrained, less crowded and colourful. This signifies class and style reflecting the differing social classes of the intended readership, in comparison with the exuberant popular culture feel of the *Mirror*'s magazine – with its carnivalesque feel.

🔍 Approaches to web-based texts

Web-based media texts are relatively new and extremely varied, both in relation to the context of their production, their consumption and their use of media language. In approaching these texts you need to be aware of moral panics over the Internet, and dystopian and utopian perspectives on new media, as well as anxieties about the effects of new technology.

The web provides a space for 'ordinary people' to express themselves by setting up their own websites, blogging or utilising a social network site such as Facebook. The Internet is also an invaluable marketing, advertising and selling tool for big businesses. An important first consideration when approaching web-based texts are the institutional and economic context in which the site is produced. Furthermore, although many texts appear to be user-generated, you need to consider the degree to which the user contribution is shaped by the confines of the hosting website. For example, Facebook has tight aesthetic guidelines and limitations on users' entries compared to MySpace.

The media language utilised in web-based texts is also influenced by the need to attract the attention of web-surfers. Goldhaber (1997) discussed how the Internet is affected by an 'attention economy'. He suggests that because there is such a mass of material on the Internet and time is short, every site struggles to get and hold an audience's attention. Think, therefore, about how the use of particular media language or the style and use of narrative in web-based texts has been constructed to gain and hold the attention of the audience surfing the web, such as the following:

■ by inviting audience input and participation

■ inter-textuality through banners and headlines that link to other webpages

■ enigma narratives, which raise speculation and questions for the consumer, often about celebrities or news stories

Key terms

Left wing: political views most often associated with the Labour party, suggesting a greater involvement by government in society and individuals' lives in order to prevent suffering and exploitation. Such views tend to be in favour of more welfare services and higher taxes to pay for them.

Right wing: political views most often associated with the Conservative party and stress the freedom of the individual and a more limited role for the government and consequently lower taxation.

Investigating media

Print off two pages or entries from two different social networking sites and make careful notes on how the institutional context has framed the aesthetic style and use of media language by the participants.

■ moving and interactive content

■ personalisation, such as addressing the surfer by name

■ membership and passwords

■ sophisticated and highly stylised visual images.

Web-based texts also raise specific issues in relation to representation. Many of the images refer to each other rather than representing the non-media world – this is part of both the appeal and arguably the danger of the Internet. It allows anonymity and identity to be played with; thus it is a post-modern space. In approaching many web-based texts consider the degree to which these texts are simulacrum and draw upon post-modern critical approaches to media.

Finally, it is important to take into account the current contemporary debates around new media: To what extent does new media influence politics and international relations? Does new media facilitate a range of different voices to speak in the public sphere?

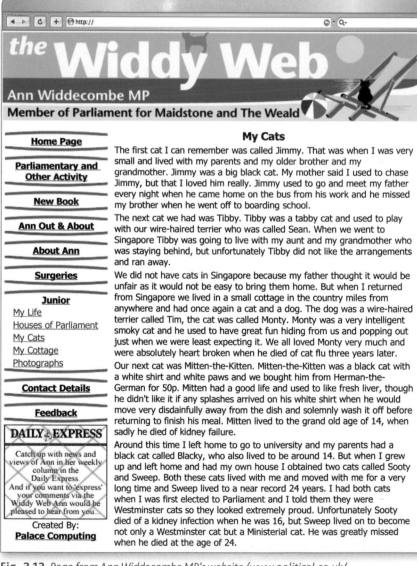

Fig. 3.13 *Page from Ann Widdecombe MP's website (www.political.co.uk/ annwiddecombe)*

Fig. 3.14 *Page from Live Leak (www.LiveLeak.com)*

Investigating media

Look at the above two texts. It can be argued that both of these texts bring politics into the wider public sphere.

■ How are the texts constructed to:
  – attract audience attention
  – encourage audiences to engage with the public sphere?

■ How important do you think the use of sophisticated web-based media language is?

■ Does the use of sophisticated web-based media language and its slick visual imagery undermine the openness of the web as a media platform in which, arguably, anyone can publish material?

💡 *Chapter summary*

In this chapter:

■ ways of investigating media texts and approaching texts were explored, which will assist you in using your knowledge of critical perspectives to complete assessments and examinations

■ the importance of the social, economic, political and historical context in which a media text is produced and consumed has been emphasised as key for understanding why media texts are constructed in particular ways

■ being aware of the economic context, media language and debates and issues in relation to specific media platforms has also been pointed out as an important part of approaching media texts analytically.

AQA Examiner's tip

The quality of your written communication will be assessed in your answers – punctuation, grammar and writing style must be clear and easily understood.

Structure your answers carefully and clearly by dividing them into paragraphs, with a clear introduction. If you are uncertain how to structure paragraphs, try to begin by making a clear point and following this with supporting evidence from the media text you are discussing. Then add further explanation or detail.

Ensure that you leave enough time to read through your answers again. When writing at speed, under pressure, it is easy to miss out a word or two and consequently change the meaning of your whole sentence. This can severely damage your mark as the examiner can only mark what is written on the paper, not what you intended to write.

Visit the exam board website and look at sample and previous exam papers. Use these as practice papers when revising. Practising questions is a good way of ensuring that you revise actively; this is a much more efficient system of revision than just reading notes from class, handouts and text-books.

4 Approaching topics critically

In this chapter you will:

 become more familiar with the format and requirements of Section B of the Unit 3 exam

 develop your understanding of how to undertake a case study on a range of potential topics

 consider how to apply your knowledge of media studies to examinations.

Section B of the Unit 3 examination requires you to have studied two pre-set topic areas. You will know in advance what these are and study them during your A2 year.

Initially these two topics are:

- representations in the media
- the impact of new/digital media.

In this chapter we also look at a range of other potential topic areas.

In advance of the examination you will need to complete your own individual case studies for each of the pre-selected topics. A case study is an in-depth area of research, involving the critical analysis of a media text, drawing upon concepts, context, theories, issues and debates.

It is important that for both case studies you study a range of texts, preferably across more than one media platform, in order to develop your own informed views about representation and the impact of new/digital media. You are expected to articulate your views upon these two topics in the exam, supporting them with evidence and examples drawn from your own case studies.

In Section B of the exam, you need to answer one question only. You will choose your question from a range of four questions, two on each case study. You will need to draw upon your case study to construct your answer. An important element of preparing for the exam will be to look at sample and/or past papers and practise answering the exam questions.

You will have one hour to answer this question including the time needed to choose your question and to check and read through your answers at the end of the exam. The question is worth 48 marks. This means that you are expected to have an extensive and detailed knowledge of your case study in order to write for approximately one hour. You will need to be able to make detailed references to specific texts you have studied.

For your case studies you will need to:

- critically analyse a range of texts and their contexts
- apply a range of theories, critical perspectives and concepts
- show an awareness of relevant media issues and debates.

Newspaper websites are helpful for getting an understanding of some of the current debates in relation to your specific case study, for example, *The Guardian* media section or *The Independent*'s arts and entertainment section.

For each text you select to investigate for your case studies you will need to know where, when, why, by whom and for whom the text was produced. The internet is a useful source of this information. For films and television programmes the International Movie Database website (www.imdb.com) is a useful starting point for a range of information on films and TV programmes. The British Film Industry website (www.bfi.org.uk) provides information on film audience statistics. The Broadcasters' Audience Research Board website (www.barb.co.uk) is an important area for television audience figures and the Radio Joint Audience Research website (www.rajar.co.uk) provides radio audience figures. You should be familiar with these websites and this material from your AS study. Each TV channel and radio station also has an internet site that gives the details of the institution's priorities, aims, finance and overall policies. This information provides the institutional context for the programme's production.

Newspapers and magazines often have their publishers' details within them, including a website address. Publishers often have two websites – one for magazine readers themselves and another aimed at potential advertisers. The latter usually contains relevant media information.

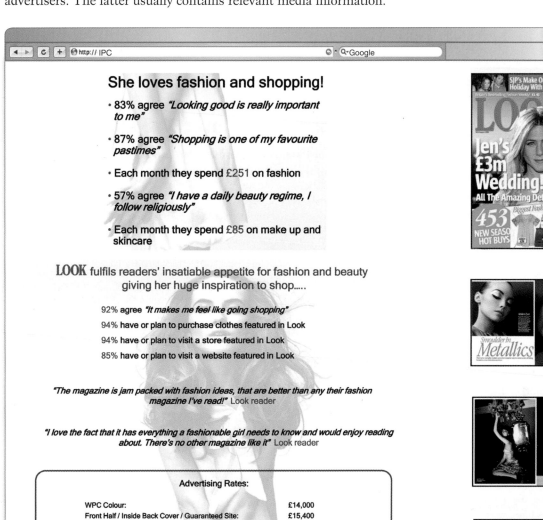

She loves fashion and shopping!

- 83% agree *"Looking good is really important to me"*

- 87% agree *"Shopping is one of my favourite pastimes"*

- Each month they spend £251 on fashion

- 57% agree *"I have a daily beauty regime, I follow religiously"*

- Each month they spend £85 on make up and skincare

LOOK fulfils readers' insatiable appetite for fashion and beauty giving her huge inspiration to shop.....

92% agree *"It makes me feel like going shopping"*

94% have or plan to purchase clothes featured in Look

94% have or plan to visit a store featured in Look

85% have or plan to visit a website featured in Look

"The magazine is jam packed with fashion ideas, that are better than any their fashion magazine I've read!" Look reader

"I love the fact that it has everything a fashionable girl needs to know and would enjoy reading about. There's no other magazine like it" Look reader

Advertising Rates:

WPC Colour:	£14,000
Front Half / Inside Back Cover / Guaranteed Site:	£15,400
Front Half DPS:	£30,800
First Ad Page / First Right Half:	£16,100
Covers	£17,500
Inside Front Cover DPS:	£35,000

For more information, please contact:

Kate MacKenzie - Group Ad Director Weeklies:	020 3148 3603	kate_mackenzie@ipcmedia.com
Lindsey Dean - Group Ad Manager:	020 3148 3668	lindsey_dean@ipcmedia.com
Donia Dacey - Head Creative Solutions:	020 3148 3698	donia_dacey@ipcmedia.com
Russell Matthew - Regional Manager:	016 1872 2161	russell_matthews@ipcmedia.com
Sarah Lock - Fashion & Beauty Manager:	020 3148 3672	sarah_lock@ipcmedia.com
Katie Sadler - Beauty & Fashion Exec:	020 3148 3669	katie_sadler@ipcmedia.com
http://www.ipcadvertising.com		

Fig. 4.1 *This is an example of the material easily available on the IPC website about the magazine* **Look** *– it provides audience figures and a useful guide to their perception of their reader (www.ipcadvertising.com/magazines/look/)*

AQA Examiner's tip

Although a useful start, simply collecting information from the internet will not provide you with enough depth and insight to revise for an exam and answer exam questions. You will need to build up an extensive and well-organised research folder on your case study. You will also need to write notes and practise writing essays in relation to your case studies. Your research will need to be highlighted and annotated so that you can utilise the material easily for revision.

The following are three useful websites to utilise when undertaking research on web-based texts:

- the 'Alexa' website (www.alexa.com) has a range of information on internet use, including lists of the most popular websites in individual countries

- the 'Compete' website (http://compete.com) allows you to compare the popularity of two or more different websites

- 'Google's trends' website (www.google.co.uk/trends) allows you to trace the trends of particular search terms and explore how often particular celebrities or moral panics are searched for on the internet.

guardian.co.uk

Setback for Murdoch over MySpace results

Networking site fails to reach advertising target
Figures call big valuations of rivals into question

Andrew Clark in New York
The Guardian, Thursday May 8 2008

Rupert Murdoch's social-networking website MySpace suffered a setback when News Corporation warned it will fail to hit its revenue target this year as advertisers struggle to judge the commercial value of making on-line friends.

News Corp revealed that its Fox Interactive Media arm, which includes MySpace, will miss its goal of an 80% increase in revenue by "about 10%". The division had been predicted to generate up to $1bn.

The news is a setback for News Corp's chairman, Murdoch, who has made MySpace the centrepiece of his media empire's digital strategy. It could raise questions over the soaring valuation of competitors such as Facebook.

News Corp's chief operating officer, Peter Chernin, said earlier growth projections had been "very aggressive" and that the group remained satisfied: "Despite the obstacles we're facing, what we're accomplishing is extraordinary."

Chernin said one of the reasons for the shortfall was the tricky task of evaluating the commercial potential of contacts in cyberspace: "It's still difficult to quantify the economic value of a friend in the social networking space." He said advertisers were accustomed to basing their thinking on long-established measures.

In spite of this, News Corp maintains that MySpace is the strongest social networking offering on the net. In the key US market, it boasts 73 million regular users compared to Facebook's 36 million, each of whom spends an average of 44% more time on the site than Facebook users.

The figures emerged as News Corp's global profits jumped by $1.8bn to $2.7bn, largely due to a gain of $1.7bn from the transfer of its stake in DirecTV to Liberty Media. The results included a $21m profit from newly acquired Dow Jones, which includes the Wall Street Journal.

Speaking on a conference call, Murdoch said his initial impressions of Dow Jones were positive: "The more time I spend working with the company, the more opportunities I see in improving and expanding its businesses."

He said he saw particular potential in Dow Jones' newswires, its cuttings service and its indices operation, which compiles Wall Street's Dow Jones Industrial Average. All of these, Murdoch said, could prosper as they serve the rapidly growing financial services industry in emerging markets. "It may take time but I'm as confident about it as I've been for any acquisition I've ever done," he added.

Elsewhere, News Corp confirmed it has tabled a bid for the Long Island-based newspaper Newsday, thought to be in the region of $580m.

Murdoch wants to combine Newsday's back-office functions with those of his New York Post title to improve cashflow by $100m annually. He brushed aside suggestions that competing buyer Cablevision might outbid him.

In Britain, earnings grew in double-digit terms at News Corp's stable of newspapers – the Sun, the News of the World, the Times and the Sunday Times – partly because of the decommissioning of older printing presses as the papers move to new colour facilities.

Annotations in margins:

Institutions advertising + social networking sites

problems for advertisers predicting value of social networking sites

multi-national conglomerate

institutions still value newspaper economic profitability

Fig. 4.2 *Example to show how you might highlight and annotate an article for your research folder (from www.guardian.co.uk)*

Representations in the media

Representations are at the heart of media studies as they convey a particular perception of the world. It is essential when you are completing your case studies to study and research how a specific group or place is represented across a range of media texts and platforms.

Making a case study

In undertaking a case study it is important to avoid selecting a group or place that is so big that it is hard to construct any arguments or observations that cannot be passed as generalisations. An example of this is the representation of women in general. It is better to focus on a sub-set, such as housewives, young girls or working mothers, for example. It can be helpful to select an area or group that is important and interesting to you, for example the area in which you live, a youth sub-cultural group to which you belong or are very aware of. Consider the images of a particular group or place across a range of media platforms and remember to include any challenges to the mainstream representations that can be found on websites, for example, or in spaces where groups are able to represent themselves.

It is often useful to focus your case study on a group or place that is the subject of political controversy or that is frequently in the news. Examples include new European immigrants, asylum seekers, inner city youth and teenage mothers. This will make it easier to give your chosen group or place the necessary context required for A2 Level.

Investigating media

The representation of new European immigrants to Britain is an interesting subject for a case study. You could compare the representation of this group across mid-market tabloids, representations in drama or television and on a website such as 'The voice of Britain's skilled immigrants' (**www.vbsi.org.uk**).

Look for debates in the press, on the internet, TV or radio about the area of representation that your case study focuses on, for example if you were looking at the representation of teenage girls, you might find a number of media debates about size zero models that would be relevant. Alternatively, you may encounter debates about your particular case study on charity or pressure group websites.

IMMIGRANTS BRING MORE CRIME

By **Tom Whitehead** Home Affairs Editor

IMMIGRATION from Eastern Europe has led to a huge surge in crime, police chiefs will tell the Home Secretary today.

The hundreds of thousands of migrants who have flocked to Britain in recent years have had a significant impact on communities and have placed fresh demands on policing, a review has found.

Pressure on police resources has soared while a lack of criminal intelligence from Poland and its neighbours has left the UK vulnerable to criminal gangs.

The damning report will be presented to Jacqui Smith in a key meeting, at which many chief constables will demand extra funds to cope with the effects of Labour's open-door policy.

It comes a day after leaked extracts from the study were used to create a positive image with claims that migration has not caused crime waves. But the full report, seen by the Daily Express, paints

TURN TO PAGE 6

Fig. 4.3 *Newspaper front page article (**Daily Express**, 17 April 2008)*

VIEWPOINT
The learning disability magazine
published by Mencap

"there should be more people like me, with a learning disability, acting because it shows that we can stand up and be counted."

Paula Sage with her on screen father Tom Dean Burn

In 2002 more than 600 representatives from 34 countries met in Madrid for the European Congress of People with Disabilities. As a result of this meeting, the Madrid Declaration was agreed upon, proposing a general vision of inclusion of people with any form of disability in society.

Article six of the Madrid Declaration states: "The media should create and strengthen partnerships with associations of people with disabilities in order to improve the portrayal of disabled people in the mass media." To do this, the declaration says that the media should focus on the positive contribution people with a disability make to society and that they should avoid patronising or humiliating comments.

Earlier this year Europe-wide project Real Live Media launched a toolkit aimed at promoting positive images of people with a learning disability in the media. Put simply, it translated article six of the Madrid Declaration for media professionals whose work features people with a learning disability.

Key points

■ There are 1.5 million people with a learning disability in the UK but they rarely feature on TV, radio or in the newspapers.

■ A number of groups have been looking at how people with a learning disability are seen in the media.

■ Media companies accept that they need to do more for people with a learning disability but change has been slow.

*Fig. 4.4 Organisations such as Mencap have been actively involved in trying to challenge stereotypes of young people with mental impairments, and provide a wide range of material that can be very useful in undertaking a case study (from **Viewpoint** – the learning disability magazine produced by Mencap, 2005)*

Approaches and investigation

In undertaking your case study you will need to:

■ analyse how representations are constructed in various media texts

■ consider the politics of representation and their production

■ consider cross-cultural factors (if relevant)

■ explore the appeal of representations for audiences and how audiences interpret representations.

Texts and contexts

There are a number of factors to consider in trying to understand why representations are constructed as they are; a necessary element of A2 Level study. Although these factors are often inter-related they can be grouped as:

■ the genre and the audience of specific media texts

■ the creators of the text, their institution and the medium they use

■ the cultural, political and social context in which the text is produced.

Genres have identifiable visual styles, themes and narrative structures which appeal to their intended audiences, guaranteeing them a predictable audience experience. For example, the audience of a sitcom such as *My*

Family (BBC, 1995–) expect a light-hearted, easy-viewing experience with a focus on family and usually a central role for women. Alternatively, the audience of an action-thriller or a gangster movie such as *Layer Cake* (2004) or *American Gangster* (2007) expect a more sinister engagement with the seedier, more threatening and violent representations of life. The perceived audiences of a text will influence the representations found within it. For example, the audience of a gangster movie is often predominantly male and may enjoy a more objectified and passive representation of women than that presented in *My Family*.

It is too simplistic to assume that all creators of media texts always have specific values and ideologies that they intentionally attempt to convey in media texts. It is sometimes the case that a media text is deliberately created to put across particular values through its representations. For example, the BBC with its public service broadcasting remit of entertaining, educating and informing the public tries to represent a wide range of social groups and the multi-cultural nature of Britain, in a positive light. One example of this is the comedy *All About Me* (BBC One, 2002–4), which attempted to create a more positive representation of disability and mixed-race marriages. Representations are often seen as positive if they portray a group or individual in a favourable light. There is much debate however about what constructs a positive representation – what appears favourable to one member of a group is not so favourable to someone else.

Often a representation that seems 'natural' to the writers, producers, directors and editors of a media text is the result of their own experiences, background and attitudes. For example, Osgerby (1998) suggests that the representation of teenagers in many television and film texts tends to operate around two main paradigms: teenager as fun and teenager as trouble. Recently, another representation has emerged – teenager as consumer. This can be seen in adverts or youth magazines, such as *Nuts* or *More*. Other, more complex representations have emerged in texts where teenagers are involved in, or in control of, the production process. For example, the script of the film *Thirteen* (2003) was written jointly with a teenage girl. Also, many teenagers construct their own websites, blogs or put their own images and text entries on their spaces on social network sites.

🔟 💭 *Effects of media regulation*

Different media institutions have their own cultures, values, priorities and perception of their audiences, which will influence representation. These institutional attitudes may prohibit certain representations – newspaper and magazine editors decide what content and representations make it to the pages we see. Alternatively some institutions try to challenge unintentional institutional bias by promoting particular representations.

Specific media platforms also have their own conventions and regulatory bodies that influence representations. Television and radio are restrained and placed under a series of obligations by Ofcom's Broadcasting Code.

However, new media such as the internet experience much less regulation. Television and radio are obliged to be 'fair and impartial' in reporting news, whilst newspapers and magazines have no such obligation and may produce an overtly one-sided approach to an event. For example, whilst both the *Daily Mail* and *Express* have carried a number of stories that represent immigration as a threat and focus on the its potentially negative effects, *New Nation*, Britain's leading Black newspaper, has alternatively explored the plight of those held within detention centres for illegal immigrants or failed asylum seekers.

3 SHOCKING CASES

Beaten to death, hurled on bonfire… by boy aged 13

A BOY of 13 battered a drunk to death then threw his body on a bonfire, a court heard yesterday.

Jamie Smith launched his motiveless attack on Stephen Croft — who was five times the drink-drive limit and unable to defend himself.

The stocky schoolboy was sent to custody indefinitely and must serve 13 years before he can apply for parole. Last night Stephen's family slammed the sentence.

His sister Sarah said Smith's parents had "dragged him up to be the monster we now know him as".

She added: "Hanging is too good for him. The punishment is for him to know he will be fed, watered, protected, educated and supposedly rehabilitated at taxpayers' expense.

"All this for him to come out bigger, stronger and still as evil."

Liverpool Crown Court heard Smith got his first conviction at 11. He was drunk when he beat Stephen, 34, in the early hours of November 6. He burnt the body to conceal the crime. Smith, of Birkenhead, Merseyside, admitted murder. His dad Gerald Murphy, 31, was given a mimimum 11-year sentence in January after paralysing an Asian man in an attack.

g.patrick@the-sun.co.uk

Girl killed with brick by raging ex-love, 17

A TEENAGER who beat his ex-girlfriend to death with a brick after she claimed she was pregnant was jailed for life yesterday.

Marc King-Bromley, 17, also stabbed Danielle Johnson repeatedly in the back and thighs.

Prosecutor Anthony Orchard told the Old Bailey it was "a terrifying and frenzied attack".

The court heard that 45 minutes later King-Bromley told a pal: "I smashed her head in with a brick until I heard it go crack."

The murder happened after hair and beauty student Danielle, 17, had run into King-Bromley and his new girlfriend.

The girls argued and later King-Bromley, of Palmers Green, North London, lured Danielle to a deserted garage and attacked her.

She was found alive but was so badly beaten her mum did not recognise her.

Danielle's life support machine was switched off 12 days later. She had told King-Bromley and pals she was pregnant, but a post-mortem showed she was not.

He was ordered to serve a minimum of 12 years.

RACE HATE VICTIM age 15

THIS is the battered face of schoolboy Imran Iqbal — who told yesterday how he "prepared himself" to die as racist thugs kicked, punched and hurled abuse at him in a park.

Quiet Imran, 15, was beaten unconscious as he walked home from class at Rochdale, Lancs, on Tuesday. He said: "I thought, 'That's it' — in a couple of hours my family were going to have to identify me. I remember feeling the tears rolling down my cheek." Cops arrested a man of 20 and boys of 15 and 17.

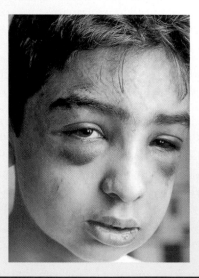

Fig. 4.5 *An interesting case study could compare this type of representation of teenagers with contemporary representations of youth from different mediums, genres and/or institutions. Consider what factors have influenced these representations. Examples of other texts might include a page from MySpace and an episode from* **Hollyoaks** *(Channel 4, 1995–) and the film* **Son of Rambow** *(2007) (extract from the* **Sun***, 12 April 2008, under the title 'Broken Britain: three shocking cases')*

Illegal migrants on our payrolls, admit hospitals

By **Tom Harper**

DOZENS of illegal immigrants have been found working with patients in National Heath Service hospitals, the Government has admitted.

Last year alone, 40 unlawful migrants – including a doctor, nurses, physiotherapists and healthcare assistants – were discovered on the payroll of the NHS, an investigation by The Mail on Sunday has revealed.

The doctor, a poorly qualified woman from Sierra Leone, was a trainee haematologist at Bath Royal United Hospital NHS Trust.

The illegal workers possessed forged passports and references to bypass NHS employment checks.

When they were finally uncovered by NHS officials and reported to the Home Office for possible deportation, most disappeared.

The embarrassing revelation comes almost a year after Prime Minister Gordon Brown pledged stringent vetting of overseas medics when three Muslim doctors were charged with attempted car-bomb attacks in London and Glasgow.

Critics claim the findings are an indictment of Britain's 'open borders' immigration policy.

Shadow Home Secretary David Davis said: 'These findings make a mockery of Gordon Brown's pledge. While he has dithered, the problem has persisted, putting the public at risk.' Using freedom of information laws, The Mail on Sunday asked all 171 NHS acute trusts in England how many illegal immigrants they had found in their employment.

Twenty-three admitted being duped by unlawful workers.

Moorfield's Eye Hospital in London hired six illegals last year, including two housekeepers from Sierra Leone and a Nigerian caterer. The Royal Free Hospital in Hampstead, North London, employed two bogus Nigerians and a Ghanaian as healthcare assistants.

Barnet and Chase Farm Hospital Trust in North London also employed illegals while world-famous Great Ormond Street Children's Hospital took on a health-care assistant and a clinician without knowing their nationalities.

Trusts in Devon, Birmingham, Berkshire, Surrey, Sussex, Dorset, Derby and the Pennines reported similar failings. Health authorities must check identities, references and immigration status before offering jobs.

Health Minister Ann Keen said: 'We are committed to tackling illegal working.' NHS Employers, which handles hospitals' workforces, said: 'The NHS has robust checks but no system is entirely secure from people with criminal intent.'

Fig. 4.6 *Look at the language and sources for this story to consider to what extent this is a one-sided approach to the story* (**Mail on Sunday**, *11 May 2008*)

Economic constraints may regulate representation on different media. Commercial television and radio channels have to fund their programmes through advertising. Their need to appeal to advertisers limits programming content. For example, in the 1980s the popular TV drama *thirtysomething* (Channel 4, 1987), lost over $1m of advertising revenue by showing an image of two men in bed together prior to an advertising break.

The lower level of regulatory and economic regulation on the internet has been responsible for a number of representations occurring on this medium that would not be seen on other mediums. For example, images were shown of Princess Diana after her fatal car crash in 1997.

Media in action

Part of Channel 4's public service role is championing alternative voices or fresh perspectives and challenging people to see the world differently. Their Statement of Programming Policy for 2008 stipulates that they have a commitment to cultural diversity, spending on ethnic minority training and improving casting and representation of disability. The policy also claims:

'Channel 4 aims to be the most ethnically diverse of the major channels on-screen and will commission programmes with multi-cultural themes.'

Highlights for 2008 include the single drama *Fallout* by black British playwright Roy Williams and a film by Hoe Bullman (*The Seven Sins of England*) about Muslim communities in Britain.

Investigating media

Visit the Department for Culture Media and Sport website (**www. culture.gov.uk**) and its pages on media regulation.

- Try to find examples of how media regulation limits media representations of, for example, teenage girls. Undertake an internet search to find out about the laws against incitement to ethnic or racial hatred.
- To what extent do you think this legislation restricts representations of minority racial groups in the British media?

One of the concerns about new media has been that it provides a platform for the circulation of extremist and racist political views and representations in the media.

- Do you think this is a legitimate concern and are there ways in which such representations can be regulated?

men. Dyer wrote about gay stereotypes nearly 30 years ago and there is much debate about the extent to which the representation of this group has shifted since then. This is an issue that would need to be explored and addressed when undertaking a case study.

Stereotyping can be seen to exaggerate difference and in doing so may increase antagonisms between groups. A problem with the media's use of stereotypes is its selectivity, as it conveys values and assumptions that may help construct the audience's perception of the world and consequently their behaviour. It is important to note that the media does not invent stereotypes, but by repeatedly using them, media can be accused of reinforcing certain values and assumptions.

Medurst (1995) has suggested that stereotypes can be seen as a type of media shorthand that provides an easy point of contact when the text needs to communicate quickly with the audience. Some genres and mediums are more prone to the use of stereotypes than others, for example, stereotypes are often seen on television in adverts and sitcoms. Other genres, such as soap opera, use stereotypes for less significant characters or when introducing new characters. Over time, both soap opera and sitcom may develop these initial stereotypes into more rounded and complex characters, which challenge the audience's first impressions and which provide for more complex enigma narratives. For example, Bianca's return to *EastEnders* (BBC, 1985–) is as a stereotypical feckless single mum, but as her character develops, more complex motivations and explanations for her behaviour are being introduced.

Perkins (1979) suggested that stereotypes are not always negative and that they often contain an element of truth. For example, the stereotypical image of the Frenchman as a riding a bicycle, wearing a beret and a striped jumper has its origins in the French garlic sellers who, in the first half of the 20th century, came from Brittany to sell garlic and onions to housewives in the south of England. Alternatively the English have been stereotyped by the French as 'Roast beefs', as this used to be the traditional Sunday lunch in England. Similarly, it could be argued that there is some truth behind the representation of Asian families, the Masoods and the Alahans, in both *EastEnders* (BBC, 1985–) and *Coronation Street* (ITV, 1960–), as running shops. The problem lies with these being the only representations of Asians within soap operas.

It can be argued that it is not the media's use of stereotypes that is problematic but the audience's assumption that this representation can be applied to all members of a particular group.

ⓘ The impact of new/digital media

The emergence of a range of new media forms in the last 20 to 30 years has become a highly contested area of current debate. There are a number of areas where new media is considered to have potentially profound effects on media by making the boundary between media producers and audiences more fluid and consequently altering the power relationships between them. For case study purposes, select an area that looks at these changes along with texts that exemplify them.

Making a case study

There are a number of areas of new/digital media that you could choose to focus on, for example:

Investigating media

Exploring the stereotypes of a particular identity group within different genres of media texts and across different media platforms is a good way to undertake a case study of representation. Analyse how the stereotypes are constructed with reference to clothing, body language or mannerisms, décor of habitat, location, accent or language, music, relationships and lifestyle. In examining a stereotype, try to consider whether Dyer's (1979), Medurst's (1995) and Perkins's (1979) arguments have any credibility.

- interactive consumers
- social networking
- blogs
- podcasts and their influence on TV and newspapers
- the changing contemporary media landscapes of TV, radio or film
- media institutions
- media and democracy
- new media technologies and audiences
- the changing role of distributors and exhibitions
- globalisation or cross-cultural factors.

When considering the impact of new media in your case study, be aware of the need to encompass all three media platforms and their inter-connectedness. This is the 'heart' of new media. Examples include websites such as YouTube that contain television clips, digital radio and newspapers that are now available online and many films that are promoted through a dedicated website or through trailers that are sent to mobile phones.

Remember that it is problematic to focus on large general areas of debate in your case study; it is important to look at a specific area and specific texts, for example, the impact of new/digital media on:

- a media organisation, such as Sky, ITV or Capital Radio Group
- a particular genre, such as soap opera or news
- a medium, such as television or radio
- an audience's consumption of media through social network sites or interactivity in computer games, such as Wii compared to online gaming.

> ### Investigating media
>
> Focusing on the impact of new media on the BBC could be a pertinent subject for a case study. You can look the BBC's website, interactive websites for its many programmes, its range of digital channels, the new BBC iPlayer and its online and digital radio stations. Your exploration could focus on one or two genres or specific areas of media.

Thinking about media

The BBC iPlayer has created a licence fee controversy – BBC iPlayer and its website are funded by money obtained from TV owners' licence fees. Some people have argued that this gives them an unfair advantage over the commercial producers of online material who have to seek advertising or subscriptions to fund their web-content.

The BBC argues that web-content must be free from advertising in order to be consistent with their public service remit – an argument they do not extend to the wide range of BBC lifestyle magazines such as *BBC Good Food*.

Other people have argued that it is unfair that television users are paying for programming that web-users can access for free. The BBC licence is arguably under threat, with Ofcom and political groups exploring whether the revenue should be shared amongst a range of media institutions – what do you think?

Newspapers may provide ideas of a range of topical areas on which to focus your case study research. Remember that it is helpful to choose an area for your case study that you already have an interest in, or know something about. Be careful, however, of merely enthusing or repeating a number of facts – you need to analyse the impact of the area of new media using concepts, theories and critical perspectives, whilst engaging with contemporary issues and debates. For example, select a music genre, celebrity or sport, explore it across a range of media and interrogate how it has been impacted by new/digital media. To do this you will need to compare the relevant media landscape before new/digital media had an impact.

THE TIMES Thursday April 10 2008 2GM

Popularity of BBC iPlayer puts the internet at risk of overload

▶ Corporation 'should share the cost of upgrade'

▶ Million programmes viewed online each week

Dan Sabbagh Media Editor

The success of the BBC's iPlayer is putting the internet under severe strain and it is at risk of grinding to a halt, internet service providers claimed yesterday.

They want the corporation to share the cost of upgrading the network to cope with the increased workload, which has been estimated at £831 million.

Viewers are now watching more than one million BBC programmes online each week.

The BBC said yesterday that its iPlayer service, an archive of programmes shown over the previous seven days, was accounting for between 3 and 5 per cent of all internet traffic in Britain, with the first episode of *The Apprentice* watched more than 100,000 times via a computer.

At the same time, the corporation is trying to increase the scope of the service.

It is making its iPlayer service available via the Nintendo Wii, allowing owners who are unable to stop playing their favourite game in time for the start of *Doctor Who* to catch BBC programmes they have missed while using the console.

Tiscali, the internet service provider, said that the BBC and other broadcasters should "share the costs" of increasing internet capacity to prevent the network coming under strain.

Ashley Highfield, the BBC's director of future media and technology, said: "We are having an impact, but we don't believe it is a great one — and it would be a unique way of using licence fee-payers' money to help internet service providers with their businessmodel."

However, a spokesman for Tiscali said that the BBC was deliberately underplaying the problem, arguing that internet providers had to "overbuild capacity in our networks" because they could predict how many people would want to watch television via the internet. "This cost would then be passed on to our customers — in effect a BBC tax levied on top of the licence fee," the company added.

The problem for Tiscali, though, isthat its concerns are not widely shared in the industry. BT, which provides a key part of the UK's internet infrastructure, said that the problem, "while real", could be solved. It said that the key was not speeding up connections to people's homes, but through improvements in "backhaul and core networks" — the links that operate up and down the country.

The iPlayer service has rapidly become a hit after it was introduced at Christmas, even though it involves either watching a programme on a computer screen or finding a way to link the computer to the television. There were 17.2 million requests to watch programmes during March, an increase of 25 per cent on February.

The Nintendo Wii tie-up means that all BBC programmes transmitted over the last seven days will be available to 2.5 million homes with a Wii — but similar tie-ups with Sony, maker of the PlayStation, and Microsoft, maker of the XBox 360, appear unlikely. It is already possible to watch BBC programmes transmitted in the past week to a PC

Most watched

1 The Apprentice
BBC One 26/03/2008

2 Louis Theroux: Behind Bars
BBC Two 13/01/2008

3 Ashes to Ashes
BBC One 07/02/2008

4 Torchwood
BBC Three 21/03/2008

5 Dawn . . . Gets Naked
BBC Three 14/02/2008

6 Torchwood
BBC Two 16/01/2008

7 Doctor Who Voyage of the Damned
BBC One 25/12/2007

8 Torchwood
BBC Three 20/02/2008

9 Gavin and Stacey
BBC Three 23/03/2008

10 Dawn . . . Goes Lesbian
BBC Three
21/02/2008

or Apple Mac, but the corporation was keen to work with Nintendo. Erik Huggers, group controller at the BBC's future media and technology division, said: "Nintendo has helped to reach a broader range of people with the Wii."

Fig. 4.8 *The popularity of the BBC's iPlayer provided free in line with their public service remit has caused some controversy because of the pressure it puts on internet providers* (**The Times**, *10 April 2008*)

THE TIMES Tuesday March 25 2008   News | 13

Plea to ban employers trawling facebook

▶ **Safeguard jobseekers, say children's charities**

▶ **Companies 'look for digital dirt on recruits'**

Rosemary Bennett
Social Affairs Correspondent

A powerful coalition of children's charities is urging ministers to make it illegal for companies to trawl Facebook and other social networking websites for information on prospective recruits.

They say that employers and educational establishments are known to be browsing the internet looking for "digital dirt" on young people who have applied for positions.

The eight charities acted partly in response to a report in *The Times* that revealed one in five employers used the internet to check on candidates, and two thirds of those who did said that their decisions were influenced by what they found.

A senior tutor at Emmanuel College, Cambridge, had also said that he used Facebook to check up discreetly on applications for a college position.

The charities, including the NSPCC, the Children's Society and NCH, said that the call for a new law is part of their wider concerns about online safety for children.

John Carr, secretary of the Children's Charities' Coalition on Internet Safety, who is co-ordinating the campaign, said that pictures or gossip uploaded during the teenage years should not be used against a young person ten years later.

"When young people put up their personal profiles they are not thinking about job or university applications. Typically, they are simply talking to their mates. Employers or admissions tutors who delve into these places are being highly and inappropriately intrusive.

It's a bit like looking at someone's diary," Mr Carr told *The Times*.

"A world where even a 14-year-old has to think twice before posting an adolescent poem suddenly looks very unappealing and increases the pressure on children and young people to conform to a set of tightly focused adult norms."

The children's charities are seeking clarification on whether discrimination legislation could be used to stop companies from using social networking sites for recruitment purposes.

Existing law requires equal opportunities for recruitment, and a system where some candidates have sites and others do not may breach that law. If that is not sufficient, the charities have been advised that data protection law could be tightened to require an employer to seek permission to access online data in the same way that they get permission to approach referees.

Margaret Moran, Labour MP for Luton South, is to lead the campaign in Parliament. She is discussing with Commons authorities the terms of a ten-minute rule Bill to tighten legislation. She has also written to James Purnell, the Work and Pensions Secretary, asking him to give his opinion on whether it is legitimate for employers to use information from social networking sites for recruitment.

"Social networking sites were never intended as a factual reference point for young people," Ms Moran said. "The technology allows unverified content to go up very easily. It is simple to load up spoof profiles and meddle with images. Companies have no way to verify what is up there."

The charities have approached the Chartered Institute of Personnel and Development (CIPD) for support. Deborah Fernon, resourcing adviser at the CIPD, said at this stage the

institute would not favour a ban, although she advised companies to be careful if they used sites for recruitment purposes.

"I wouldn't want it to become illegal because in some industries, advertising and IT for example, personal sites have become almost a CV in itself, and that might become more commonplace," she said.

"But we would warn companies that in the quest to find the right person for a job, social networking sites could be at best irrelevant and at worst misleading. Also, good practice requires that every candidate is treated equally, which means all candidates would have to have similar profiles before information is used, otherwise it would be discriminatory."

Recently the charities won a powerful backer when Sir Tim Berners-Lee, the British scientist who created the world wide web, said that online data and web history belong to the individual who put them there. But he warned young people to think carefully about what they put on their sites, because others saw it as common property.

David Smith, the Deputy Information Commissioner, has also pointed out that despite the privacy settings offered by service providers, more than half of young people make their profile pages public. Mr Smith said: "The cost to a person's future can be very high if something undesirable is found by the increasing number of education institutions and employers using the internet as a tool to vet potential students or employees."

Keeping a cool profile on Myspace could just cost you your next post

GET IT FIR

The Times report on February 4

Fig. 4.9 *Article on the use of Facebook by employers (**The Times**, 25 March 2008)*

■ **Investigating media**

This article in *The Times* (25 March 2008) raises questions about privacy and censorship on the internet alongside issues of children's use of new media. This article can be used as a base for a case study that looks at the changing media landscape – how what was once private is now in the public sphere of the internet – alongside an exploration into how different audiences interpret texts differently. A focus on three social networking sites, which operate differing levels of control, such as GossipReport, Facebook and MySpace, would provide a good focus and provide scope for detailed analysis of texts.

Approaches and investigation

In undertaking your case study you will need to consider the following questions.

■ Has new/digital media democratised the production of media texts by shifting the control of media content away from large media institutions?

■ Has new/digital media changed the way media texts are consumed and what are the social implications for this?

■ Has new media technology provided new cross-cultural, global media texts that communicate across national and social boundaries?

■ How active or interactive are consumers of new media and how significant is this in terms of power?

- How has new/digital media impacted on traditional media production and consumption?
- To what extent does new media escape some of the constraints of censorship that traditional media encounters?
- How is new media interacting with, using and changing traditional media platforms?

◣ Texts and contexts

In looking at new/digital media it is important to consider the context of both its production and its consumption. Some people argue that the impact of new/digital media technologies is so profound that it has changed the historical, social, economic and political context of the society in which it is produced. Castells (1999), for example, emphasises that the contemporary internet society, with computer-generated communication, is focused around networks and flows of information that disregard the constraints of time and space. For example, social networking websites provide a network over which information flows between groups of friends. The information flows without friends actually meeting. The social networking website provides an imagined community of participants who are not restrained by time and space.

crème

Need a team? Get on the network

Corporate social networks are the new recruiting grounds. JACKIE COSH explains

Social networks are part of modern life — but what about *corporate* social networks? Increasingly, companies are realising the benefits of using these to keep in touch with employees and clients.

Each week a million searches are conducted on IBM's Blue Pages, a corporate social network set up long before MySpace or Facebook became popular. The aim was to connect employees and contractors, to help sales people with leads, and to ensure that everyone felt part of a cohesive team.

Ethan McCarthy is editor-in-chief of IBM's Intranet. "Blue Pages is an essential part of IBM," he says. "Each employee has his own page which is full of information. It enables managers to find workers with the skills and experience they require, which makes building teams easier."

Rather than banning Facebook and MySpace, some employers have decided that it could be better to compete with them and provide an alternative.

Eric Didier is the CEO of Viadeo, a corporate social networking site. His company offers to host and update networks for clients. "The smartest companies are providing these sites," he says. "When they are looking for expertise within a company, the HR department may not have all the information required — a good corporate social network site can provide the solution. And when you are meeting partners or clients, it can be useful to have information from the site before the meeting."

J4b, which offers grants and funding information for small and medium-sized companies, has the largest network on Viadeo, with 1,200 members. Peter Crosby, J4b's business development manager, explains why: "As well as looking to us for information, companies want to talk to other businesses that have been there before, to find out what mistakes to avoid."

When the network was set up last September, it immediately proved popular. "We e-mailed our clients to tell them we were setting it up," Crosby says, "and overnight a thousand of them signed up. People go on and ask questions. It is a way of getting the grants community together." But could the information get into the wrong hands? "There is always the fear that head-hunters may use the site to find employees," Eric Didier says. "But as an employer I think the benefits outweigh the risks, and I would prefer employees to be in the network."

Richard Jordan, of Ernst & Young, adds: "A corporate social network site is a different route for having the same conversation we've been having at career fairs for years — a shiny new channel which doesn't say anything new. But it's speaking to people using a media *they* want to use, rather than one *we* want to use."

Fig. 4.10 *Social networks are not restricted to social interaction; they have become an essential element of the contemporary working world (***The Times***, 2 April 2008)*

Similarly, players in an online internet game are not restricted to players who live near them, but can play with people in other countries, unregulated by time constraints.

In many respects Castells's argument is a **technologically determinist** argument, suggesting that technology influences and dictates the nature of society. This argument has been challenged by other theorists, such as MacKay (2001), who stress the importance of the way in which technology is utilised and incorporated into society, for example, the way in which the personal computer and the internet have been incorporated into home and family life.

It is interesting to note that although internet and social networking sites offer global interaction they often have a strong local focus, for example, MySpace has regional networks such as the one in Brighton and Hove. The local Brighton and Hove Facebook network has 175,000 members, which implies that many of the participants resist the urge to transcend national boundaries, but cling to an imaginary community based upon place.

The rise of locally based websites, which interact and challenge local newspapers or radio, provides an interesting example of the ways in which the social significance of the internet may be reliant upon the users who are also active producers of web-based text themselves.

■ **Key terms**

Technological determinist: argues that technology dictates or determines the nature of society.

■ Case study: Chidham and Hambrook website

An analysis of West Sussex villages Chidham and Hambrook's local website (www.chidhamandhambrook.info) indicates that not only is its focus geographically local, but it also serves as a focus for interaction within the local community who contribute a range of material to the site. The site provides a public sphere for locally based politics and debates about environmental issues, advertisements for local businesses, organisations and events.

At one level it can be seen as taking local news to a new micro-level, but its interaction with local newspapers is also significant.

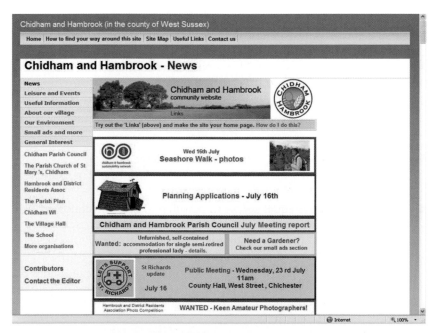

Fig. 4.11 *Front page from Chidham and Hambrook website (www.chidhamandhambrook.info)*

Another potentially interesting case study is one that explores the impact of new/digital media technology on local media. This case study could explore how local radio, newspapers and websites have changed as a result of their interaction in the contemporary media landscape. Most newspapers and radio stations, for example, now have websites, and radio can be listened to online. In some areas small-scale local cable TV stations or pirate radio stations have been facilitated by new media technology.

A number of stories posted onto the website are reproduced in local newspapers; for example, a story of a local dog that had eaten an LSD tablet found at the local bus stop was on the front page of the local *Chichester Observer* in February 2007.

Careful analysis of the site's use produces an even more complex relationship between the local and the global. Although the majority of uses are from the UK the site has a significant number of hits from the USA, Asia and Australia. Within this framework it is interesting to note how the website represents an image of what it is to be English, southern, rural and quaint. For example, there are a number of images of fields, tress, local animals, rural roads, houses and the church.

Using a critical framework

There are a wide range of theories, concepts, critical approaches, debates and issues that are useful in constructing a critical framework for a case study on the impact of new media. These include:

■ moral panics around new media

■ debates about post-modernism, cyber culture and virtual reality

■ issues of globalisation

■ censorship

■ audience theories and the active audience

■ issues of gender, race, sexuality and who is empowered by or participating in new/digital media

■ Marxist debates about media organisations: conglomerates and alternative media

■ liberal pluralism

■ new media youth and music

■ questions around who controls the media, whether audiences or producers.

Many of the debates about the impact of new/digital media focus on its potential democratisation. These debates argue that it breaks down the control of media by media producers and large media conglomerates as 'anyone' can set up a website or blog, upload their contribution to a social network site such as YouTube or MySpace and place an entry on Wikipedia.

There are a number of debates that have emerged surrounding this utopian perspective on new/digital media. These need to be addressed when completing a case study on this topic.

■ How much control remains in the hands of large media organisations, many of whom have bought into new media platforms? For example, Rupert Murdoch's News International owns MySpace.

■ Does everyone have equal access to new/digital media technology? For example, there are significant divisions in terms of expertise to cope with software and the money to buy hardware.

■ Is the democratisation of publishing on the internet necessarily a positive move? Are all the entries to Wikipedia as significant and what are the associated problems of people uploading sometimes inaccurate or offensive views or information?

There have been a number of controversies in recent years concerned with the 'offensiveness' of material posted on the internet. For example, online gambling sites are now illegal in the USA, many pro-anorexia websites have been closed down and police are attempting to monitor the 'dark web' websites that promote terrorism.

APRIL 13 · 2008 **The Mail on Sunday**   **41**

By **James Tapper**

UNDER FIRE: Sarah has been criticised by listeners for airing her own opinions on her show

Listeners who attack Sarah Kennedy on BBC website

SHE'S the radio presenter who likes to give listeners the benefit of her own views on all manner of things . . . but now the BBC has banned criticism of Sarah Kennedy from its website after a barrage of complaints from listeners.

People seeking to post negative messages about the controversial early morning Radio 2 host have been warned they may be guilty of 'harassing' her and that their actions risk being seen as 'cyber-bullying'.

The 57-year-old, who hosts the Dawn Patrol show between 6am and 7.30am, has provoked anger by talking over records, promoting her personal beliefs and deliberately mispronouncing words, as well as making them up.

Last year she sparked a race row when she said she had seen a black pedestrian in the dark only because 'he opened his mouth'. And there were fears for her health last August when she apparently began to slur her words on air.

The ban on online criticism of Kennedy comes after Bill Oddie complained last week of 'abuse' about him on the Springwatch messageboards, and some users of the BBC messageboards believe the crackdown may be linked to his concerns.

The BBC employs staff to monitor

THAT'S ENOUGH: Peta's ban and, top, an angry post

comments posted on its website but they usually act only if the posts are abusive. But last week a BBC moderator known as 'Peta' wrote: 'There are a number of people who come to this board to repeatedly post negative comments about Sarah Kennedy, using various accounts.

'We're now having a little hiatus on the "Sarah knocking" because it's seen to be a form of online harassment.

'I'm sorry to learn that you can't bear the SK programme and don't listen to it. Perhaps you'd like to comment on some of the programmes that you do like? 'I'm closing this thread now, as it's at risk of attracting those that just wish to post nasty personal comments ...'

After shutting down a further discussion, 'Peta' wrote: 'As I've posted on a number of the other threads about Sarah Kennedy, it's very obvious that people have opposing views about Sarah, but we're not running any more "SK knocking" threads. It's boring, it's repetitive and some people posting have been – literally – doing it for years. Enough.

'If you want to be rude about Sarah and just post the same old negative comments time and time again, then please find another board, outside of the BBC, to do it on.'

Some contributors to the website have complained about Ms Kennedy's presenting style. One listener's tirade read: 'Sarah Kennedy ... talks over the vocals at the start of a track, interrupts a tune halfway through (most annoying if you are enjoying the track) to relate information, which many of us would prefer not to hear, frequently gives her own beliefs much more prominence than she should as a presenter on a major Government-funded radio station, seems to have little interest in, or knowledge of, music, deliberately mispronounces words or uses annoying malapropisms.'

Last week Springwatch presenter Bill Oddie said some viewers made 'hurtful' comments about him.

The 66-year-old former Goodie said: 'I've got to the stage where my work is taking the edge off the enjoyment. Some of it is actually deeply hurtful.'

A BBC spokeswoman said: 'On the online messageboards, we do reserve the right to remove messages that break our house rules, for example if they cause offence, or are harassing or defamatory towards any of our presenters.

'We do not restrict our users from talking about any BBC presenters, and no discussion has been closed because a presenter has requested it.'

Fig. 4.12 *Some websites, such as that of the BBC, carefully monitor the material that is posted on them; this however undermines the democratisation of new/digital media (***The Mail on Sunday***, 13 April 2008)*

🔆 *Media production and consumption*

New/digital media is seen as changing media production and consumption, leading to a greater level of interactivity and the opening of boundaries between producers and consumers. For example, many news and weather reports on television rely upon images sent in by viewers, online newspapers invite readers to give their views after reading an article and websites invite audiences to vote on issues as a way of expressing their views. For example, the *OK!* magazine website asked its readers (21 April 2008) whether they were:

> ... excited for Mario Lopez to perform on "Dancing with the Stars".

The website gave them two options:

- ■ Yes, he's such a good dancer
- ■ No, focus on the actual show

Controversy has however occurred in relation to the place of journalism and new/digital media. For example, ex-editor of the *Daily Mirror* Roy Greenslade resigned from the National Union of Journalists because he saw it as too slow to embrace the world of new/digital media. Other journalists have argued that new/digital media is undermining journalistic values and integrity by allowing material, which is unreliable, inaccurate and misleading to be published.

■ Investigating media

Another interesting area of exploration for a case study is the impact new/digital media has on the news. The case study could explore the interconnectivity of media platforms through a national newspaper and its websites, looking at the impact of digital 24-hour TV news channels and internet news on specific newspapers. It could also consider the significance of user-generated content sites and blogs for giving alternative versions of the news and also look at the importance of new media technologies, such as mobile phones, for enabling ordinary citizens to provide content to broadcast news.

Moral panics and new/digital media

Finally a number of moral panics around the impact of new/digital media on audiences, particularly children, have presented a dystopian view of new/digital media and are strongly influenced by the media effects debates. Many of the concerns focus on the lack of supervision or protection of children using new/digital technology, as well as its apparent addictive qualities.

Arguably these concerns are influenced by the degree to which new/digital media crosses the boundaries between domestic and public spaces. All media brings the public world into the domestic world but new/digital media does so in a particularly individualised way. Instead of an idealised image of a family or group watching television or listening to the radio together, web-based media are often consumed individually and often by children in the privacy of their own rooms. This is seen as having an effect on family and group dynamics, but is also seen as particularly threatening because parents are not able to censor their children's media consumption. The growth in the number of children having televisions in their rooms has already erased this ideal of media consumption and the internet can be seen as leading to a more interactive attitude towards television. However, the internet, due to its global nature and vast size, is less regulated and seen as potentially more dangerous than television.

Insomnia curse of Generation X-Box

Number of children with sleep disorders rockets as parents let them stay up late playing computer games in their rooms

By **Jo Macfarlane**

MEDICAL CORRESPONDENT

COMPUTER games and fast food have been blamed by doctors for a startling rise in the number of children being treated in hospital for sleep disorders. The problem is especially pronounced among young boys, with thousands now being treated every year.

Experts say parents are at fault for failing to enforce strict bedtimes and allowing children to play computer games and watch TV in their rooms late at night. Eating too much sugary food is also blamed for preventing children from dropping off to sleep.

Newly released NHS figures show that the number of under-11s referred to hospital specialists for insomnia, sleep-walking and sleep-related breathing problems has rocketed by 26 per cent over the past five years.

But the true numbers affected could be much higher because the figures reflect only those seeking medical help.

Studies have linked poor sleep to Attention Deficit Hyperactivity Disorder (ADHD). And lack of sleep harms children's ability to learn at school. Psychologist Chireal Shallow, of the Naturally Nurturing clinic for children's sleep disorders in London, said: 'There are likely to be thousands more children whose parents do not seek treatment. A lot of the problem is guilty parenting where kids are allowed the rule of the roost because Mum and Dad come home from work late.

'Increasingly, we also don't let children play outside because of modern dangers and instead put them in front of a screen to keep an eye on them.

'The light, sound and movement of television or computer screens is stimulating and keeps children awake and there should be at least an hour's gap before going to bed.'

Nick Seaton, chairman of the Campaign for Real Education, said: 'It's absolutely crazy for parents to let their children go to bed any time they like.

'It's obviously going to create problems for youngsters later in life and is part of the general problem of poor discipline in homes and schools.

'Parents need to exert more authority and remove computer games from bedrooms to make sure kids have the best start in life. I'm sure teachers would be delighted.'

CASE HISTORY

Jane Howell, 34, from Morden, South West London, struggled for years to get her son Marcel, now 13, to sleep.

After spending most of the day at school in front of a computer, Marcel would spend the evening watching television but then found it hard to drop off, often not falling asleep until just a few hours before he had to be up again.

Eventually the problem got so bad that Jane approached a sleep clinic.

She said: 'The clinic asked me about his routines and said computers, televisions and mobile phones were a distraction.

They told me to minimise the time he uses computers and after 8pm it's now wind-down time.

'He now has much more energy and is sleeping better. As parents you have to be hard on your kids. They want to do their own thing but you have to be strict.'

Fig. 4.13 *Moral panics about media use have accompanied the introduction of all media platforms – do you think the issue here is about the technology or the way it is being used?* (**Mail on Sunday**, *13 April 2008*)

▪ Investigating media

A case study that looks at the impact of new/digital media on a TV genre such as soap opera could explore online texts, websites and chat rooms that accompany television texts. It could discuss the debates around an audience's relationship with these different texts and the degree to which it is interactive and democratic.

This case study could also explore the ways in which some TV texts have become more complex in order to stand up to the challenge of being watched and re-watched online. One of the initial examples of this phenomenon was *Buffy the Vampire Slayer* (Fox, 1997–2003), which had numerous complicated plot narratives that could only be accessed through repeated viewing and discussion with other fans via websites.

There are a range of examples that indicate that new media audiences are active, entering their own material, playing with Wiis or using the technology as part of their social interactions with friends and families.

When looking at your case studies you will need to consider carefully the space for interactivity that different web-based texts offer their audiences and the extent to which power lies with the producer or consumer of web-based media texts.

Genre: audiences and producers

Genre is a way of categorising groups of texts. Genre operates, as Neale (1980) argues, by a process of similarity and difference – a genre text has many similarities with other texts in the same genre, but it is also different in significant ways.

Genres may be identified by the following typical key conventions.

Narrative structures:

■ types of plots, for example, continuous serial action or enigma narratives

■ plot situations and issues

■ characters and character relationships.

Visual iconography:

■ props or costumes and signifiers

■ shots and camera movements

■ locations and backdrops

■ lighting, styles, themes and background music

■ mood and tone.

Ideology and themes:

■ representations of gender, race, sexuality and place

■ values and ideologies

■ themes.

Making a case study

In order to make a case study based upon genre, you will need to begin by selecting a genre and using the categories listed on page 118 as a guideline to identify the typical components of texts that belong to that particular genre.

Importantly, you need to choose a genre that can be explored across all three different media platforms (moving image, print and web-based media). You may find that one of these platforms is more important and you may find it useful to familiarise yourself with how the genre operates within one medium before exploring how conventions are adapted to other media platforms.

To think of cross-media genres is not as difficult as it may seem at first. For example, comedy can be identified on television in sitcoms, on internet websites such as YouTube and in a range of magazines and comics. Lifestyle media are found in magazines such as *Country Living* and *House Beautiful*, in Sunday newspaper supplements, on television, in programmes such as *Relocation, Relocation, Relocation* (Channel 4, 2005–), on various websites such as that of Channel 4 and Primelocation or on kitchen and garden design CD-Roms.

The following are general examples of genres:

■ *war media* – including films, TV programmes, websites and magazines

■ *hip-hop or other music genres* – investigating music press, the music itself and websites of bands, individual musicians, fans and those used to promote and review music

■ *news* – looking at press, television and internet news

■ *children's programming* – looking at websites, games, TV programmes, comics and magazines

■ *sport* – looking at TV, web and newspaper coverage.

💡 Case study: the gangster genre

The gangster genre can be used as the subject of a case study. The case study can begin with an investigation into the gangster films, such as *Little Caesar* (1930), *Public Enemy* (1931) and *Scarface* (1932), which became popular during the great depression and the rise of organised crime that accompanied the ban of alcohol during the 1930s prohibition. The case study could include a brief investigation into why the gangster genre returned to popularity during the economic crisis of the late 1970s and early 1980s when there was again a rise of organised crime in relation to drugs, in particular with films such as the *Godfather* trilogy (1972, 1974 and 1990) and *Goodfellas* (1990). There are also a range of more contemporary gangster films such as *Layer Cake* (2004) and *American Gangster* (2007) that can be included in the discussion.

Some of the identifiable genre characteristics of gangster films include:

■ a narrative structure based upon the rise and fall of the gangster who is usually from an immigrant or marginalised ethnic group

■ visual iconography of guns, urban places, cars and family gatherings

■ themes of violence

■ an ideology that hard work can temporarily bring financial success even if the hard work is put into criminal activity.

In addition, there are a range of gangster-focused computer games, including *The Godfather* and *Mafia II* and the *Grand Theft Auto* series, as well as newspaper and magazine coverage of the type shown in Figs 4.14 and 4.15, which can be considered.

Approaches and investigation

As well identifying the narrative structure, visual iconography, ideology and themes of each genre, you will need to investigate the producers and audience of your chosen genre. As particular genres catch the mood and preoccupation of the social, economic, political or cultural context in which they are produced, it is important to consider the context in which a genre was produced.

The following are key questions to consider in your research and investigation into a particular genre.

■ How is the genre adapted and developed between media platforms and over time?

■ How and why does the particular genre appeal to audiences and producers?

■ Are there issues of gender, race, sexuality and age to be considered in relation to the audiences to which the genre appeals?

■ How is the particular genre a product of the context in which it is produced?

■ Is genre still a useful concept in the post-modern media world?

BRITAIN'S most notorious gang lead lives that mimic the fictional heavies from The Sopranos or Lock, Stock & Two Smoking Barrells.

Among the most notorious is crime lord Terry Adams, who was jailed for seven years last year after he admitted money laundering. This week he lost an appeal against the sentence.

Adams was outwardly a dapper gent in his velvet-collared overcoats. He lived in a £2 million house in North London crammed with stolen antiques, a far cry from his upbringing on the rough Barnsbury estate in Islington.

But his family and associates are reputedly worth £200 million and are feared far more than the Kray twins ever were.

Bugs placed by MI5 agents in Adam's home caught the gangster sounding like Marlon Brando in The Godfather.

In one tape, recorded in July 1997, Adams was heard discussing a dispute over a missing sum of £50,000.

He told jeweller Solly Nahome, his "financial adviser", who was shot dead in 1998: "Let Simon give the geezer a good hiding . . . tell him to use the family name." In another conversation Adams said: "When I hit someone with something I do them damage."

But unlike in the gangster movies, the sickening violence is horribly real.

In a third he told how he dealth with a row over cash. He said: "100 grand it was, Dan, or 80 grand, and I want crack."

"On my baby's life, Dan, his kneecaps came right out there . . . all white Dan, all bone and white . . .'"

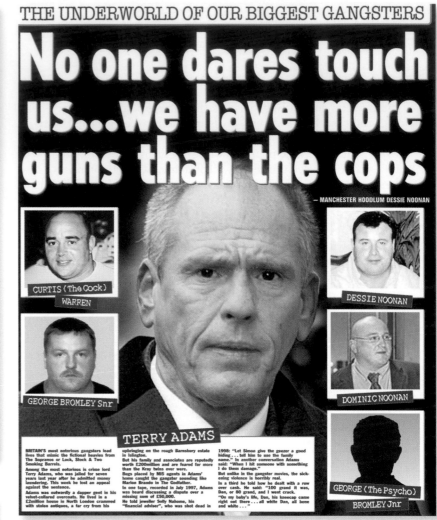

Fig. 4.14 *Notice in this and Fig. 4.15 how the newspaper narratives of 'organised crime' reference gangster films* **a** *in the drama of the overall presentation above and* **b** *in the text printed in the margin alongside* (**Sun**, *12 April 2008*)

'Ocean's 11' safe gang get 20yrs

A gang of Ocean's 11-style safe-crackers was jailed for a total of almost 20 years yesterday after a series of raids on betting shops.

The syndicate broke into 24 bookies in three months – and got so skilled cops called their technique "a fine art".

The seven men made off with more than £300,000 and left branches of Corals in London and Kent looking like bomb sites.

Initially they spent hours attacking the heavy duty safes with angle grinders, drills and other tools.

Later the gang, led by career crook John Robinson, 30, used safe-cracking techniques more suited to the 1950s and could spring safe doors open from the inside.

After destroying metal armour on the outside, they drilled through up to six inches of concrete at a particular spot on the safe that triggered the door mechanism.

They became so expert they could crack a safe in half an hour.

Detective Constable Steve Marshall told Woolwich Crown Court: "The damage and debris they caused was quite phenomenal, like a bomb had gone off. They got better and better at doing it until it was almost a fine art."

But the gang were trapped by hidden CCTV cameras. In one raid, Robinson was filmed attacking a cash machine with a pick axe and jemmy for 45 minutes.

Last night Detective Inspector Peter Highley, of the Met's Territorial Police Crime Squad, said: "If they had put their skills to better use they would probably have become good tradesmen."

The raiders admitted conspiracy to commit burglary between May and August last year.

Robinson, of Bethnal Green, East London, has 36 previous convictions. He has since told Corals how to improve their security. He was jailed for five years and four months.

Fellow Londoners Michael Mehmet, 31, from Peckham, got three years; Edward Cairns, 29, of Rotherhithe, three-and-a-half years; Kingsley Daniel, 20, from Poplar, two years plus a further year for unrelated offences; Brian Donnelly, 27, of Bow, 15 months, and Derek Johnstone, 27, from Bermondsey, 21 months. Terry Fraser, 18, from Southwark was sentenced to two-and-a-half years youth custody.

Judge Charles Byers said: "This was a story of sophisticated banditry."

Fig. 4.15 **a** *The text from the article '"Ocean's 11 safe gang get 20yrs',* **b** *shown in its complete form in the margin alongside* (**Sun**, *12 April 2008*)

'OCEAN'S 11' SAFE GANG GET 20YRS

Raiders' skill stuns cops

A GANG of Ocean's 11-style safe-crackers was jailed for a total of almost 20 years yesterday after a series of raids on betting shops.

EXCLUSIVE by ANTHONY FRANCE, Crime Reporter

The syndicate broke into 24 bookies in three months – and got so skilled cops called their technique "a fine art".

The seven men made off with more than £300,000 and left branches of Corals in London and Kent looking like bomb sites.

Initially they spent hours attacking the heavy safes with angle grinders, drills and other tools.

Later the gang, led by career crook John Robinson, 30, used safe-cracking techniques more suited to the 1950s and could spring safe doors open from the inside.

After destroying metal armour on the outside, they drilled through up to six inches of concrete at a particular spot on the safe that triggered the door mechanism.

They became so expert they could crack a safe in half an hour.

Detective Constable Steve Marshall told Woolwich Crown Court: "The damage and debris they caused was quite phenomenal, like a bomb had gone off. They got better and better at doing it until it was almost a fine art."

But the gang were trapped by hidden CCTV cameras. In one raid, Robin-

Crack job . . . old-style

son was filmed attacking a cash machine with a pick axe and jemmy for 45 minutes.

Last night Detective Inspector Peter Highley, of the Met's Territorial Police Crime Squad, said: "If they had put their skills to better use they would have become good tradesmen."

The raiders admitted conspiracy to commit burglary between May and August last year.

Robinson, of Bethnal Green, East London, has 36 previous convictions. He has since told Corals how to improve their security. He was jailed for five years and four months.

Fellow Londoners Michael Mehmet, 31, from Peckham, got three years; Edward Cairns, 29, of Rotherhithe, three-and-a-half years; Kingsley Daniel, 20, from Poplar, two years plus a further year for unrelated offences; Brian Donnelly, 27, of Bow, 15 months, and Derek Johnstone, 27, from Bermondsey, 21 months. Terry Fraser, 18, from Southwark was sentenced to two-and-a-half years youth custody.

Judge Charles Byers said: "This was a story of sophisticated banditry."

a.france@the-sun.co.uk

For more cracking crime reads head to thesun.co.uk/justice

Texts and contexts

It is important to consider genre products in relation to the social, historical and political context in which they are produced. For example, significant contextual factors leading to the increased popularity of cookery shows in the 1990s and 2000s are:

■ the rise of consumer culture

■ an increasing focus on lifestyle, taste and domestic style

■ anxieties about diet and health.

From when Michel Boulestin first appeared in a programme entitled *Cook's Night Out* (1937) cookery programmes have been the mainstay of television daytime schedules. More recently cookery shows are being aired in the more popular 6–9pm slots, albeit on the less popular channels, and are accompanied by a growing number of print and web-based related texts.

It is important to identify the conventions of your chosen genre, for example, for TV cookery programmes these include:

■ Todorov's (1997) theory of narrative structure – equilibrium, disequilibrium, new equilibrium – is identifiable in shifts from ingredients to mess to new food

■ an educational or instructional, direct style of address has changed to an interaction between one or more people

■ the mode of address

■ a focus on the preparation of food

■ food preparation as skill

■ men's expertise rests upon their role as restaurant chef and women's on their role as wives and mothers

■ middle-class cultural values, tastes and milieu

■ a celebrity focus

■ a visual style that was originally a three tripod style, replaced by active camera movement

■ an expandable series format that enabling further series to be produced.

It is also important to identify the institutional motivation for producing the genre at a particular point of time. Thus, in institutional terms, TV cookery programmes can be seen as an option for cheaply produced TV that can compete in the environment of contemporary multi-channel digital television. They also offer a range of related streams of funding including product placement (technically illegal in UK at present), related advertising and through the sales of books and DVDs. Furthermore, cookery programmes are able to fulfil institutional remits for public service broadcasting, providing information, education and entertainment.

Similarly, you need to identify the appeal of the genre for a particular audience at a particular contextual moment. It is not coincidental that cookery programmes have increased in popularity at a time when less and less cooking is being done in the home. Arguably, the appeal of TV cookery programmes can be understood in relation to, on the one hand, cookery being seen as a domestic chore and somewhat mundane, versus the image of food as pleasure, leisure or sexual fantasy. For example, eating is placed, in *Nigella Bites* (2001) and *Nigella Express* (2007), in a sexual and pleasure category, with a focus on indulgence and consumerism.

■ **Investigating media**

The cookery genre can produce an interesting case study. This can be done by initially selecting at least three very different TV programmes, from different channels, times in the schedule and audiences for analysis and investigation. You can include at least one cross-genre text, such as *Ready Steady Cook*, as well as explore the extracts of TV cookery shows on YouTube. The analysis can be taken further through two or three related print media texts, for example, magazines such as *Olive*, *Delicious* and *Observer Food Monthly*, as well as by analysing two or three related websites, such as the BBC cookery website (www. bbc.co.uk/food) and Jamie Oliver's website (www.jamieoliver.com).

Finally, it is important to be aware of shifts in the genre that is being dealt with in a case study. In recent years there have been significant shifts in genre as different institutions produce programmes for different audiences. A number of genre hybrids have appeared as a result, for example, the merging of reality TV with the cookery show in *Ramsay's Kitchen Nightmares* (Channel 4, 2004–), the merging of game show and cookery show in *Ready Steady Cook* (BBC, 1994–) and the merging of travel show with cookery show in *Hairy Bikers' Cookbook* (BBC, 2004–). Each of these hybridisations aims to increase the audience of the genre, by pulling on established audience loyalty to both genres.

Using a critical framework

Genre theory, based upon structuralism and the work of Neale (1980), see page 117, provides the basic critical framework for genre study. This framework suggests that genre can be understood as an implied contract between audiences and producers. This means that the audience knows what to expect from a genre product and that the media producer is able to ensure a regular audience for their particular genre product, for example, a specific genre of computer game or a film of a particular genre. Thus media institutions tend to produce media texts that are known to be popular with audiences, so that they can maximise profit and minimise risk. In addition, standardisation of production can result in particular media producers acquiring the skills, facilities, enthusiasm and a reputation for a particular genre product.

Genres are also a by-product of the way audiences work, as audience pleasures may be enhanced by the mixture of expectation and differentiation in genre texts. Thus audiences often like a sense of predictability in choosing a media text; they enjoy having their expectations met and seeing how the format is adapted so that the text is distinguished from others in the genre. Furthermore audiences may get pleasure and a sense of status from their knowledge of a particular genre and recognition of its features and stars.

Genres go through cycles of popularity; their success leads to over-production with audiences becoming bored. This is often followed by media producers creating parodies of genres, which render the original genre texts ridiculous. For example, *Shark's Tale* (2004) can be seen as a parody of the gangster genre as it utilises the narrative structure of a gangster film and the voices of actors known for playing gangsters to make a cartoon about fish.

A range of other theories, critical approaches, concepts, issues and debates may be useful in undertaking a genre case study. These may include:

■ the politics of representation – specific genres may have particular representational practices

■ moral panics – certain genres are more likely to evoke moral panics

■ media effects, audience theories and the active audience

■ post-modernism and globalisation.

It can be argued that in the contemporary, media-saturated, post-modern world genre is no longer a relevant way of analysing media texts. Some arguments that challenge genre theory include the following.

■ Genres are often not identified by audiences or producers, but by media critics at a latter time.

■ Texts are often categorised and marketed by the stars and celebrities utilised, rather than the text's narrative structure, visual style, ideologies or themes.

AQA Examiner's tip

In undertaking case studies of genre you will have to critically engage with debates about whether you see genre as a useful tool for analysing media texts, across media platforms, in a fluid and changing contemporary media landscape.

- The idea of genre has been taken to extremes by sequels such as the *Harry Potter* films (2001–), and even prequels.
- Many media texts are now genre hybrids – mixtures of more than one genre.
- Media texts often contain a *bricolage* of inter textual references to other texts.
- Innovative texts defy genre categorisation.

Collins (1992) argues that contemporary Hollywood films take two approaches to genre.

- *Eclectic irony* – whereby traditional elements of genre are used in a completely new and very different setting. For example, the *Star Wars* movies (1997–2005) can be seen as Western genre movies set in space.
- *New sincerity* – where a sincere attempt is made to rediscover lost generic conventions. For example, the Coen brothers film *The Man Who Wasn't There* (2001) can be seen as a sincere attempt to recreate the generic conventions of Film Noir.

■ Audiences' participation in construction of the media

In the contemporary media landscape there are an increasing number of areas where the audience can play a part in the construction of the media. This is especially true for web-based media where audiences can, for example, construct videos to be uploaded onto YouTube or create their own profiles on MySpace. Audiences contribute to the construction of both print and moving image media in a variety of novel ways, for example, as a contestant on a reality TV show, on a radio phone-in or by sending a letter or problem into a newspaper or magazine.

Audiences' participation in the construction of media texts is an important area of study for media theorists. These theorists debate the extent to which an audience's participation shifts the balance of power between media institutions and audiences.

Making a case study

In order to undertake a case study that looks at an audience's participation in the construction of media, it is important to look at topics that can be explored across all three media platforms. A focus on a particular theme, genre, area or issue will enable you to do this. Examples that you might like to consider are:

- *documentary and 'true life' stories* – on TV, in print media and websites
- *audience participation in music* – in TV talent shows, on YouTube and MySpace and in reviews for print media texts
- *problems and relationship issues* – on talk shows, in print media problem pages and through website networks
- *local issues* – local TV, radio and internet sites
- *audiences' views* – in letters, phone-ins and website posts.

Approaches and investigation

To complete an in-depth case study on audiences' participation in the construction of media texts you need to:

- investigate the texts that you have chosen in relation to production, audience and context

Investigating media

The quiz and game show genre can be successfully analysed in a case study format. Once thought of as outmoded, they have had a revival since the launch of *Who Wants To Be A Millionaire?* (ITV, 1998–) by the independent production company Celador. Having been sold to over 100 countries it is now the most internationally popular television franchise of all time.

Fig. 4.16 *First person, true-life narratives not only appear in a range of print media publications, but are also the mainstay of mass-market consumer publications, such as* **That's Life** *(24 April 2008)*

■ Investigating media

For an interesting case study you could select a marginal group, such as single parents, and explore the range of media texts where audiences from this group participate in media construction. For example, documentaries, reality TV, such as *Young Mum's Mansion* (BBC, 2008), *The Jeremy Kyle Show* (ITV, 2005–), true-life stories of single parents in women's magazines or interviews and problem pages in print media texts and web forums such as YouTube (www.youtube.com) and Netmums (www.netmums.com).

The key questions to consider are as follows.

■ To what extent do single mothers control their representation?

■ How do institutions or media producers control the image and voice of single mothers through the process of media construction, for example, through editing voice-overs or the views of experts?

■ How do these issues shift between different genres and media platforms?

■ undertake a close comparative textual analysis

■ consider the following questions:

– How is the balance of the power between audience and producer influenced by the audience's participation in the production of media texts?

– How and to what extent is the audience's participation structured by media producers?

– Does the audience's participation in the construction of media texts produce different representations?

– How does media language and editing represent the audiences and their contribution to the text?

– What are the advantages for media producers in constructing texts with a significant degree of audience participation?

– Are groups that were once excluded from participation in the media now getting a voice?

– Are there different social groups participating in and consuming specific media texts?

– What is the appeal for audiences in media texts where the audience has participated in the construction?

Fig. 4.17 *Many television audiences dream of taking part themselves in the construction of media, potentially becoming celebrities; the gap between producer and audience becomes to them more blurred (www.thecastingsuite.co.uk/newfaces)*

Texts and contexts

It can be argued that the rise of audience participation in media texts is due to a number of factors. The most significant of these reasons relates to the cost of producing media. For example, talk shows such as *Trisha* (ITV, 1998–2005 and Channel Five, 2005–), reality TV such as *Wife Swap* (Channel 4, 2003–) and talent contests such as the *X Factor* (ITV, 2004–) all provide relatively cheap TV programming. Similarly, the use of images of readers' wives in adult magazines, such as *Fiesta* or girlfriends in *Nuts* and *Zoo*, saves expenditure on models.

Audience participation in phone-ins and online voting can raise significant amounts of money for media production companies and this has an obvious financial appeal for institutions. However, in the mid-2000s, there were a number of accusations aimed at television companies regarding the collection of voters' money after voting had closed and audience's votes in online polls being overridden by producers. For example, the children's television show *Blue Peter* (BBC, 1955–) issued an apology to viewers in September 2007 when it was discovered that, in the previous year, the winning name voted for by viewers (Cookie) was ignored and the new *Blue Peter* cat was named Socks.

Even with the tighter controls on making money from audience participation, for media producers there is a perception that audience participation can be translated into audience loyalty. For example, if the audience takes part in the construction of a media text by phoning a radio station, adding a post to an online newspaper article, voting for a contestant in TV show such as *I'd Do Anything* (ITV, 2008) they are more likely to develop a sense of loyalty to this media text and remain part of its audience.

Alternatively the greater involvement of audiences in media products can be seen as a reflection of the contemporary 'confessional culture' in which media is now produced. This culture shows a preoccupation with personal relationships, with a tendency to discuss and confess in public what would once have been a private matter. For example, the make-over television programme, *The Sex Inspectors* (ITV, 2004–), focuses on a couple's sexual problems. An expert then provides advice and guidance to help the couple improve their sex lives.

Using a critical framework

A wide range of the theories, critical perspective, concepts, debates and issues introduced in earlier topics may usefully be drawn upon to assist you in developing a critical perspective to texts where the audience participates in their construction. These include:

■ reality TV
■ realism
■ the politics of representation
■ celebrity
■ censorship
■ new media youth and music
■ debates about the audience's use of media and the extended audience
■ who controls the media, audience or producers?

Shuttac (1997) focuses upon audience participation in the construction of media texts by looking at the popular TV talk show host, Oprah Winfrey and her show *Oprah* (Harpo/ABC, 1986–). She argues that *Oprah*

Investigating media

An interesting potential case study dealing with audience participation in the construction of media texts could focus on gambling within the media. The case study could look at websites, such as PokerRoom (www.pokerroom.com) and TV programmes, such as *Quiz Call* (Channel Five, 2005–). A number of virtual reality poker game sites are available online where participants can enter 'rooms', and construct and participate in virtual games. Similarly, audiences phone in, chat and participate in gambling programmes, such as *Sky Poker* (Sky, 2005–) and contribute to their construction, increasing the producer's profits. Note that Ofcom has now reclassified gambling channels along with teleshopping and advertising.

operates as public sphere for the discussion and debate of a wide range of ethical issues rarely covered in other areas of the media. Shuttac went on to argue that working class and black participants' representation on the show was very controlled by the production company, experts and Oprah herself. Despite this control the show was valuable as it served as one of the only areas that such groups were able to participate in television culture and ensure they had some cultural representation.

■ Media and democracy

It can be argued that in a democracy the media has a vital role to play in keeping citizens informed of government actions, questioning these actions and providing citizens with all they need to know in order to make an informed choice in local and national elections. However, there is much debate about whether the selectivity of media representations influences the operation of democracy in a prejudicial way, favouring some political groups and marginalising others.

To many media analysts, the growth of media texts, facilitated by new technology, offer the potential for a wide range of different political viewpoints to enter the public sphere.

Making a case study

In selecting a case study that deals with the issues that surround media and democracy, there is much benefit to be gained from focusing on a topic that is subject to controversy and/or you have some interest knowledge or concern about. A good place to start is by looking through print or web-based newspapers. The following are also worth considering as potential case studies:

■ the Iraq war
■ immigration and race relations
■ terrorism
■ an American or British election
■ animal rights
■ immigration
■ ASBOs (Anti-Social Behaviour Orders)
■ celebrity and politics
■ charities or pressure group politics in a democracy, including charity records, press campaigns and TV extravaganzas.

Approaches and investigation

In your case study you must include a careful exploration of the production and audience with reference to the historical, economic, social and political context of the selected media texts. There are also a range of questions that you will need to consider to ensure that you approach your selected media texts in a critical fashion.

■ To what extent does the media operate as a public sphere, enabling the formation of public opinions critical of the government?
■ Does the media encourage the sensationalism and trivialisation of political issues?
■ Which groups are able, and not able, to get their views across in the media and why?
■ What regulation of the media is permissible in a democracy?

■ Investigating media

The debate around democracy and the media is a general topic that is too broad for the scope of your case study. You could refine your focus onto the issue of the punishment of criminality and prisons, for example. To do this, you could explore films and TV documentaries focusing on prisons, soap operas or chat shows that represent criminals such as *Bad Girls* (ITV, 1999–2006) and *Prison Break* (Channel 4, 2005–) and debates in the press about sentencing and prisons. There are a range of relevant websites for local prisons and debates held in Parliament are published through Hansard. There are also websites produced by interested pressure groups, such as the Howard League for Penal Reform (www.howardleague.org) and the Prison Reform Trust (www.prisonreformtrust.org.uk).

- How has new media shifted the workings of democracy?
- What role does the media play in constructing hegemony?

Texts and context

In adopting critical approaches to a case study dealing with media and democracy, you need to carefully consider the context of production and audience. For example, a comparative case study looking at the role of the media in an American versus a British election; or in a national versus a local election, requires careful investigation into the context in which the media texts are produced. An important element of this context is the nature of the media institution that creates the text.

The screening of debates between the American Democratic presidential candidates in 2007 and 2008 via both television and YouTube is an example of the democratising potential of new/digital media – 'ordinary' citizens sent in questions rather than watching questions framed by a TV interviewer.

The context in which a media text is consumed, by whom, how, when and where, are important questions to consider in relation to the role of media in democratic nations. Although there are a range of media spaces where information about the workings of democracy is available, their place in the audience's everyday life may limit the degree to which any

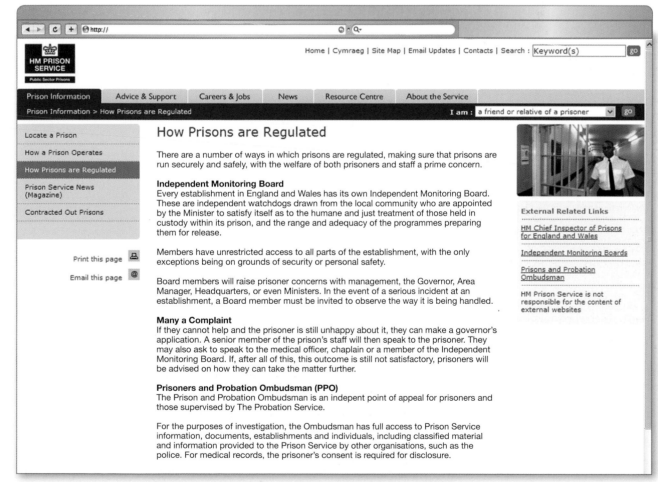

Fig. 4.18 *HM Prison Service's website appears to present an informative and ideologically free representation of prisons. What do you think this site contributes to the debate about the place of prisons in a democratic society? (www.hmprisonservice.gov.uk/prisoninformation)*

complex political debates can be explored. For example, many newspapers are only glanced at or flicked through, people often use the television news as a break and many informative, politically engaged websites have a limited number of hits or time spent reading their material. For many people the sheer quantity of media material results in information overload. People become 'informed citizens' through small sound-bites of news or information on the radio or on the entry page of their web server.

One of the key debates that you will need to consider in relation to media and democracy is whether the contemporary media landscape has led to a focus on sensationalism and trivialisation of serious political issues. In addition some media critics question the extent to which politicians have become media-savvy celebrities, at the expense of serious political debate.

Censorship is also a significant area of debate for this issue, especially as media regulation of content is dependent on historical economic, political and social context. Different regulations operate in different countries at different times, for example, web-users in China have been blocked from accessing the term 'Human Rights' on internet search engines. You cannot buy or watch the pro-Hitler documentary *The Triumph of the Will* (1935) in Germany.

There are very different national perspectives on how much citizens have a right to know about government departments and institutions or about MPs and people with power in a democracy. For some people knowing if a married MP has an extra-marital affair, employs family as part of his or her parliamentary staff or claims parliamentary expenses to complete house renovations are issues of public interest, which should be freely available in the media. Others see this as an intrusion into a political figure's private life or symptomatic of a culture fixated by gossip, scandal and trivia.

guardian.co.uk

Debate brings Youtube to centre of 2008 presidential campaign

Old media enter into an uneasy alliance with new media tonight to grill the Democratic candidates in the United States's 2008 presidential race.

CNN and YouTube, the video-sharing website, are holding a joint debate in which the public have sent in video-recorded questions for Hillary Clinton, Barack Obama and the other candidates.

Hours before last night's deadline, more than 2,300 videos recorded on webcameras and mobile phones had been submitted.

Among them is a 30-second clip from a cancer survivor who removes her wig and says her chances of survival are not as good as they would have been if she had had health insurance.

"What would you, as president, do to make low-cost or free preventative medicine available for everyone in this country?" she asks.

The event is being hailed by the organisers as a breakthrough for the new media, comparable to the impact of television on politics when Richard Nixon debated with John Kennedy in 1960.

But some bloggers, who see the internet as a democratic free-for-all, have expressed unhappiness about the involvement of CNN. The candidates will meet in a military college in Charleston, South Carolina and watch the questions being displayed on a 7.6 metre by 5.5 metre screen.

Allowing CNN to select the 25-30 questions has upset many bloggers.

Questions submitted so far cover climate change, immigration, gay rights, welfare and foreign policy. The ratio of questions about Iraq is low in comparison with the extensive daily coverage it gets in US papers and on television.

Although CNN is filtering the questions, there is the potential for the quirky or emotional question that might unsettle a candidate.

Steve Grove, head of YouTube's news and politics section, told the Washington Post: "These YouTube questions - a lot of them, anyway - are intimate, emotional, personal. That person is in his/her surrounding, and that person is bringing you into their world, their reality. That makes it a very powerful experience."

Some of the videos do not ask questions at all: in one, a man plays guitar and sings a song about potential vice-presidents; another includes a talking duck; one man, making a point about the impact of petrol on the environment, is shown driving a 1987 Chevy convertible.

Phil Noble, founder of PoliticsOnline, told Reuters YouTube's increasing coverage of politics was significant. "In the past, the campaigns sort of stuck their toe into technology and innovation - it was a small detail of what was going on. The difference in this election is that technology has become fundamental. Every campaign has figured out ways to use YouTube all the time."

The internet played a small but short-lived role in the 2004 presidential election, with online donations funding the sudden rise of the Democrat Howard Dean. Online Democratic bloggers played a bigger part in last year's Congressional elections.

But the internet is shifting into a central position in this campaign in terms of disseminating ideas, fundraising and mobilising support, particularly among the young.

YouTube, which did not exist during the last presidential campaign, has already had an impact on this one. More than 2.5 million people have viewed the video I've Got A Crush ... On Obama since it was posted last month and a follow-up about women fighting over Mr Obama and Rudy Giuliani, the Republican frontrunner, has been watched more than 500,000 times since it appeared last week. A Hillary Clinton campaign spoof on the final episode of the Sopranos was also popular.

YouTube effectively knocked the former Republican senator George Allen out of the race . A video of him last summer referring to a dark-skinned Virginian as "macaca" cost him re-election to the senate and a tilt at the presidency.

CNN and YouTube are to join forces again on September 17 for a Republican debate.

Fig. 4.19 *The influence of a large conglomerate such as CNN on these debates and their framing raised questions about the representations produced (www.guardian.co.uk/media/2007/jul23/broadcasting.digitalmedia)*

Another area to consider is the extent to which freedom of expression contributed to the operation of a democracy, and when and where it should be constrained. For example, is it right to censure some political views from television or the internet?

Using a critical framework

Debates about representation are important to an exploration of the relationship between media and democracy. If, for example, a constructionist approach suggests our sense of reality is constructed through media texts, then the reality through which we assess our governments and make decisions as informed citizens is entirely constructed by the media.

Many of the other theories, critical perspectives, debates and issues you covered in Chapters 1 and 2 are also of relevance to a critical investigation of media and democracy, for example:

■ censorship and media regulation

■ moral panics

■ news values

■ Habermas and the public sphere

■ audience theory and the active audience

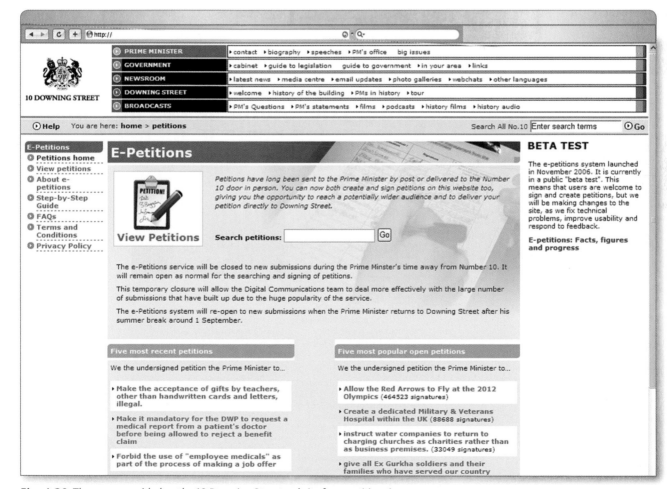

Fig. 4.20 *The space provided on the 10 Downing Street website for e-petitions is supposed to enable citizens to feed their views and requests for action to the government – do you think it is an effective process? (http://petitions.pm.gov.uk)*

- media organisations
- Marxism and liberal pluralism
- the politics of representation
- celebrity
- who controls the media – audiences or producers?

According to Curran and Seaton (2003), the media should have a key role in society. Media should work with Parliament, the government and the legal system to form the fourth essential element of a democratic system. It should provide a link between the government and the people and keep citizens informed about what the government is doing. It can be argued that in recent years the widespread growth of new/digital media has made connecting the government and citizens easier and less mediated. Most politicians have their own websites, as do all government departments and the Prime Minister's office at 10 Downing Street. In the first two years of its operation (up until March 2008), the 10 Downing Street website has had over 29,000 petitions formed by visitors to the site, many of which have several thousand votes recorded in support of them.

In addition, records of all Parliamentary debates are published on the internet, many politicians and political parties upload videos onto YouTube and the BBC broadcasts Parliament proceedings on its digital channel: BBC Parliament.

Media's engagement with important issues in a democracy does not only occur within serious genres such as news or documentaries. Political groups require support, consensus and hegemony – all of which are as likely to be developed from issues debated in soap operas or chat shows as in newspapers.

Investigating media

There is the potential for an interesting case study of how political blogs and websites are being used in political campaigning in contemporary political culture. The case study could focus on a particular political event. One example is comparing the celebrity status of two leading candidates in the 2008 US presidential election campaign, as constructed through YouTube and mainstream media. This comparison could also explore the role played by informal political bloggers such as John McCain's daughter.

'Bittergate' storm shows how blogs have spread panic in US journalism

The net-led furore over Barack Obama shows that radical change is contorting the world of political reporting, writes Edward Helmore

At 61, Mayhill Fowler, a San Francisco housewife, Obama supporter and part-time contributor to OffTheBus.net, a campaign journal published by the neo-liberal commentary website the Huffington Post, is an unlikely source for a breaking news story that briefly looked as if it might derail the Illinois senator's presidential campaign.

The instant sensation of Obama's comments about bitterness, God and guns in small-town America, and the inference that he was an elitist, supplied his rivals with ammunition and the US media with almost a week of news, commentary, counter-reaction and expectation of further excitement to come.

If Obama is beaten in Pennsylvania's primary vote on Tuesday then his comment that small-town voters bitter over their economic circumstances 'cling to guns or religion or antipathy to people who aren't like them' may come to be seen as pivotal to his campaign.

For the media, the episode shows how the internet is changing the reporting of politics. The event was closed to journalists; Fowler was only invited because she had given generously to Obama. 'We had a fundamental misunderstanding of my priorities,' she told the New York Times.

Fig. 4.21 *Candidates in the 2008 American election discovered that new media meant that nothing they said was off the record; anything could turn up videoed and on a website* (**Observer**, *20 April 2008*)

☑ Approaching the examination

The assessment objectives for Unit 3 outline exactly what is expected of students in the exam:

■ *AO1* – demonstrate knowledge and understanding of media concepts, contexts and critical debates

■ *AO2* – apply knowledge and understanding when analysing media products and processes (and evaluating own practical work) to show how meanings and responses are created.

The examination has two sections:

■ *Section A* requires you to respond to two unseen media texts in relation to three questions

■ *Section B* requires you to answer one essay from a choice of four topics, using one of your case studies in relation to one of the two pre-set topic areas.

Your investigation and the knowledge and understanding gained from your case studies should also inform your response to the unseen texts in Section A, which will relate to the two case studies.

Sample examination paper

Read carefully through this paper and any past papers available online via the AQA website, ensure that you thoroughly understand what is required of you in the exam and if uncertain about any of the instructions on the front of the sample paper discuss this with your teacher well in advance of the exam.

Unit 3 Sample paper

General Certificate of Education

Advanced Level Examination

Specimen Paper

MEDIA STUDIES
Unit 3 Media: Critical Perspectives

For this paper you must have:

an 8-page answer book

Time allowed: 2 hours (including 15 minutes reading time)

Instructions
Use black ink or black ball-point pen.

Write the information required on the front of your answer book. The Examining Body for this paper is AQA. The paper reference is MEST3.

Answer all *three* questions in Section A.

Answer *one* question from Section B.

Information
The maximum mark for this paper is 80.

In this paper you should explore and make connections between the different elements of your study of the media. You should refer to a range of media issues and debates.

In this paper you will be expected to show that you understand media concepts; how meanings and responses are created within media products and processes and the relevant contexts of production and reception.

Advice
You are advised to read the question paper carefully first.

You are advised to spend 15 minutes reading the texts and making notes. These notes will not be marked.

You should then spend 45 minutes writing your answer to Section A.

You should spend 1 hour planning and writing your answer to Section B.

Quality of Written Communication
Quality of Written Communication will be assessed in all of Section B. You are required to:

- ensure that text is legible and that spelling, punctuation and grammar are accurate so that meaning is clear;

- select and use a form and style of writing appropriate to purpose and to complex subject matter;

- organise information clearly and coherently, using specialist vocabulary where appropriate.

SECTION A

You have *15 minutes* in which to study the texts on pages 132 and 133 and make notes.

You should then answer *all three* compulsory questions below.

You are advised to spend *45 minutes* answering the questions.

1   Compare and contrast the two texts, with particular reference to the representation
     of teenagers.   *(8 marks)*

2   Consider the view that the current press treatment of teenagers is simply another
     'moral panic'.   *(12 marks)*

3   There are always concerns about new technology. In your view, what are the possible
     benefits and problems attached to social networking, particularly on the Internet?   *(12 marks)*

SECTION B

You should answer *one* question.

You are advised to spend *1 hour* on your answer.

You will be rewarded for detailed reference to specific media texts and to your own case study.

Representations in the media

1   (a) It has been said that media representations often reflect the social and political
         concerns of the age in which they are created. Discuss.   *(48 marks)*

OR

1   (b) "Media representations favour those with power at the expense of those without".
         To what extent do you think this statement is true?   *(48 marks)*

The impact of new/digital media

2   (a) "Digital media have, in many ways, changed how we consume media products."
         Who do you think benefits most – audiences or producers?   *(48 marks)*

OR

2   (b) "Media institutions are right to feel threatened by new/digital media." Consider
         this statement and show how media institutions are reacting to technological
         developments.   *(48 marks)*

END OF QUESTIONS

END OF THE SPECIMEN QUESTION PAPER

Text One

This text is the front page of *The Metro*, published on 21 Febrary 2007 by Associated Newspapers, London

FREE **METRO**

Wednesday, February 21, 2007   www.metro.co.uk

WIN
A short
break in
Monaco

Page 34

The YouTube gangsters

Exclusive: How armed teenage thugs recruit over Web

BY JOHN HIGGINSON

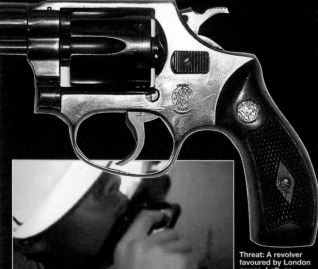

Threat: A revolver favoured by London gangs. Left, an image taken from a YouTube gang video

VIOLENT street gangs are using Internet networking websites to advertise and recruit members, Metro can reveal.

Teenage thugs post videos on YouTube and MySpace showing themselves brandishing firearms, taking drugs and speeding along suburban streets in powerful cars.

Other clips appear to commemorate gang-members who have 'fallen in combat'.

The revelation comes days after 15-year-old Billy Cox was shot dead in his South London home.

One video shows members of the Younger Woolwich Boys, from South-East London, posing with weapons.

One youngster, who looks no older than 14, even cocks a pump-action shotgun before pointing it at the camera.

A film recently removed from MySpace showed a boy with blood oozing from the side of his mouth, being forced to strip by members of a South London gang called Don't Say Nothing.

He is then slapped and told to identify himself, show his gold teeth and repeat the name 'DSN'.

A spokesman for London-based charity 100 Black Men yesterday claimed Internet sites are being used by gangs to 'send out messages to each other'.

He said: 'Gang members are putting these messages up to make themselves visible to their rivals. But innocent and naive kids are getting caught up and drawn into it.'

The Metropolitan Police say they are aware of gangs using YouTube and MySpace.

Both websites ban footage which is deemed to be 'threatening or offensive', but regulation is difficult with tens of thousands of videos being uploaded each day.

Text Two

This text is taken from the website for *The Daily Mail*.

Daily Mail

Why this gang of young yobs must now be called a 'group'

By **Steve Doughty**
Social Affairs Correspondent

ANYONE who has been a victim of their contempt for the law or menacing behaviour might find it a little difficult to swallow.

But on the orders of a government agency, gangs of teenage criminals should no longer be called 'gangs' because it might offend them.

Instead they should be referred to as 'groups' and their crimes described as 'group-related'.

The instruction comes from the Youth Justice Board, which organises probation, training and detention for under 18s.

It echoes the decision by the Metropolitan Police three years ago to drop the phrase 'gang rape' and replace it with 'group rape'.

Officers reasoned then that the word gang can wrongly suggest clearly-defined membership.

The YJB sets out its case in a 200-page report on 'gangs' and how teenagers are drawn into them. It

'Dislike being labelled'

states: 'Many young people interviewed for this study resented the way in which the term had come to be used to describe any group of young people involved in anti-social behaviour. They felt adults attached the label to them simply on the basis that they were young and met in a group, assuming that crime was their main purpose for meeting.

'In fact, the label conjured up an image with which they might not want to be associated, even where they were involved in offending – not least because in some cases they knew from their own local experience what real gangs were and several of the young women in particular had suffered at their hands.'

The report said that some youngsters could find the idea of a gang seductive because of crime films and TV programmes and black 'gangsta' music.

It added: 'There has been a noticeable trend toward referring to groups of young people indiscriminately as gangs.

'This is not appropriate and it could exacerbate the extent and seriousness of group-related

Watch your language: Teenagers resent the word 'gang'

Posed by models

offending or create problems where none previously existed.

'Juvenile gangs do exist in some urban areas, but most young people involved in group offending do not belong to gangs – even if others label them in this way.'

Examining the broader issues behind youth crime, the agency said that chaotic family lives and the lack of role models were frequently to blame.

It found that youngsters drawn into gangs overwhelmingly come from family backgrounds characterised by disruption, conflict and single parenthood.

Young men follow brothers or more distant adult relatives into crime as they look for someone to emulate.

For many from the worst backgrounds, a gang provides a home life better than their 'chaotic and unstable' families, it added.

The findings are further evidence linking broken family life with crime.

Children of single parents are far more likely to do badly at school and drift towards vandalism and crime. In particular, boys who grow up without fathers are at risk of falling into criminal behaviour.

The report said: 'Teenagers could gravitate toward gangs and group violence as a result of poor family relationships, exclusion from school, absence of positive role models and a lack of youth facilities.'

It found that among 25 girl gang members interviewed, only two lived with both parents.

■ The Oxford English Dictionary says a gang is 'any band or company of persons who go about together or act in concert (chiefly in a bad or deprecatory sense, or associated with criminal societies)'.

s.doughty@dailymail.co.uk

Section A: responding to the unseen texts

The unseen texts are likely to be from different media platforms; it is therefore important to carefully consider what the significance is of each platform to the production, text and audience.

The examination allows for you to spend 15 minutes studying the texts, reading or viewing them. Use this time actively. If the unseen text consists of a video or DVD extract, it will be shown to you three times, with pauses in between for you to write notes. Under the pressure of an exam it is easy to forget the finer details of what you have seen on a video, so do ensure that you write notes.

In your answers do not just give common-sense personal opinion, but incorporate what you have learned from your case studies and write from a theoretical, critical perspective. Show the examiner what you know, but make sure you answer the question that has been asked. Show that you have studied the key concepts by incorporating the concepts into your answers and not by listing each concept and its relevance in turn.

Use theories, critical perspectives, current media debates and issues and media terminology only if they are appropriate to your argument and can be applied to the specific media texts presented in the questions.

It is important to plan your answers by initially writing notes, in a list or jotted across a page, on each question and then constructing your answer. Below there is an example of the sorts of notes, comments etc. that you might write in relation to Question 1 of the sample paper.

Keep all three questions in mind as you make notes and construct your answer; you don't want to get carried away with answering Question 1 only to discover that you have covered areas that need to be addressed in Question 2. Underline the key words in the question.

Section A, Question 1 *Compare and contrast the two texts, with particular reference to the representation of teenagers*

Example notes:

	Text 1	Shared issues	Text 2
Production	■ Freebie newspaper – relies on adverts and circulation	■ Crisis in newspaper industry – ageing and falling readership	■ Newspaper website – needs advertising
Text	■ Visually more striking ■ Ideology/values internet suggested as cause of youth problem ■ Use of black background and gun to signify threat and trouble ■ Image of gun and reference to gangsters utilises gangster genre ■ Representation of black youth as threatening gangster – issues of race and 'otherness' ■ Emotive language	■ Representation of teenagers as trouble ■ Signifiers of youth as trouble ■ Importance of tag lines to other parts of paper or website	■ Image of group of youths – baseball cap, drinking from can and congregating in a public space – the street – signify trouble ■ Attack on political correctness and sense of antagonism to experts' views on language etc. ■ Appeal to notions of common sense – assumed knowledge of single parents and the breakdown of the family, focusing on gangster rap and crime TV as cause of problems ■ Ridicules the problems of emotive language
Audience	■ London-based commuters (social groups?), paper needs to appeal to them in order for them to pick it up		■ Web-browsers who are actively looking for newspaper or topic ■ Silver surfers? As *Mail* has an older audience than many papers
Context		■ Post-modern, insecure and uncertain world ■ Risk society	

You will need to structure your response carefully. The opening sentence should ideally respond to the question. Use the following opening sentences and the notes above as a starting point to construct three paragraphs to answer Question 1.

> There are significant similarities between these texts; both are products of relatively recent responses by newspaper producers to carve out new markets...
>
> Both texts represent teenagers as trouble and as threatening ...
>
> However, the media language utilised by these texts to do this and their representation of what causes teenagers to become troublesome, differ...

Section A, Question 2 *Consider the view that the current press treatment of teenagers is simply another 'moral panic'*

The notes you made on each text will be useful in answering this question, but you need to tap into a range of media debates and issues:

■ moral panics

■ media effects

■ debates about audiences.

You could also discuss the politics of representation, who is representing who in the press? It is important to define concepts in the introduction and then show that you can utilise them.

Use the following paragraph beginnings to construct an answer to Question 2. Although each of these openings to paragraphs presents an argument it must be elaborated on using examples, quotes and specific references to the stimulus texts.

> Cohen (1972 and 2002) argues a moral panic occurs when society sees itself threatened by: the values and activities of a group who are stigmatised as deviant and seen as threatening to mainstream society's values, ideologies and/or way of life. In recent years there have been a number of moral panics about teenagers, for example: gun crime, gangs, drinking and anti-social behaviour leading to the introduction of ASBO's. It could be argued that much of this has been caused by the press, these two texts are examples of this...
>
> However, these texts also tap into a number of other moral panics in the contemporary risk society. For example, there is a sense of panic in both these texts around the effects of media and the perception that youth are passive, vulnerable consumers of the internet, gangster rap and crime...
>
> There is also evidence of a moral panic around 'family' in these texts. The <u>Mail</u> website suggests ...whilst the <u>Metro</u>...
>
> News values suggest that bad news sells newspapers and this may lead to moral panics, that the press often treat teenagers in this way is an indication of who owns, writes and are the readers of these papers...

Section A, Question 3 *There are always concerns about new technology. In your view, what are the possible benefits and problems attached to social networking sites on the internet?*

This question invites you to account for both a utopian and dystopian perspective on social networking sites. Making notes on this is a good starting point towards constructing and answering the question.

Example notes:

Utopian perspective on social networking sites	Dystopian perspective on social networking sites
■ Democratising publishing – everyone can be a media producer ■ Less censorship and control by large institutions of broadcasting means scope for otherwise marginalised groups to represent themselves ■ The web brings people together and provides scope to build new communities – this may be particularly important for groups marginalised from mainstream media and society	■ There is little control over the quality, content, values and ideologies perpetrated on social networking sites ■ The material produced may have harmful effects particularly on vulnerable young children who, because of the privatised nature of such media consumption, are not regulated by their parents ■ The web may bring together communities whose values, ideologies and actions are threatening or morally reprehensible to the society but is being legitimised through social networking spaces

It is useful to expand on the utopian and dystopian arguments above in the first two paragraphs of your essay. Remember, however, that the texts are supposed to act as a stimulus and so it is important to link your answer to the texts and use some of the examples therein to support your points. For example, you could point out that many of the criticisms of the 'effects' of social networking sites are also voiced against traditional media. You could directly refer to both articles or suggest that the iconography of new/digital media, such as social networking sites, often comes from traditional media, for example, 'gang' referred to in the *Metro* article, mimics gangster movies.

You could also point to the problems of the polysemic nature of these texts, especially when taken out of context. For example, you could discuss whether the teenage members of a gang posing with weapons described in *Metro* were merely playing at producing their own gangster-movie images, perhaps involved in a post-modern ironic pastiche.

Section B: preparing and presenting your case study

Section B is made up of four questions (two on each of the topics) from which you will select **one.** Respond to this question using your case study and by referring, in detail, to the texts you have studied in it. Remember that you cannot take any notes into the exam with you.

You will need to show that you have studied these texts and your chosen topic from a critical perspective. Make sure you draw upon theories and concepts and engage with the relevant current media debates and issues. Simply listing facts about platforms and the texts is not enough to gain a good mark (your understanding developed from the case study will help you in answering questions in Section A of the examination, too).

Section B carries the highest proportion of marks, so ensure that you leave enough time to produce a well-crafted essay.

Read all the questions carefully before making your choice and stick with the question that will enable you to really utilise the thought and analysis that has gone into your case study. You should not answer a question because it looks interesting if you have not got the research and textual reference to support your answer.

Remember that you should discuss all three media platforms in your answer and discuss a range of media texts in detail. There is only space here to consider two of the questions in Section B, one of which is discussed in full and the other in brief.

Section B, Question 1b *'Media representations favour those with power at the expense of those without.' To what extent do you think this statement is true?*

This question invites discussion around the politics of representation, including:

■ Marxism and liberal pluralism

■ feminism

■ Queer theory

■ post-colonialism and race.

Debates about stereotypes may also be of relevance. The question should be answered with reference to at least one group or place focused on in your case study. There are a number of different responses that you could take to this question, such as:

■ *yes* – media representations do favour those with power

■ *no* – media representations do not favour those with power.

However, the use of the word 'extent' in the questions suggests that you are expected to engage in a debate that explores how much representations favour those in power, as well as what factors influence the extent to which representations favour those in power.

Your introduction should respond to the question, provide any relevant definitions and explain to the examiner what case study you will be drawing upon in your answer. For example:

> To a large extent media representations do favour those in power, for, as some Marxists argue, the powerful tend to control the intuitions which produce media texts. Indeed Dyer (1979) argues that stereotypes (a form of media shorthand) are made by the powerful about the less powerful. However, the advent of new media has provided potential sites for groups to represent themselves. In this essay I shall discuss the extent to which media representations favour the powerful with reference to the representation of gay men.

You may want to follow your introductory paragraph with a brief paragraph that covers some of the historical, cultural, economic and social context in which representations take place. For example, if you were using gay men as a stereotype, you might consider the legal changes in relation to homosexuality since the 1960s, the sin and sickness paradigm within which representation takes place and the significance of civil partnerships in recent years.

In planning your answer, you have probably got the scope to make three or four points really well. The following are suggestions of points and opening statements using teenagers as a case study example.

Osgerby (1998) argues that the term 'teenager' only occurred after the Second World War and that teenagers are represented in terms of trouble, freedom or consumer. For example...

One of the problems that surrounds the issues of representation of teenagers is that in traditional media they are rarely part of the process of producing representations. For example, newspapers and documentaries on teenagers...

However, the audience for which a representation is produced do exert some power over representations. In texts with a primarily teenage audience there is a greater variation in representations, which may therefore represent the teenager as less powerful teenager for example...

New media texts including blogs and social networking sites provide scope for teenagers to represent themselves. For example...

Finally, it is important to point out that representations cannot always be easily defined as favouring one group or another; they may be polysemic. For example...

AQA Examiner's tip

Keep updating your case study by following the current media. Contemporary examples earn marks and show critical autonomy. Always give real and recent examples to support your views and your learning. Form your own views and be prepared to argue your case in an examination.

Section B, Question 2a *'Digital media have in many ways, changed how we consume media products.' Who do you think benefits most – audiences or producers?*

In answering Question 2a you will need to draw upon your case study – for example News and New Media – and to consider what theoretical debates will be of relevance, such as:

■ utopian and dystopian debates about new media

■ questions about who controls the media – producers or audiences

■ marxist and liberal pluralist debates about audience theories.

You will need to structure your answer into an argument, responding to the question in your introduction and aiming to make three or four points which are supported by examples from your research. Remember that you need to discuss all the different media platforms – perhaps referring to television, newspapers or radio in an initial historical paragraph.

Chapter summary

This chapter has emphasised the importance of utilising the theories, concepts, critical perspectives, ideas and debates about the media to undertake Unit 3 of the examination.

The format and requirements of the two parts of the exam and suggested ways of approaching the questions in the sample exam paper have also been considered.

For the exam you will be undertaking case studies in two of the following:

■ representations in the media

■ the impact of new/digital media

■ genre: audiences and producers

■ audience participation and the construction of media texts

■ media and democracy.

Suggestions for case studies, concepts, theories and debates that will be of relevance and ways of undertaking these case studies have therefore been explored.

4 Research and production

5 Independent research

In this chapter you will:

- become confident in choosing a topic for both your critical investigation area and your linked production

- understand what is required when undertaking primary and secondary research to prepare both elements of your coursework

- know how to formulate a title or hypothesis for your critical investigation and ensure that your linked product is appropriate

- feel ready to plan the structure of your own critical investigation

- become aware of what the examiner is looking for and how to maximise your grade potential.

Key terms

Synoptic: showing a breadth of view that demonstrates learning in different areas of media study.

Link

Remind yourself about the basics of media forms, representations, audiences and institutions by looking back to your AS textbook, Topics 2 and 3.

Chapters 5 and 6 are linked, and together will support your study of Unit 4, Research and production. Chapter 5 will take you through research skills, while Chapter 6 will help you to build on the learning and experience of practical work you gained at AS Level. The introduction to this unit in the specification states that:

> 'In this **synoptic** unit candidates will build on their skills from AS study to investigate a media theme/text in more depth and realise a production piece reflecting this research.'

Following your reading of these chapters, you should feel confident in demonstrating your learning from across the specification in this manner.

Linking research and production

Identifying a topic with good assessment potential

Unit 4, Research and production requires you to produce a critical piece of research (approximately 2,000 words in length), together with a piece of practical work inspired by your critical findings. It is useful to complete the research component first, followed by the practical work and final draft of your investigation. The critical investigation must contain integral references to the media you have produced. It is advisable to write a number of drafts to ensure that references are incorporated appropriately alongside the making of the practical work. The written aspect of the study is worth 48 marks and the linked production is worth 32 marks.

You will be expected to:

- *AO1* – demonstrate knowledge and understanding of media concepts, contexts and critical debates

- *AO3* – demonstrate the ability to plan and construct media products using appropriate technical and creative skills

- *AO4* – demonstrate the ability to undertake, apply and present appropriate research.

For AO1, you need to show that you are confident in exploring the key concepts specific to your field in your written work. This includes media forms, representations, audiences and institutions. You will also be expected to show knowledge of narrative, genre and semiotic analysis, using them to draw conclusions about the ideological values of particular texts, and critically evaluate how their meanings may vary according to factors identified by exploration into the concepts.

You must also be able to explore your area of focus within its broader cultural context. This means considering your topic within its political, economic, cultural and social contexts. You should also be able to account for how audiences respond to or interact with the text or texts you identify as part of your study.

■ Link

You will need to use the knowledge you gained of media platforms in Chapters 1 and 2 of this book to assist you, particularly where you are evaluating the links between institutional, audience and technological factors.

■ Link

For further information on the linked production, see Chapter 6.

AQA Examiner's tip

Try not to choose something you're a 'fan' of unless you're absolutely sure that you are able to maintain sufficient critical distance from your text. Many of the best studies are chosen with the head not the heart. If you decide to choose a text you really like, think carefully about exploring a second, contrasting, but linked text as part of your secondary research – this will help you reflect on the first text.

AQA Examiner's tip

Remember that your choice of text must be contemporary – this means it must have been first printed, broadcast or made available digitally in its present form within the last five years.

Being aware of critical debates means you will need to use not only your knowledge of current debates surrounding media production, such as regulation and censorship, but also be able to select relevant theoretical perspectives you will have encountered elsewhere on the course, particularly in Unit 3, Critical perspectives. Your research will carry much more weight if you are to show that you can confidently apply, for example, the ideas of feminist or post-colonial theorists or refer to the different ways in which genre debates have evolved recently.

For AO3, unlike in Unit 2, in Unit 4 you will not be expected to provide physical evidence of your pre-production planning, as it is expected that the quality of your pre-production work will be implicit in the quality of your final product.

For AO4, the critical investigation and the linked production provide an opportunity to explore an area of the contemporary media that really captures your interest. However, you must remember that this is a critical investigation. This means that it is essential to maintain a critical distance from your topic and to ensure that you will have undertaken appropriate research to support your findings from a variety of sources. This means being able to 'stand back' from your chosen text or area and see it from a Media Studies perspective rather than that of a media consumer.

Regardless of the format in which you choose to present your research, it is good practice to provide a detailed bibliography. However, in reality, the quality and range of the research you have undertaken will be just as evident in the practical work you produce. It will be clear from the meanings you offer and the methods by which you choose to convey them just how much your critical writing has informed your technical and aesthetic choices in creating practical media for this unit.

🔍 *How do I choose a topic?*

To meet the requirements of the module, you will explore, in-depth, a text, theme, issue or debate relevant to the contemporary media landscape. This exploration will inform your production piece. This means basing your arguments on real media texts. The following examples illustrate how you can transform an initial interest in a text into a workable and rich research area, together with a linked production.

An initial interest in the contradictory messages about the fashion industry and its associated media offered in the US TV series *Ugly Betty* (Channel 4, January 2007–) can be explored further. Or an investigation

Fig. 5.1 *Screen shots from* **Ugly Betty** *(Channel 4) and* **Ross Kemp on Gangs** *(Sky One)*

as to whether representations of groups of men in the media are always portrayed as negatively as in the programme *Ross Kemp on Gangs* (Sky One, 2007, Series 3) might be considered. You could use these initial points of interest to begin to identify a research angle.

Some of the initial research could involve considering whether other contemporary texts that are linked in some way offer some possibilities for comparison, even if you still decide to use the text you originally identified as being of interest as your main focus. Below is an example.

 ## Case study: *Ugly Betty*

Text	Point of comparison	Notes
The Devil Wears Prada, dir. David Frankel, 2006. A mainstream Hollywood literary adaptation following the fortunes of a young woman trying to launch a career in journalism, who ended up as a PA for a high-profile fashion editor	This film text presents the audience with a similar narrative proposition; a supposedly non-conformist and clever but unfashionable young woman lands a high-profile job as an assistant to an editor on a fashion magazine, each hoping it will further their more noble aspirations for a career in journalism. Each then exposes the values of the industry as shallow and materialistic.	Demonstrates through similarity the popular appeal of such narratives, but may be too similar to be really useful.
Next clothing advert, Autumn 2007	This advert references the opening sequence of *The Devil Wears Prada* and uses the same soundtrack.	Could be really interesting with the above text; would need to reference the above if using this as a text with *Ugly Betty* anyway.
Features from fashion magazines, such as *Marie Claire* or *Vogue*. Any appropriate current issue	Texts that exist to promote the fashion industry would make an interesting comparison with one that on the surface appears not to condone its values but may covertly promote them none the less.	Can't see too much of a problem with this – nice to use a text from another platform, too.

Case study: *Ross Kemp on Gangs*

Text	Point of comparison	Notes
Tribe, BBC documentary fronted by Bruce Parry, series 3, 2007	This documentary predominantly examines the behaviours of male groups in tribes around the world, as well as the role of women in the tribe. Women's experiences of everyday life tend to get less coverage than the men.	Might be interesting – more positive representations of men in this anthropological documentary. Too rich in other areas for comparison?
Local newspaper report on a teen gang crime spree. Selected from a local paper, 2008	An extremely negative representation.	Quite good to use news to contrast with documentary. This forms a really nice cross-platform link.
Top Gear, current series, 2008	A more subtle text; 'laddishness'?	Could be a challenge to compare, but if managed successfully could really tell me something about attitudes.

■ Key terms

Hypothesis: an informed assumption you make about a topic area of your choice in order to focus your line of enquiry during your research.

Fig. 5.2 *Student undertaking primary research into both a moving image and print text*

Conducting research

The distinction between primary and secondary research is not always clear in Media Studies and may depend on the title or **hypothesis** you formulate. Essentially, for the purposes of the critical investigation you should consider primary research to be your own analysis and ideas concerning the text(s) you are investigating. This may also be undertaken to a lesser degree with secondary texts – those that you are using for comparison or to illuminate your main text. These might be either contemporary or historical texts, but you must always ensure that the main focus of your debate is on contemporary texts.

Secondary research, which is equally important, involves researching your text, debate or issue using other sources such as relevant academic text-books, internet sites, magazines, journals and newspapers. This can get a little confusing – if a magazine or newspaper article is your primary text, a documentary that references your topic could easily become a secondary source. The important thing is that you are clear when planning your study, which sources you are using and how.

Primary research

Primary research is research that is undertaken by you into the text or texts themselves (which are your primary source), using the tools of analysis and theoretical frameworks you have encountered in other topics. It could also involve the acquisition of appropriate production skills, such as creative camera-work, radio directing techniques or web-design, during the linked production. Once you have decided on the text(s) you wish to make the centre of your study, you should study it/them carefully and begin to organise your ideas under conceptual headings, as illustrated in the case study that follows. Remember that in primary research you must support each point you make with evidence from the text.

■ Case study: *Water Voles*

> *Water Voles* is a short wildlife documentary that was shown on BBC Two at 9.50pm on a Friday during October 2006. It followed the documentary *Galapagos*.
>
> **Media forms**
>
> - Gentle soundtrack of guitars and strings is used to mediate mood and the changes in seasons – generally unobtrusive.
> - 'Voice-of-God' style voice-over – documentary mediated by an unseen and unnamed authority on the voles' activities.
> - Close-up shots allow privileged, detailed views of wildlife usually glimpsed at a distance.
> - Establishing shots (long) of canal signify the change in seasons.
> - Diegetic sounds of the canal recorded to connect us with the environment.
> - Cycle of seasons used to organise the narrative – spring associated with beginnings.
> - Simple chronological and linear narrative structure constructed through straightforward visual grammar and aural codes.
> - Binary oppositions – world of man versus world of nature.
> - Villains are the predators – grass snakes, mink and pike all threaten our heroes, the voles (Propp, 1928).

- Sets up the enigma (Barthes, 1968) as to why these endangered creatures are thriving in this unlikely place.
- The audience expects this genre to expose it to things they don't usually see (in this case the voles of the Cromford Canal).
- Text follows the fortunes of a particular group of animals, in a particular place, over a particular time period.
- Voice-over used to make sense of the behaviours of animals, sometimes **anthropomorphising** – seen here in the references to 'Ratty' who can obviously speak and has other human characteristics in the book T*he Wind in the Willows*.
- Informs the audience of surprising, dramatic, moving or interesting facts about the creatures.
- Operates within a framework of behaviours the audience can understand, for example tolerating cold weather, finding food, mating, having families etc.

Audience

- Uncontroversial content – wildlife documentaries are popular with a broad target audience.
- Mode of address straightforwardly didactic, again supporting family viewing (although maybe not on this occasion – 9.50pm).
- British – produced by, for and about British environment.
- Audience likely to have viewed quite demanding 50-minute documentary about a less familiar environment (*Galapagos*) – this is a nice 'wind-down'.
- Offers Utopian solution of transparency (Dyer, 1992) (we get to see what the voles get up to), community (they are a 'family'), energy (the voles are constantly on a quest for food, the seasons are compressed into a very short period of screen time) and intensity (the voles live short lives, apparently filled with feasting and sex).

Representations

- Tone is optimistic in spite of creatures being endangered.
- Voles represented as being busy, resourceful, greedy, yet fluffy and cute, chosen for mass appeal.
- Shows voles as part of an eco-system, which also includes their predators and other wildlife, such as birds with which they share the canal.
- Behaviours, which might not otherwise make coherent sense, are mediated to us by the voice-over.
- Humans represented as unobtrusive, harmless and ignored by the voles.
- Assumes a familiarity on part of audience with the character of 'Ratty' in the story *The Wind in the Willows* (written in 1908 by Kenneth Grahame – considered a children's literature classic), which is referred to several times.
- Man and nature can co-exist.
- British wildlife is represented as important, valuable and worth conserving.
- Suggests that the natural world can be surprising and much around us is hidden.

Media in action

Diegetic sound – sound that appears to be produced within the world of the documentary.

Non-diegetic sound – sound that is added afterwards, such as a voice-over or music. This is a complicated distinction with wildlife documentaries – with foley sounds such as broomsticks used to make antlers sound as if they're clattering and so on!

Key terms

Anthropomorphising: giving an inanimate or non-human subject human-like qualities to create a particular effect.

Link

For more information about Dyer's theory of Utopian solutions, see the Media in action box after this case study.

Institution

- The BBC has a public service remit to 'inform, educate and entertain' – in this documentary an attempt is made to do all three.

- This kind of programming is relatively cheap to produce – small production team, no outlay on cast or sets etc. Differs from the expensive, large-scale Attenborough documentaries in this respect.

- BBC Two – alternative Friday night programming to the more lively fare offered by BBC One and other terrestrial channels that may seek more to entertain – a good programme of 'wildlife wind-down' after a busy week.

- *Galapagos* (the preceding programme, a high profile 'quality' nature documentary) could be 45–50 minutes long because the BBC intends to sell it on to other channels, which may carry at least 10 minutes of advertising in the hour.

- Used here as a schedule 'filler'. Short films and video diaries have been used in a similar way over the years by the BBC. Will not date – has been broadcast at least once before as a short series.

■ Media in action

Richard Dyer's theory of Utopian solutions

This is a great theory for thinking about what media audiences get from almost any media text. Dyer (1992) proposed that media texts helped make up for some of the deficiencies of modern life. These were as follows.

Community – media texts often present us with groups of people working towards common goals, and constructed communities that we can vicariously enjoy. This is in contrast with real life, where increased population movements and other societal pressures such as increased isolation, the breakdown of the extended family and fear of crime have diminished real-world communities. Social networking online is an interesting phenomenon in this respect!

Intensity – most people's lives consist predominantly of routine, such as going to work or college, raising family etc. Media texts offer worlds where exciting things happen as a matter of course, and this is pleasurable for the audience. Consider the age-old complaint about soap operas not being true to life (as if they had a duty to be!) and think how dull they'd be without all the dramatic events that befall characters and families within them.

Abundance – one of the key pleasures of many media texts is seeing worlds where people can drop whatever they're doing and pursue adventures without any apparent financial cares. We also love to see glamorous and exotic locations and lifestyles that contrast with our own. Abundance may not just be about money – texts can offer an abundance of other desirable things such as open landscapes as well as material wealth.

Transparency – the narrative cohesion and privileged positioning of the audience in many texts allows us an experience of media consumption where motives are laid clear and, unlike in real life, all the answers are (usually) provided. This is one of the appeals of news consumption in that it helps us make sense of the real world by rendering it comprehensible through familiar narrative codes and news values. Transparency is also evident in the popularity of long-running TV series such as *Spooks*, *Casualty* or *The Bill*, which give us fictionalised insights into the operation of our nation's institutions (MI5, the NHS and the police force).

Energy – the daily routines of most people's lives, as suggested under the heading *Intensity* (above) are tiring. They are so tiring, in fact, that the energy many people have left at the end of the day is just about enough to turn on the TV and watch others looking less exhausted! Texts that harbour energy are not just about people, but also about editing style, colour, *mise-en-scène* and the sense of spectacle contained within many media texts. Print media texts with a lively and bright/colourful layout can equally be said to have energy.

Secondary research

Effective secondary research should perform a number of functions.

It should:

■ provide you with evidence to support claims made in your primary research

■ add layers to your argument that you may not have previously considered

■ allow you to discover more in-depth information about your topic, providing you with contextual information about institutions, historical contexts etc., which you can include in your discussion

■ provide more information that adds to your argument by showing it is not limited to a single text

■ provide you with the tools needed to test your hypothesis

■ make you aware of issues relating to your investigation that you may not have time to cover in detail. You can show an awareness of them by raising them.

Part of intelligent research is being able to select the most appropriate materials from the many you come across and not trying to include everything.

Using secondary texts

For the *Ugly Betty* case study on page 141, there are number of potential secondary texts that could be explored, which would broaden the argument. All of the following could provide interesting wider referencing:

■ *Absolutely Fabulous* (BBC, 1992–6 and 2001–5) – a long-running sitcom about the lives of two women, Edina and Patsy, who work in the fashion industry

■ *Fig Leaves* (Howard Hawks, 1929) – one of the earliest films about the fashion industry

■ *Zoolander* (Ben Stiller, 2001) – a comedy film about a male model

■ *Prêt-à-Porter* (Robert Altman, 1994) – another satirical film about the superficial nature of the fashion industry

■ *What Not to Wear* (BBC One, 2005) – reality TV make-over show where participants are given heavy-handed style advice from 'experts' Trinny and Susannah.

Investigating media

Choose one of your favourite media texts. Using the format shown here, conduct your own primary research and present it in the form of bulleted notes, as above.

Link

The critical investigation case study on pages 152–160 includes a bibliography and a commentary, giving an examiner's perspective that will aid you as you develop your own.

AQA Examiner's tip

It is very important that you acknowledge any sources that you use, in order to avoid any accusation of plagiarism. Regardless of whether you write a traditional essay or not, you should provide a complete bibliography, which should include:

■ titles of the books with their author, publisher and publication date

■ articles from journals, magazines and newspapers

■ websites, including the dates accessed, and a one-line descriptor describing the site content and usefulness.

Fig. 5.3 *Using secondary texts for research*

Viewing a couple of other texts that explore similar issues to your chosen text can help you to find new angles that you might not have otherwise considered. Through repeated observation of narrative shape, content and flow, stereotypes or elements of mise-en-scene, you may find new layers in your existing text.

Using books and journals

You are expected to read some academic books that relate to your research topic. Some topics will have a number of relevant articles and books that deal with them, such as the older genre forms of soap opera or science fiction. A digital media topic may have fewer. A college or school library or media department may have single or multiple copies of a range of older A-level Media Studies text-books; they may also have some books on advertising or film genres and other topics, which may prove very useful to you.

There are however a number of other research possibilities that could make your critical investigation even more authoritative and confident. Consider (if you have the funds) buying second-hand books via the internet – these can be resold after you have finished with them. A website such as Amazon can be surprisingly useful in identifying available books relevant to your topic. Put words from your study into searches, see what comes up and read the reviews. You can order these books from your local library, through inter-library loans, if you do not want to buy them new or second-hand. Libraries can also help you search for similar relevant titles – all for free or a small charge.

Universities that offer media-related degrees will have many relevant books and journals. While private membership can be expensive, many university libraries offer a service where you can buy photo-copying credits for educational purposes. The advantage of this is that you may find many texts relevant to your topic on display, or you can read, make notes and take quotes from them while you are at the library.

Journals are periodicals relating to specialist areas of academic study. Your best chance of finding useful journals is, again, a university library. However, keep looking out for electronic journals on a range of media-related topics online. Good examples include 'SCOPE' (www.scope.nottingham.ac.uk), which is the well-established online journal of the Institute of Film and Television Studies at Nottingham University and 'E-Media Studies' (journals.dartmouth.edu), which is a newly created journal (2008) dedicated to the study of digital media and also considering aspects of television consumption.

Using the internet

Using the internet effectively for research is a real skill. The main area that presents difficulties is differentiating between the varying levels of quality of information found on the internet. Film reviews and fan-sites or forums are unlikely to be of much use to you, unless you are specifically studying audience interactivity or the functions of the user-generated review.

Using sources and quotes with no credibility of any kind actually damages your investigation more than simply leaving them out. This looks as though you can't tell the difference between research that genuinely adds something to your study and the ramblings of an opinionated blogger three time zones away.

AQA Examiner's tip

It is clear when a student has not taken enough time over their web research. The information used is often simply a repeat of the student's opinions and the quality can be poor – badly written, opinionated and inaccurate.

Make sure you don't copy and paste or otherwise plagiarise *anything* you find on the internet. This is easy for teachers and moderators to spot, and could jeopardise your marks for your whole critical investigation.

So how do you go about sifting through all the information on the internet?

Some examples of good and relevant web resources to use are:

- ▪ *industry websites* – e.g. www.mediauk.com/tv/news, news site for TV industry professionals
- ▪ *promotional sites owned by media organisations* – e.g. ABC.com, home of the US TV channel
- ▪ *online or electronic journals relating to media study* – e.g. www.scope. nottingham.ac.uk, film and TV journal
- ▪ *examples of undergraduate or post-graduate work on university websites that show-case some of the best work* – eg.www.aber.ac.uk/ media, the Media and Communication Studies site at Aberystwyth University
- ▪ *media education sites* – e.g. www.filmeducation.org, which provides a range of interesting resources on various film texts
- ▪ *archives of online versions of newspapers* – e.g. www.guardian.co.uk, which allows you to search for relevant stories.

If you refer to websites from the above categories you will be able to filter out a certain amount of poor quality information, but you must still be very careful. Think about what you're reading and don't take everything at face value. For example, Wikipedia is an incredible cultural and intellectual phenomenon that offers a good starting point for research into a lot of topics. However, only use it as a starting point. Do not rely on it even when an entry is very appropriate to your investigation and is clearly written by an academic expert in your field.

> ### Investigating media
> Find an example of both a useful and a less useful Wikipedia entry that relates to two media topics of your choice. Write a short evaluation of each, explaining why the entries either are or aren't useful.

Using magazines and other print media

Don't forget to keep an eye out for anything in the press or magazines you read that relates to your topic and may prove interesting from a cross-platform perspective. It's a good idea once you've settled on your text and topic to compile a list within your Media Studies class of the texts and topics you're all hoping to explore. This means you can be each others' eyes and ears – other students are often very willing to help you out by collecting and bringing in or alerting you to anything relevant they see coming up in TV schedules or on the magazine shelves in the supermarket.

Linking the investigation with a production

The linked study should not be treated as an afterthought, but should be an integral part of the planning stage even though it is recommended that you complete the research stage of the critical investigation before you go into production. The specification offers a number of examples of suitable linked productions. More detailed support on this area is available in Chapter 6 (pages 173–175).

When initiating your independent research planning, you may or may not have a clear idea of what you hope to produce. Try to avoid a situation where you have put a great deal of energy into your critical investigation with no idea of what form your linked production is likely to take. The four examples offered below will hopefully give you some inspiration for the possibilities offered both by particular texts and the productions to which you could link them.

Critical investigation 1

How and why do wildlife documentaries such as *Water Voles* (BBC Two, 2008) and *Life in Cold Blood* (BBC One, 2008) sustain the interest of BBC audiences in the digital age?

Possibilities for linked productions

■ The opening three minutes of a conventional new wildlife short documentary for the BBC, which establishes the environment and habitats to be explored in the documentary, complete with voice-over.

■ A website for a new 'diary-style' documentary based on an aspect of British wildlife.

■ Front cover, contents and feature articles from a new magazine that encourages younger children to look for wildlife in the city, town or countryside.

Critical investigation 2

Ugly Betty: what are the problems inherent in portraying a world of fashion, aspired to by many people, in a negative light?

Possibilities for linked productions

■ Front page, contents and three-page feature article from a new alternative fashion magazine promoting real women and high fashion looks, on a low budget.

■ A website and blog by a mystery industry insider debunking myths associated with the fashion industry.

■ The first three pages of a new weekly newspaper targeting employees of the fashion industry.

Critical investigation 3

Boys don't cry: how do the contemporary documentaries *Ross Kemp on Gangs* (Sky One, 2007) and *Tribe* (BBC Two, 2007) represent masculinity?

Possibilities for linked productions

■ A series of three 30-second TV adverts from a public information campaign designed to warn young men of the dangers of gang culture.

■ A four-minute documentary produced for the FourDocs website (www.channel4.com/fourdocs) where women of different ages are asked to express their views on what they think today's men are like.

■ Five-minute segment from a talk radio discussion and phone-in about whether there is still a place for 'the gentleman' in the 2000s.

Critical investigation 4

How does the BBC Film Network website (www.bbc.co.uk/filmnetwork) function as both distributor and exhibitor in the digital age and what does this mean for the future of the short film as a media form?

Possibilities for linked productions

■ A short narrative fiction film suitable for submission to the Film Network website.

■ A new website set up to showcase short film-making by A Level students of Media and Film.

■ Three one-minute comedy films designed to be disseminated by mobile phones.

🔆 🔍 Research study

Hypothesis and titles

It is recommended that you conduct some of your primary research and possibly some secondary, before you write your title. This will then

---

Investigating media

The early stage of preparation is the best time to explore your options. Look at the following five possible topics for critical investigation. For each topic, try to think of three possible linked production outcomes.

■ An exploration of representations of British identity in three promotional trailers for British films produced in the previous year.

■ A study of the contemporary TV news landscape, including the interactive features of *BBC News 24*, BBC Three's *60 Second News* and the 'your news' feature on Channel Five's evening news.

■ An examination of current trends in car advertising, with a focus on three different strategies represented by three different adverts.

■ The iPod as a marketing phenomenon – its current advertising campaigns and the impact the device itself has in shaping popular media consumption.

■ Curbing consumerism: *Spendaholics* (BBC Three, 2008) and the *It Pays to Watch* TV series (Channel Five, 2008) and website (www.moneysavingexpert.com).

need to be submitted by your tutor to a coursework adviser for approval. It's important that you do actually do some research prior to this stage, because, once agreed, your title can't be changed without specific approval from AQA. This means that if you find yourself suddenly at a dead end, it becomes more awkward to get permission to change your study and you'll have wasted valuable time in the process.

The more care that is put into formulating a title and identifying an appropriate linked product, the more likely it is that the coursework adviser will approve your title with only small amendments. The benefit of getting a coursework adviser's advice and input before you have done too much work on the topic is that they can help to make sure you're on track and support you in obtaining the best chance of success.

Although many people choose to submit this assignment as a traditional essay, there are other formats that can be used such as:

- a Wikipedia-style entry on your topic or text
- a DVD commentary
- a podcast
- a feature in a magazine for media students.

Whatever format you choose, the wording of your title is very important. There are no hard and fast rules, but it should be worded so that it:

- defines the text or area of investigation you have chosen
- identifies your approach to this text or topic.

Often your title will contain a question or hypothesis – as this is a critical investigation and not a descriptive overview your aim is to find something out! Your study must be lively, exciting, and test ideas, whatever the format it is presented in.

Look again at the case study *Ugly Betty* on pages 140–141 and the related texts. There are a number of different angles that could each emphasise particular texts, conceptual areas or concepts. The examples below are best suited to a more traditional, essay-style approach. They demonstrate, through seven different titles, how it is possible to vary your angle and the emphasis on different aspects of the text in order to find the focus you really want.

- Why is the deadly serious world of fashion so often a target for comedy? Exploring *Ugly Betty* (*Absolutely Fabulous* and *Zoolander* as secondary texts).

  Possible angles:
  - ideology
  - representations
  - media forms.

- Cultural imperialism in *Ugly Betty* and *The Devil Wears Prada* – how and why does fashion travel?

  Possible angles:
  - institution
  - representations.

- Fashion travels – assessing the relative conformity of the mainstream media product in *Ugly Betty* and *The Devil Wears Prada*.

  Possible angles:
  - institution
  - media forms.

■ Representation and the fashion world – how does the audience relate to a world so far removed from the experience of most? Intertextuality in *The Devil Wears Prada* and Next's recent TV advertising campaign.

Possible angles:

– audience

– representation.

■ Why do we both celebrate and denigrate in media texts what we love in the real world? *Marie Claire* and *Ugly Betty*.

Possible angles:

– representation.

■ What are the inherent problems in portraying a world of fashion that people aspire to in a negative light? Wilhelmina; Amanda and Miranda; Emily and friends in *Ugly Betty* and *The Devil Wears Prada*.

Possible angles:

– audience

– representation.

■ How important is a sense of spectacle in media texts, which present to us an image of the fashion world? The uses of *mise-en-scène* and montage in *Ugly Betty* and the recent Next advertising campaign.

Possible angles:

– media forms

– representation.

◤ Structuring the study

Regardless of which format you choose to present your critical investigation in, you will need to ensure that similar ground is covered, with an in-depth level and quality of research. A word of warning – the specification states clearly that:

> The focus of the investigation should be on content, not format and marks should be awarded for content, not presentation.

It is in the linked production where you will be able to demonstrate your media production skills. If you choose to produce a recorded or web-style piece to present your critical investigation, spending a lot of time on the design or sound editing issues is really a waste of your time as for this part of the assignment these issues are not considered. Remember, it is the content that matters.

The following are some of the elements that make up a good critical investigation.

There is not one formula for structuring a critical investigation successfully and it is also not desirable that everyone's work looks the same. However, the following are some recommendations that will help you structure your critical investigation.

■ Try not to present your study in 'chunks'. An investigation that first deals with media institutions, then a section on debates, then describes each concept one by one and ends with an evaluative section on the linked production will not read fluently. It is also not likely to score very highly in the mark scheme, since the ideas presented within it will not be linked together.

■ Avoid describing your primary texts or your linked production. A brief comment, which should most often be only part of a sentence, is enough to identify the narrative context of a point. This is an area

---

Investigating media

In pairs, come up with a shortlist of three media texts, from any platform that you are both familiar with. Compete to see how many different titles you can each write for the same three texts.

Fig. 5.4 *The 'ingredients' of the critical investigation*

of confusion for some students, who perhaps are concerned that their tutor or the moderator won't understand what they're trying to say about a text if they haven't seen it themselves. There is no need to worry about this. Those responsible for the marks awarded to your study are looking for your understanding of where the text fits into the media world, namely contextualisation, not description. This means that if you make your points clearly your argument will make sense without needing to describe the texts.

- The opening of your investigation should outline its main focus, preferably by establishing a research direction or line of enquiry. Realistically, this could be a more detailed explanation of your hypothesis or a series of questions that you raised during your research. It could quite effectively take the form of a 'problematic', where you set out to resolve a seeming problem or contradiction you see in your text or texts. It should also state, briefly, what you feel your linked production brings to the debates you have outlined and how you feel it connects with your research focus.

- The central part of your study aims to integrate research, theories, debates, textual analysis and a clear conceptual focus, with numerous concise references to your linked production. Throughout, it should maintain a tight focus on the areas you outlined in your opening.

- In your closing section, go back to your original hypothesis, title, question or problematic. Ensure that you have either answered it fully or partially; it is often the case that research opens some difficult questions you may not be able to answer. Identifying and discussing why these issues are difficult to address is the mark of a strong investigation, especially as you only have 2,000 words available. Your final paragraph must summarise how the investigation informed the choices you made for the linked production. If there are critical problems you can see within the linked production, state here what these are.

Investigating media

An example of a case study is provided on page 151. Photocopy the pages and annotate them to show:

- use of media theories
- critical debates about the contemporary media landscape
- evidence of secondary research
- close textual references to media institutions, audiences, representations and forms
- comments linking research to production.

Critical perspectives

In Chapter 3, the importance of approaching texts critically was discussed. At A2 Level, it is vital that you explore critical perspectives in your research and use them to inform your practice. This has several implications for your research strategy.

■ You will need to ensure that you use appropriate critical theories in your investigation. These might be generalised, such as an awareness of how a feminist, neo-Marxist or post-colonial theorist might read the text you are studying. This could mean outlining the reasons for taking a particular approach to the texts and why using it allows you to deepen your understanding of your chosen topic. You might also wish to apply the ideas of specific theorists, for example Barthes (1968), Gramsci (1971) or Dyer (1992), without explaining the wider context of their work.

■ You will need to consider the social, historical, political and economic contexts of your texts. These might be discovered through wider reading and your own ability to evaluate the key influences that you feel impact on the production and reception of a particular text or texts.

Linking with production

The link between your critical investigation and the production itself must be absolutely clear. On pages 147–148, you began to think creatively about what kinds of productions might be suitable to link with a variety of investigations. The linked production is intended to demonstrate that you can adopt a knowledgeable stance as a media producer and that you can apply practically what you have learnt.

Remember that you are limited by the 2,000 words requirement. This means that each reference to your product needs to be concise and carefully integrated into the rest of your study. This could be by way of comparison or practical demonstration of a theoretical point.

Investigating media

The critical investigation of the BBC Film Nework site is based on a real student's work and together with the examiner's comments provided, should help you develop your own study. The linked product, in this case a short film, is discussed in Chapter 6.

Case study: a sample critical investigation

How does the BBC Film Network site function as both distributor and exhibitor in the digital age and what does this mean for the future of short film as a media form?

The short film is a medium that has never really achieved the recognition it deserves. At the beginning of the 20th century all films were short, due to the limitations of technology. The short film is a neglected form that is now experiencing a resurgence of interest. This is primarily because of both the possibilities and the limitations of new technologies available now. The linked product I have created, a short (five minutes) fiction film entitled *Lutey* demonstrates some of the possibilities of digital film-making. It also illustrates the contribution that can be made to the medium via user-generated content on a web-based platform. Today, we no longer have to attend a film festival, stay up late to catch a midnight slot on Channel 4 or go to an independent cinema to see a short film. The use of personal computers, MP4 players and a new generation of mobile phones can be seen as redefining the exhibition space and potentially bringing short film to a whole new global audience.

Short films offer a true spectrum from compressed versions of recognisable genres, such as horror or romantic comedy, to films that resist definition and would be much less widely understood by a mass audience. Some push the limits of what might be considered fiction film at all and are better labelled 'video art'. One of the short films I researched on the BBC Film Network site, in addition to analysing the homepage itself, was a quirky romantic comedy called *Sweet*; my own film could be described as a supernatural horror film. The way in which categories are organised on the site recalls Neale's (1991) work on genre where he states that:

'Genres do not consist only of films. They consist also … of specific expectations and hypothesis that spectators bring with them to the cinema.' ('Questions of Genre', Screen, 1991)

In this case, the website is the exhibition space, but that is all that differs. These categories reflect the content of the site and therefore the predominant range of films submitted. They differ considerably from the major film genres of feature-length films. For example, there is a large range of animated films available that seem to follow Cooper's (2000) assertion based on old Disney features that such shorts:

'… used established narrative forms – the tale, the fable, the journey – to convey, and at times to frame, the narrative.' (3: 2000)

Many of the best-known and award-winning short films are animated and are not targeted at children only.

Short films often have a limited number of characters and many do not offer the same narrative trajectory in pace or concept, due to their limited length. Some, like *God Talks to Dave*, make limited use of location and rely on interesting scripting of dialogue. Conversely, my own film makes extravagant use of location to determine its feel. Some very short films, such as *The End*, are based on a very simple conceit, vignette, visual joke or idea. This was important in planning my own film, as I had to ensure that the narrative was not too complex for the running time.

The short film has always had a place in British film-making. Here, it has long had a role (as in the US) as a way of getting noticed by the industry and a way of showcasing new talent to be picked up by the big studios. Gillespie, for example, shot to fame for directing the mainstream horror film *I Know What You Did Last Summer* (1997) – he was offered this work on the basis of his short film *Joyride* (1995). Many US-based film-makers use short film exclusively as a marketing tool to promote their capabilities and once their careers are established they rarely return to the form. In Europe, the short film is used in a similar way, where a win in one of these categories at a festival often precipitates a 'break' into the industry for a film-school student. However, it would seem that in Europe, with its rich tradition of non-mainstream and art-house cinema, there is a greater appreciation for the short film in its own right and dedicated festivals such as those organised by Future Shorts are held that celebrate short films and have:

'… created a much needed link between the film industry and the short film world.' (www.future shorts.com)

In recent years, there has been an explosion of websites where enthusiasts can go to view short films. User-generated content is free to website owners, making it a desirable market for generating advertising revenue. The success of YouTube (see Appendix 1, below), which is a user-generated forum where anyone can upload content, has popularised the practice. YouTube is not generally restricted or regulated for quality, making it a relatively democratic exhibition tool. As is often the case with new technologies and

Fig. 5.5 *Sample investigation: student's full-page screenshot of BBC Film network site*

digital media, the demand and the first products on the scene were driven by users themselves. With increased access to digital technologies, there is more incentive for audiences to become media producers themselves, and innovative sites are created as exhibition spaces for these.

'Online video isn't just about the latest ways to make and share movies; it's also about getting viewers involved in something they really love … recognition isn't the goal, having a voice is.' (Matt Hanson, Guardian, 2008)

The internet is still revolutionising and providing an alternative to more traditional models of film distribution (either handled by specialist distributors who manage the exhibition strategy as well as the marketing of a film) and exhibition (usually as cinema space or video rental or purchase).

Two examples of websites carrying short film content that have capitalised on the spirit of YouTube for public service purposes are the BBC Film Network Site and Channel 4's FourDocs site. The latter exists specifically to encourage the making and sharing of documentaries by amateur film-makers. Anyone around the world can contribute a documentary to the site; however, their work must abide by strict documentary ethics, evidence of which, such as signed permissions letters from documentary subjects and music clearances, must be provided. In addition the four-minute documentaries will only be posted on the site after being subjected to a review procedure by a moderator. In the UK, cheaply-priced weekend workshops are held to encourage people to make their own FourDoc. Contributions are all reviewed publicly online by the site editor and the best are selected periodically to be broadcast on Channel 4's 6.55pm Three Minute Wonder slot. There is also the facility for any casual viewer to watch the documentaries and for

Fig. 5.6 *Sample investigation: student's screenshot of FourDocs website*

members of the site to review films, either giving them a star rating or comments.

The BBC Film Network site exists to promote the industry (its own branding states that it is 'showcasing new British film-making') and the 'magazine' features articles that covertly promote two British comedy films, which are currently doing well in terms of both critical and box-office success, Mike Leigh's *Happy-go-Lucky* (2008) and Garth Jennings's *Son of Rambow* (2008). The site also functions as an archive of hundreds of short films that audiences can view and, if they join the site (of which membership is free), review for their own entertainment. This audience sense of community (Dyer, 1992) and the opportunity to participate offered by new media is a crucial audience pleasure provided by user-generated forums. The films on the site range from nearly 25 minutes in duration, such as *Map with Gaps*, to around a minute, for example *The End*. More common lengths are 10 and five minutes.

'Broadly, we look for films that meet a certain standard both in terms of ideas and technically and that are innovative, have a strong coherent narrative and use the cinematic medium effectively.' (Submissions page, www.bbc.co.uk/filmnetwork)

The film I have created is five minutes long, making it ideal to submit to the site. Whether it would fulfil the technical standard

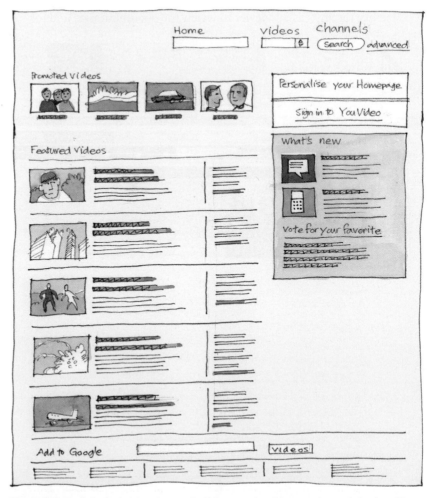

Fig. 5.7 *Sample investigation: impression of a popular video-posting website (used by the student in screenshot form)*

required is questionable, since the production values of the many films viewed seemed very high even on projects that were probably contributed by film students. This means that the producers of the films either have free access to high-quality equipment as part of their education or the film has had a reasonable budget. Interestingly, both the FourDocs and BBC site offer free film-making guides to encourage participation.

One of the popularly viewed films, *Sweet* is a romantic comedy. This is signified by the centring of the narrative around youthful characters (the Pete Sweet of the title, his imaginary girlfriend Poppy and his best friend Stitch) and their romantic problems. The fact that the lead roles are played by the then less well-known alternative comedians Noel Fielding and Julian Barrett probably contributes to the popularity of this film, which offers intertextual pleasures for fans of the sitcom *The Mighty Boosh*. In terms of representations, it presents modern and liberal values and ideologies concerning homosexuality, as well as sexual relationships in general. This may make the film popular with a youth audience who may share these values, since the preferred reading is that the film will amuse rather than shock or offend its audience with its content. I also used comparatively young actors for the two roles in my own film, since I felt their youth made the narrative more poignant and raised questions about the innocence or naivety of youth.

Sweet is voiced over by the main character, securely anchoring the narrative throughout and for the greater part the film deploys a conventional continuity editing style. For the majority of my film, excluding the dream sequence in the middle, I employed a similar editing style, but restricted dialogue in favour of a more mysterious soundtrack featuring the sound of the sea and gulls, which was more in keeping with the genre I was trying to evoke. I hoped that my basing of my story on a real Cornish supernatural legend might work for a youth audience in the same way as many Japanese horror films draw on traditional tales as their source.

The BBC Film Network homepage provides a stylish and attractive interface with a predominantly neutral and fresh-looking aqua blue and grey colour scheme as part of its presentation. Three new shorts, which constitute dynamic content, change regularly to appeal to the site's many frequent and returning visitors. They are promoted with a single striking image and one-line synopsis, which employs enigma codes (Barthes, 1968) to engage the reader. A different user-generated film is selected each week for the main profile and a promotional still from the film is prominently positioned near the top of the page, which lists categories of film on colour bars signifying those used on video for colour balance, which will be familiar to many digital camera users. Several award-winning shorts are also profiled, perhaps in order to convince the visitor to the site of the quality of its content.

Many of the films presented on the site have Film Council support or funding from various regional arts organisations. This serves as a microcosm of the wider debates concerning how film funding operates in the UK, where rather than being funded by one major studio, producers need to secure funding from a variety of sources before production can commence. My own short film was made on a very limited budget of around £50 in total and relied upon quite basic equipment and the goodwill of a small amateur cast and crew.

From an audience perspective, even though the BBC website may seem very democratic, in reality its users too are limited at present economically by the need to have broadband access and a personal computer powerful enough to view the films.

During the period from April 2006–7, the site ran a free digital downloads trial. Members were able through peer-to-peer networking to download a small number of high resolution downloads of films per fortnight to watch at home for a period of 30 days, after which the download would expire. This has been replaced by the ability to have a selection of the films sent to your mobile phone. This costs the price of the text to download, so is very affordable. FourDocs can also be downloaded as 'vodcasts'. The digital rights to enable this have been individually obtained on a film-by-film basis. iTunes is another, much higher profile organisation, which goes to extraordinary (and often contentious) lengths to protect its digital rights over both music and video content. The BFI have created a 'shop' along the iTunes pay-per-download model where users can download short films made by known film-makers for a fee by film, for example £1.99 for an early 10-minute short by Shane Meadows (*Where's the Money, Ronnie?*), comparable with the £1.89 charged by iTunes for one of their Pixar animated shorts *For the Birds*. Both of these prices have fallen in the last year by more than a pound.

The distinction is now blurring because of the availability of new technologies for both media production and exhibition between the amateur film-maker and the industry professional. My investigation into the area allowed me to create a real media product using quite basic equipment, which I would be free to submit to the site and gave me the confidence that this was achievable on next-to-no budget. Cooper (2000) said:

'… it is possible that a new and longer term interest in the short film may develop; recent cable programming initiatives and speciality market developments suggest that it may experience a renaissance.'

Every day, more content is added to sites that show short films and every day the global audience for short films distributed via the internet is growing. At the time of writing, the BBC Film Network have suspended submissions to the site due to an overwhelming deluge of content, forcing them to plea for a break to catch up on their promise that every film submitted will be seen. The trend looks set to continue for the foreseeable future.

[Word count 2117 (excluding quotes)]

Bibliography

Books

Burton, J. and Stevenson, E. (2008) *AQA Media Studies AS*, Nelson Thornes: Cheltenham

Cooper, P. and Dancyger, K. (2000) *Writing the Short Film*, Focal Press: Oxford

Corrigan, T. and White, P. (2004) *The Film Experience: an Introduction*, Palgrave Macmillan: Hampshire

Figgis, M. (2007) *Digital Film-making*, Faber and Faber: London

Frensham, R. (2003) *Teach Yourself Screenwriting*, Hodder Headline: London

Kruger, S., Rayner, P. and Wall, P. (2001) *Media Studies: the Essential Introduction*, Routledge: London

Magazines and journals
The Guardian Guide to Making Video, January 2008
Hanson, M. 'A New Era in Video' *Guardian*, January 2008
Neale, S. 'Questions of Genre' *Screen*, 1991
Media Magazine article: 'Why Study the Short Film?'

Internet
www.bbc.co.uk/filmnetwork (Accessed 3.2.08–27.4.08) Main focus
of study, where all shorts referred to may be found.
www.futureshorts.com (Accessed 3.2.08) Useful information about
short film festivals and lots of links to great shorts and sites of
interest to new film-makers.
www.bfi.org.uk/filmdownloads.html (Accessed 7.3.08) Used for
research into paid-for downloads.
www.channel4.com/fourdocs (Accessed 18.3.08) Contrasts with film
network site by specialising in one genre.

Examiner's commentary

This investigation is quite large in scope and looks at the changing
face of short film production and consumption. The topic is well
researched and this is implicit in the authoritative grasp of the subject-
matter and debates, in addition to the explicit references made to
secondary research. It falls well within the spirit of the specification
and shows evidence that prior learning from Unit 1 in the cross-media
study and the Unit 3 topic of digital media has been put to good use. It
is an issue-based study, which shows a strong awareness of the nature
of the contemporary media landscape and demonstrates primary
research in its use of a particular example of a digital platform as
interface, as well as an example of the material it carries. It effectively
explores the link between the digital production and exhibition and
consumption of the short film and its historical contexts. A number of
media theories are referenced and subtly integrated into the text and
the candidate also shows confidence in the handling of critical debates
surrounding the development of digital media. It is likely that this
response would be placed in Level 4 (37–48 marks) because:

- it is a 'fluent and analytical investigation'
- it has a 'clear autonomous and critical perspective'
- it provides 'a very detailed bibliography and source list'
- it demonstrates 'sophisticated knowledge of media concepts'
- 'the link between the investigation and the production is cogent,
  clear and evident'.

This is not a perfect study. At times there is a sense that the candidate
is allowing their enthusiasm for the topic to dominate at the expense of
solid conceptual exploration. There is a slight imbalance in integration
of textual analysis with debates and at times the investigation wanders
slightly, tending to lead to some digression within this huge topic.
There is a stronger focus on debates than on concepts at times, with
representation as an area left relatively under-explored although not
ignored altogether. The study is also, by the candidate's own admission,
about a hundred words over the word limit. This could have perhaps
been remedied by, for example, spending less time considering YouTube
and the FourDocs site and focusing more on the two texts stated as the

focus of primary research. Time could also have been spent refining the written style during drafting to make the investigation more concise. The candidate might have considered the use of footnotes or the Harvard system to reference their research sources more precisely. For these reasons, it seems likely that this investigation would be placed in the lower end of the band.

Additional examiner's comments on bibliography and appendices for case study

This candidate has provided a bibliography that is not extensive, but shows the ability to select judiciously from the range of available material on a topic upon which there is both a great deal written on some aspects and very little on others.

Academic and more practical guides to media production are both acknowledged as part of the secondary research. It is clear how the texts included in the bibliography have informed both the critical investigation and the linked production. The fact that the candidate has restricted their reading on the short film and film history has probably assisted the investigation in this case, as it is already rather broad in scope.

Two familiar A Level Media textbooks have been referenced and these are used in the bibliography to show the source of media theories used where the original reading may not have been available to the candidate or even appropriate at this level of study.

The internet sources are all appropriate and in addition to the date accessed, the candidate has also provided a helpful single-line summary of the site content, which helps the reader to differentiate between the uses of the Film Network site as text and the sites used mainly for secondary research.

Two of the magazine and newspaper sources referred to have perhaps contributed less to the study and there is a sense that these have been included to show a range of research, rather than because they really informed the study. One of these is also not properly referenced with date of publication. However, their inclusion is satisfactory.

The appendices show screen shots from the primary and secondary texts discussed during the course of the investigation, providing a useful visual reference for a moderator unfamiliar with the websites studied.

Chapter summary

In this chapter:

- how to choose a topic for the research and production unit was explained
- how to undertake and use primary and secondary research was explained
- details on writing a title for the critical investigation and identifying a suitable linked product for it were given
- how to organise the structure of a study was illustrated
- outlines of what the examiner is looking for were provided.

6 The production

In this chapter you will:

- discover how to research the practical skills needed for your production

- be able to plan your production as effectively and creatively as possible

- understand the production and post-production processes in each medium.

Link

In the AS book, we discussed the importance of pre-production work and of the planning required. It will be useful to revise the topics relevant to your skill in the *AS Media Studies* book, Topic 8 Using technologies and Topic 9 Creating products.

AQA Examiner's tip

Remember not to submit any production piece that fits into any of the production tasks set at AS Level from the current or previous two examination series.

This chapter will help you to focus on building upon the technical skills you acquired at AS Level during Unit 2, Creating media. When choosing the medium in which you want to work, remember the following:

> Since this is A2 and candidates will have already completed a production at AS Level, there is an expectation that they will make more use of media technology and produce a production piece to a higher standard than expected at AS Level.

AQA specification, 2008

This means that if you choose a new skill to work within, you must be aware that you will still be expected to produce work of an equal standard to that of other A2 candidates. It is recommended therefore that you to continue to develop the technical skills you are already familiar with in order to get the most out of this unit.

This chapter focuses on improving the skills you have already gained at AS and seeking to hone and innovate with those skills to reach an even higher technical and aesthetic standard. There are checklists in this topic to remind you of key learning that has already taken place at AS. On pages 176–180 is a case study of a student's experience of making a linked production. This case study serves to illustrate the processes of producing a broadcast product – one of the more technically demanding and multi-skilled disciplines in media production.

During the course of your critical investigation, you have conducted primary research into one or more texts. This involved observing the characteristics of a particular media form, as well as how representations have been constructed within it and the messages these convey. The linked production that you make may not always be in the same medium as the text that you analysed, so be prepared to undertake further primary research. If you investigated representations of masculinity in *Ross Kemp on Gangs* for your critical investigation but chose to do a public information advertising campaign to discourage gang involvement for the linked production piece, you would need to conduct some primary research into existing recent public information campaigns about responsible drinking or raising literacy levels, for example.

You will also need to conduct research into the wider production skills needed. Books are available on many aspects of practical media production, as are a number of websites that offer free advice on the effective use of media technologies.

Research and investigation

This section is presented as a series of case studies, one on each mass medium:

- broadcast media tasks (page 162)
- digital media tasks (page 163)
- print-based tasks (page 165)
- audio tasks (page 166).

Fig. 6.1 *Screen grab from* **Rave Dog**, *a user-generated submission on FourDocs*

Media in action

Some documentary-makers say that the true subject and story of their documentary often only emerges post-production, when they find out what the most interesting parts of their footage are. Sometimes in making a documentary you may discover quite a different 'truth' or representation to the one you thought you would offer the audience when you set out to film!

Technical tip

- If you are not recording sound externally, place the camera as close as you can to the subject.
- Allow talk-space within your frame and compose shots of subjects carefully. Can you get them doing a task, in a suitable location?
- Record atmosphere (background noise at an event or location) and room tone (the ambient noise in the room when no one is speaking) on location.
- Film cutaways of the environment and your interview subject or mix up your questions and use more than one angle or distance – someone just talking can be visually boring.

Each case study illustrates how to use primary research for the purposes of production. Each demonstrates, in a practical way, how to use academic skills and learning gained from the critical investigation to research a linked production, as well as the kinds of information you should be looking for about technical skills.

Investigating media

Each mass medium related case study in this chapter has a focus text for you to look at as a starting point.

When you begin to investigate a text, write a bullet-pointed primary research analysis of the text itself or a similar one. Two examples are shown in Fig. 63 on page 164.

You can use these brainstormed points about audience expectations provided for soaps and websites that promote a film to help get you started. Write your own for documentaries and TV spin-off magazines. The examples of mass media used are:

- *broadcast* – Rave Dog, a short film from FourDocs (www.channel4.com)
- *digital* – *Brick Lane* official movie site (www.bricklane.com)
- *print-based* – *Torchwood* magazine
- *audio* – *Silver Street*.

However, for this task you could use other examples. For example, although *Silver Street* is freely available each week to download as a podcast from the BBC website, you could also use *The Archers*. There are hundreds of FourDocs to choose from on the website – but remember to choose one that has received a high rating from viewers and a positive review from the site editor. You could use any film promotion website and if you can't find *Torchwood* magazine, find another science fiction broadcast fiction spin-off, such as the *Doctor Who* or *Heroes* magazines.

Broadcast media

Case study: broadcast media, creating a 'FourDoc'

Focus text

Rave Dog

Pre-production planning

- Write interview questions (but don't let your subject see them!).
- Visit the location in advance, if possible, to help you plan shots.
- Make contact with your subjects by telephone or email, outlining the purpose of your documentary and how you see them contributing.
- Draw 'thumbnails' of a basic storyboard that includes the kinds of shots you need to get or write a shot-list.

Issues of style

- Commentaries should be written and recorded after the shoot. Be aware they can sound heavy – a light touch is best.
- Avoid too many 'talking heads'.
- Use a tripod for pans, establishing shots and any slow zooms, but be aware that interviews using a tripod can look too 'newsy' and static.

Digital media

Case study: Digital media, creating a website to promote a film release

Focus text

Brick Lane official movie site

Visit the site for the above film, released in the UK in 2008. Using a diagram similar to the one provided in Fig. 6.3, brainstorm your own practical observations about layout, media forms and conventions, audience etc.

Pre-production planning

- Decide on the media content of your site and plan how you will create any content such as video clips and MP3 recordings.

- List the technical issues and skills you will need to check against your web-design software, for example how to embed a Flash animation or QuickTime file.

- Draw a site-map for the complete site, before deciding how much of the content you need to produce for your actual production. This will vary depending on whether you work in a group. See the specification for precise guidance on this issue.

- Draw a layout of your pages, including clickable sections and the pages or events they manage.

Issues of style

- Consider using slideshows rather than single still images.
- Theme your images across the webpages.
- Try to ensure your site is 'sticky'.

Key terms

Sticky: a web designer's term that refers to webpages with dynamic content, pages that people want to come back to repeatedly.

Fig. 6.2 *Screen grab from* **Brick Lane** *website*

■ Make sure that any other media content matches the overall style and look you have created for the site. Keep in mind the look of the whole project even when videoing, recording or photographing its individual components. Pay as close attention to *mise-en-scène*, quality sound recording and other aspects as if you were making a broadcast product.

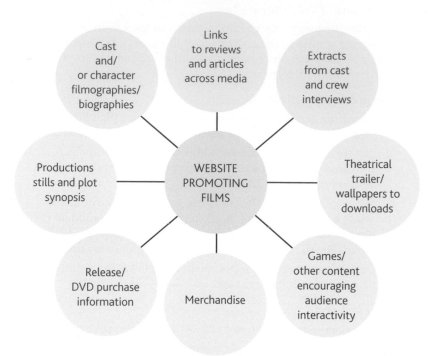

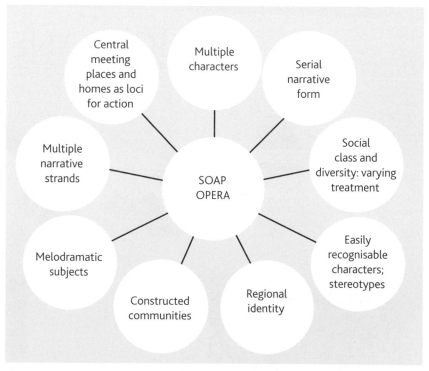

Fig. 6.3 *Brainstormed observations about media forms and conventions for websites promoting films and soap operas*

Technical tip

■ Try to keep your media content files as small as you can without impacting significantly on quality.

■ Use the technical components and conventions of your site securely such as breadcrumb trails and navigation bars, dropdown menus and search bars to make sure your site is easy for the audience to use.

Print based

Case study: Print based media, creating a spin-off magazine for a TV series

Focus text

Torchwood magazine

Pre-production planning

- Produce a detailed, actual size, mock-up of your page layout and plan your layers with sketches.
- Select fonts and check style drawers on your DTP program.
- Write your copy, type-set into columns and stick onto your mock-up. Finalise your copy length before you begin to finalise your designs.
- If you are creating a print product in a group, and will be creating quite a substantial number of pages, it may be worth creating a flat plan showing all of these plans in detail to help everyone keep track.
- Take a good range of carefully composed photographs, preferably at different distances and angles.
- Create a shot-list so you don't forget something crucial.

Issues of style

- Ensure that all the elements of your page layout merge to create your intended meaning and that nothing jars.
- Look for a near range of colour and tonalities to unite different features between pages. Consider repeating some fonts, a logo or two colours.
- Decide on a house style for photographs. For example, heavily colour-saturated and energetic? Black and white and arty? Slightly over-exposed in appearance with cool-colour temperatures? Warm and homely? Use a **colourise** tool to find the look you want and match it to your text.

Technical tip

- Use Photoshop or a similar software package to combine some of the graphics, scanned backgrounds, photographs and text to import to your DTP program for a really professional finish.
- Make use of a photo-editing package with your digital photographs to create the correct style and feel by using saturation, cropping etc.

Fig. 6.4 Torchwood *magazine*

Audio

Case study: audio, creating a radio soap

Focus text

Silver Street (BBC, Asian Network)

Available online as a daily listen at any time, or as an omnibus.

Pre-production planning

- Write character profiles with brief back-stories and map their relationships with one another.
- Create a key locations list that will provide the listener with a range of aural contrasts.
- Create a narrative for your first episode with at least three separate strands to fully engage the audience.
- Familiarise yourself with radio play script format and learn how to use your script-writing program before writing your script.
- Write the script for your first episode.

Key terms

Saturation: the amount and shades of colour used in a print media text and the resulting effect. High saturation is very bright, bold, and unrealistic. Low saturation will have a more subtle effect.

Colourising: using a tool to change the colour range of a particular photo or set of photos, e.g. to have greyer tones, sepia, or be warmed using reds and oranges.

Cropping: removing unwanted areas of a photograph or focusing the reader's attention on a particular aspect of it by selecting where its borders are positioned.

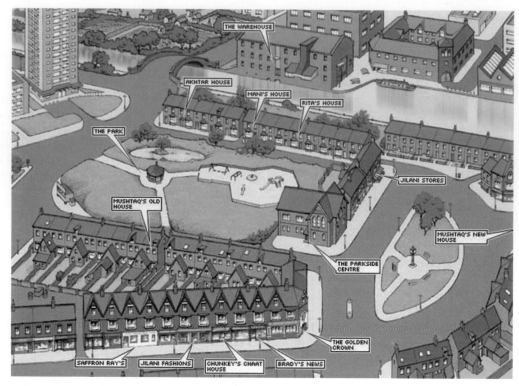

Fig. 6.5 *Locations map for* **Silver Street** *from webpage*

Technical tip

- Encourage your actors to begin their conversation walking towards the microphone at the beginning of a scene for a more realistic radio recording. If they're supposed to be lifting something together, consider actually providing them with something to lift!

- Remember that a naturalistic delivery of dialogue that is appropriate to TV where there are visual cues may need slowing down for radio.

Issues of style

- Make sure you match your storylines to the regional setting and social class of your characters and character stereotype.

- Select a brief clip of music for your signature tune, which is lyrically and musically appropriate for both the setting of the soap and its target audience.

■ Pre-production and production planning

Summary of prior learning from AS Level

Broadcasting tasks

- *Scripting* – make sure you can produce a working script or script outline for your project, which resembles industry practice as closely as possible.

- *Storyboarding* – remember all the elements that need to be included on a storyboard. Pay close attention to details such as shot type and duration, camera angle and movement, framing and transitions.

- *Shot-lists, thumbnails and shooting scripts* – are all valid alternatives to traditional storyboarding, depending on the type of project. The important point is that you decide on a location, what to film and that you have thought it through in detail before turning up.

- *Common pitfalls* – try to avoid the most common technical and aesthetic errors, such as zooming in and then out on the same shot.

- *Health and safety* – remember to be conscious of safety issues all the time and that videoing in particular is a very distracting activity.

Keep it creative – there are five classic but underused shots and techniques that look great.

- *Multi-level action* is a nice way to compose shots that suggest a narrative link. It basically means having two things happening in different parts of the frame, which the viewer then connects in meaning. Perhaps someone is sitting in a café, but over their shoulder and unseen by them, an argument has broken out between a man and a woman.

- *Montage* is a hugely underused area. It can be used for title sequences, showing the passage of time or an emotional response to an event such as memories or surreal dream sequences. This can be seen to wonderful effect at the end of the film *Donnie Darko* (dir. Richard Kelly, 2001), as other characters in the film are shown in their bedrooms, one after the other, at the moment when Donnie dies. They cannot really know what has happened, yet each is shown to have an emotional response which makes sense to the audience. This is an extraordinarily powerful use of montage.

- *Multiple takes* can be used sparingly to signify a dramatic or exciting event. A plate of food being dropped on the floor in a shock reaction can be filmed three times from three different angles and cut together for added emphasis.

- A *searching pan* or *tilt* can be used to slowly reveal an object, person or scene. These take confidence, a tripod and a steady hand to control, but can add extra tension or a moment's stylish 'breathing space', depending on how they are used. This can be effectively used to control the moment when a villain is revealed, or to drift away from a key event, letting a powerful soundtrack do the work. This technique was used controversially in a torture sequence from *Reservoir Dogs* (dir. Quentin Tarantino, 1991), where audience imagination was allowed to do all the gruesome work. This was so effective that there was a moral panic about the scene in the press, even though the crucial part of it was never actually shown!

- *Visually matched shots*, where a shape or image in one frame at the end of a sequence dissolves into a similar shape or image at the beginning of the next. These shots are aesthetically pleasing and can add subtle dimensions to your narrative (Note: this is not the same as a matched cut, which is a standard unit for constructing screen space in the continuity editing system.) When a door slowly opens in one scene, to be matched to another closing behind a character in a subsequent scene, this is a visual match. The type of shot and therefore the proportionate size of the door are preserved between shots, providing an interesting transition for the audience.

Digital media tasks

- *Crossovers with other media disciplines* – web design will involve you using similar skills to print media but also has its own specific rules and quirks, which you need to be aware of. Don't forget that video, photography and sound can all be important elements of web-design and will all need careful planning.

- *Problem-solving* – different web-design programs have different capabilities, particularly when it comes to embedding other media. It's vital that you do your problem-solving and technical research early on to prevent disappointment later.

- *The three-click rule* – most people want to accomplish what they went to a site for in, at the most, three clicks.

AQA Examiner's tip

Groups for practical media work may not have more than four candidates. You can of course consider using fewer than four, or working alone. Be certain of your own skills and other people's commitment to your project if you do choose to make a broadcast product alone. You do not need to count actors etc. in your group number; only those who have a production role and are expecting to be marked for their contribution to the assignment.

Thinking about media

Make a list of your own top five shots. You could use favourite films or TV programmes to do this, identifying perhaps dramatic moments that appeal to you, and then working out how they have been constructed visually through camerawork and editing.

■ *Keeping it creative* – web design is a creative new medium with no rules!

  – Creating links to fictional characters on Facebook or MySpace, games relating to site content or fan forums offering ticket privileges are all ways of making your site exciting. Although these ideas are not new, you can still use them. You can also reassemble them into a new and refreshing combination for your own site.

  – Sometimes with websites, less is more. Some people find a musical or spoken accompaniment to their web-browsing more of an irritation than a pleasure. They like to feel an element of control and love clicking the mouse! So, if you want to avoid alienating your audience, give them the option of using sound or not and get across any audio and video content by encouraging them to click to listen or see it. This will make them feel they are doing it voluntarily.

  – Introducing a strong design element, such as a series of short animations with related stills, clips or banners, positioned in other aspects of your design, could really add to the personality of your site. Flash is a useful tool to create these elements.

  – Think about what elements from more traditional media might be appropriate for your site, such as comics that exist solely in cyberspace, as many people appreciate good graphics and original artwork.

  – Think about the pleasures people get from other media forms. For example, can the aesthetic pleasure of a series of beautiful photographs convey a narrative through a slide show, which uses subtle slow dissolves?

Print-based tasks

■ *Generating copy* – remember to read plenty of style models to assist you in finding the correct journalistic style for your target audience. Don't forget that all copy must be original and produced by you, and that writing good copy should be an absolute priority and is important as design considerations.

■ *Working with graphics and digital photography* – check that you have access to suitable equipment and software and can use the relevant programs. Learning how to work with layers can be quite complex.

■ *Design considerations* – try to work to a realistic size for your publication type and bear this in mind when working on screen. Find out how much flexibility there is in templates offered by any DTP package and preferably design your own to suit your exact requirements.

■ *Avoiding and fixing problems* – remember that you need to be able to print off your work in colour. If you need to save and transport your work to another computer for printing, check that it has the same version of software program and is able to open the files. Plan ahead how you will retrieve the work to present it and back up your work as you create it, preferably in more than one place.

■ *Keeping it creative* – use the 'rule of thirds' (where you imagine the photograph as divided into nine boxes and important elements of the image are positioned in these boxes and along these lines rather than in the middle, which can look boring) to compose your photographic images confidently, especially when you're first starting out, to ensure they will be pleasing to the eye.

Thinking about media

Make a list of the top five most creative things you have seen on a webpage. List the features or elements that have really enhanced your experience of the site. Think about how and if you can use one or two of them in your own way.

- Keep your photographs simple by avoiding busy backgrounds and ensuring that your subject has somewhere to move into within the frame if they're moving to bring the image to life.

- Use diagonal lines, which are very strong, and s-curves in your images. Both of these make for bold and eye-catching photographs, so consider some unusual angles to try and capture these.

- Look for ways of framing your subject, through trees, archways; anything which can be built into the edges of the frame to give a context and depth to your subject.

- Use a range of shot types. Many people forget how effective macro shots can be in allowing the audience to see fascinating patterns and perspectives and sometimes surprising details. Sometimes, even with people, we do not need to see 'the whole picture'.

Audio tasks

- *Scripting* – see the advice given for broadcast media on page 168.

- *Health and safety* – see the advice given for broadcast media on page 168.

- *Technical issues* – use good quality headphones, microphones and digital sound recorders, but remember that these are not a substitute for a good ear. A sound recordist needs to be constantly sensitive to background sound, levels of voices and any interference such as jewellery dangling on a microphone cable and so on.

- *Keeping it creative* – a bank of sound resources for you to consider and how to use them.

  - Is recording an interview or scene on location going to be too difficult? Visit the location separately and record the background sounds to mix in later underneath the 'studio' track.

  - Think of alternative ways to get the sounds you want. If you need the crackle of a police radio but can only download ones with American accents, ask around. Perhaps your college caretaking team use walkie-talkies or you have a friend whose younger brother has a set.

  - It may seem obvious that you should use music that's appropriate to your text. Examples are panpipes used in the background of an environmental documentary, a sea shanty in a feature about the coast and a child singing a nursery rhyme used eerily in a radio drama.

  - Incidental sound that underlies action is often neglected and can really bring a radio piece or podcast alive for the listener. For example, in a garage, a car repeatedly failing to start in the distance can add depth to the media, as do metallic hammering and the sound of a spanner being dropped. In the kitchen, some crockery or cutlery being moved, a kettle boiling, vegetables being chopped on a board and gas ignition being lit are all realistic sounds to add to the media. This kind of attention to detail will bring your audio recording to life and if done properly won't sound obtrusive.

  - There are many inexpensive and even some free sound effects available to download from the internet. Make sure you preview them first. A good tip is not to use more than three library sound effects in a five-minute piece. In radio, you can add a few more, given that aural codes are all your audience have to go on. The point is to mix the sources you get your sound from, and don't put too many artificial sounding studio recordings into one text.

Thinking about media

Choose five striking images from a range of newspapers and magazines. Using tracing paper, trace over the outlines of the main elements of the picture. Observe how the picture has been composed from these to have such an effect. Write a short analysis of the image, commenting not only on composition, but the possible interpretations by the reader of colour, dress codes and other signifiers.

Thinking about media

Listen to the first five minutes of a radio soap or radio drama. The afternoon play broadcast on Radio Four 4 might be useful for this activity. List all the sounds you hear on one listen, and compare your list with others in the group. Discuss how these could be replicated through a combination of library and real sound recordings.

The production process and post-production

Broadcasting

Broadcast products may vary hugely in their range, but the processes are essentially the same. Whether you're working within a small team collaborating on the project or with a small team who are helping you out, effective organisation is the key to a smooth shoot. Everyone must be absolutely clear about their roles and responsibilities

On the shoot, wherever you're filming and whether you're working in interior or exterior surroundings, remember the following four points:

- prioritise health and safety issues
- bring all the necessary recordable media and appropriate equipment, including storyboards and scripts
- log or check off everything as you go along
- be 100 per cent focused on getting what you came for and preferably do not leave until you have it.

When you're concentrating on shot types and framing your subject nicely as well as the action happening within the frame, it's easy to lose sight of some other aspects of *mise-en-scène*. These might include what's happening in the background, the quality of the lighting and whether you have a horizon that is tilting queasily. Remember that at A2 Level the examiner is looking for a high level of competence in your handling of media technologies. If you're filming a piece of single-camera drama, for example, you will need to keep a very tight focus on all these things as you change angle and repeat the sequence.

For drama that includes dialogue, an effective and level sound recording will need to be taken. It is easy to forget about sound when you're concentrating on the visual action. Make sure you know what your requirements are and how important sound will be at different points in the shoot. There is a limit to what can be done with poor sound at post-production, for example, volume levels can only be raised to a certain level and can become very 'noisy' as they have an exaggerated hiss behind them and a weak quality to the voices. Wind noise is almost impossible

Link

For further guidance, refer to the *AS Media Studies* book, Topic 8, Using technologies.

AQA Examiner's tip

The specification states that moving image and audio work is not expected to be longer than five minutes, and that many productions such as animated products and audio or video adverts will only be 30 seconds. Work which is over five minutes in length almost always deteriorates in quality and loses marks. You don't have to make a complete programme for TV – you can make, for example, the opening five minutes.

Media in action

In the film industry, it was traditionally the job of a person known as the 'script-girl' to record continuity issues between takes. This is a highly demanding job, requiring great levels of concentration, focus and professionalism and is often not very well paid! A whole sequence could be rendered unusable if an error of continuity was made. If your shoot is quite complex, it may useful to nominate someone to check the continuity.

Fig. 6.6 *Location filming*

to eliminate entirely on semi-domestic equipment and difficult even for professionals to do much about. However, if you have to film outside on a windy day use the following simple tricks.

- Choose a sheltered spot and if you are using a small camera with a built-in microphone, take a strong umbrella with you and someone to hold it out of shot so that the level of wind hitting the sensitive microphone is reduced. Make sure that the umbrella is not blocking the light!
- If you're using an external microphone rather than a built-in one to record sound, make sure you have a wind-shield. This might be made of foam or a more heavy duty, furry contraption.

If you have access to portable lighting, make sure you know how it works, and be very careful with trailing cables and the lights themselves, as they can get extremely hot. Remember to take any gels with you. If you know any photographers, you could ask to borrow a **reflector disc**. Many low-budget film-makers use 100 watt light bulbs when they need bright light or even large hand-held torches, so experiment.

Post-production, it's helpful to name your video clips. This will help you find your way through your footage, particularly if you have lots of takes of one sequence. Remember the advice you were given at AS Level in Topic 8 on page 127–8, about avoiding and fixing problems: don't be tempted to overkill the effects and spoil the work and never, ever surrender your original tape with footage for recycling until you have finished your work and made two hard copies of it – one to hand in; one for your own safe-keeping.

Digital media

When designing your website, experimenting with labelled pencil sketches of content organised in various ways is the best way to begin. Sketching out a plan on several large A3 sheets of paper stuck together works well and allows you to develop a site-map at the same time and a clear vision of how the pages will work together.

When dealing with e-media production and web-based sound and video, sometimes you might require a different production style. Some websites use video content, which has more in common, stylistically, with that of a corporate video or even a videoed instruction manual. Here, someone may demonstrate something or talk about something from a seat behind a table. You may also want to use much shorter video clips, but do not forget that not everyone has broadband access. Try to be inventive – simply using a clip does not make the site more interesting; the clip itself needs to add to the content of the site.

Podcasts currently tend to fall into two categories. Some, such as excerpts from radio programmes may have to have high production values and lots of different aural codes that engage the listener. These will generally have the usual codes and conventions of the relevant radio genre. Others can be more like a blog read aloud! The first is not always superior to the second – often they have very little editing and make effective use of diegetic sound (see Chapter 5 for more on this) to engage the listener, for example, when someone works in an interesting environment or is somewhere that is exotic to the listener.

Try to use the classic rules of print media production in designing layout; for example, structuring your text to be read from the top left-hand corner of a page. Other things people notice include bright graphics in bold shapes or blocks and faces. Faces bring a webpage to life, so try and include a human somewhere in your design, especially if they are attractive or interesting-looking. Web designers also make use of grids in the same way newspapers and magazines have historically used the column.

Remember to be prepared to have patience when looking for solutions.

Print

When you begin your designs, try to consider and experiment with the **elements** and **principles of design**. It may take some time to get used to considering all the principles of design; it's a highly specialised area and can involve looking in detail at contrast (in shape, colour and size), the dominance of some elements over others, their scale and balance, the repetition of parts of an image or shape in different areas of the layout etc. Think carefully about the links you want to establish between images, copy and graphical elements of your design, and pay close attention to anchorage.

Consciously manipulating all or even some of these details in your design means you should have the beginnings of a print media piece, which will have real impact on the audience. Think, too, about how you are going to use white space – some is always good for the eye. When you are designing your pages remember what you have learnt about the way that people read and interpret images.

Taking original photographs that have real impact is a learnt skill. Initially follow the 'rules' of composition, but then try breaking them and learning to trust your instinct. If you can use the manual settings on a camera to good effect, go ahead; if not, you can still take perfectly good photographs on an automatic setting.

Audio

Audio work could seem like an easy option compared with the complexity of video work. However, audio work is very demanding. Technically, you may not need a great range of skills to use the most basic of audio equipment, but you will need to develop an excellent ear for issues relating to sound balance.

One of the biggest problems with linked productions, which are intended for radio broadcast and to some degree podcasting too, is a loss of **verisimilitude** for the listener due to inappropriate casting, interviewing or presenting. This means that while the content of the text may be fine, there is a poor choice of actors or contributors. Sometimes this is due to the wrong level of formality of language register or someone leaving their natural accent behind. It is very important that everyone speaks clearly in an audio text, but this does not necessarily mean using an overly-exaggerated style of received pronunciation.

Sometimes you need to script sections of a show that would usually be spontaneous contributions. These can sound awful read aloud, unless your contributors are really good! See whether you can rely on your participants to make it up on the spot under your clear direction to ensure that it sounds natural. Remember that you will edit the recording so you have the chance to correct any mistakes. Another problem can be the youthfulness of your participants – try to utilise friends and acquaintances with a good tonal range and variety to their voices, and if you want an elderly lady to participate, go out and find one!

Think about your target audience and representation issues when you are writing your script or script outline. Direct all the participants in your

---

■ **Key terms**

Elements: the basic units you want to include on the page layout. It also applies to the composition of a photograph.

Principles of design: refers to balancing the elements in different ways so that they are aesthetically pleasing.

Verisimilitude: means 'seeming real' or 'like the truth' and refers to what an audience expects from a text in terms of content, but also forms and conventions. If your linked production has verisimilitude, this means it is convincing enough for an audience to accept it as a real example of the genre even if its production values are not as high as in the real industry.

radio show according to the expectations of this audience. You have a difficult job if you're sitting in a booth alone – you may have to be sound recorder and producer. It's very easy when you're concentrating on the technical quality of the sound recording to forget to direct your actors or host and guests appropriately. Sometimes, when people are giving up their free time to take part in a project, it can be hard to ask them to re-record sections of the programme until they get it right. One way around this is to warn them this will probably happen and to direct them throughout, firmly but courteously, until you are satisfied. They will hopefully be impressed by your professionalism and really enjoy the experience.

If you're recording interviews, **vox-pops** or sound effects on location, train yourself to listen carefully for background noises and ensure that the sound balance of your microphone is good. You will get much better, clearer results if you are wearing a good set of headphones and can hear what the sound levels are like through your recording device. It is essential to do a sound test before you begin the take, rather than trying to adjust levels part way through a recording. If you're using a hand-held microphone, experiment to find the best distance and angle from your speaker or sound effect.

Fig. 6.7 *Capturing effective sound on location using a hand-held digital audio recorder*

Fig. 6.8 *If you are unable to access a sound studio facility with equipment for radio broadcasting, this is a more basic, but perfectly good solution; using a USB microphone to record directly into sound editing software*

■ **Key terms**

Vox-pops: short for *vox populi*, meaning voice of the people. In news bulletins and documentaries in particular, this technique involves editing together short clips of people's responses to the same question asked by an interviewer to give an impression of a range of public opinion. These can be very easily manipulated during the editing process to convey the desired view of the programme-maker.

Whether you upload your sound separately or record straight onto a computer, you'll need to give all your files sensible names to keep track of your progress. Most sound editing programs are non-destructive and will allow you to undo actions and to preview effects and mixes before you apply them. However, it's still a good idea to keep your original files separately to the main edit as a backup.

💡 **Case study: a student's experience of a linked production**

The case study provided here is the recorded experience of a real student and the way their linked production was made. It should be noted that to assume sole responsibility in this way for a five-minute piece of video work is an enormous amount of work for one person and very ambitious. It is more likely that many students will undertake a production on this scale in a small group, with clearly defined roles and responsibilities for different stages of the production process.

```
                    GIRL

                    What can I get for you?


                    LUKE

                    Just a coffee, please. Black.

        The GIRL smiles and writes his order down. As she
        turns to leave, LUKE notices the comb in her hair, but
        only half registers it with a slight frown.

        LUKE continues to look out to sea, tired and still
        disturbed by his dream.

        Presently, the GIRL returns with his coffee. She sets
        it down on the bench in front of him, and rests her
        elbow on the table as she leans in, half flirting with
        him.

                    GIRL

                    Are you okay?

                    LUKE

                    Just on the hallucinatory
                    side of tiredness. I was up
                    early, trying to catch the
                    tide still in.

        The GIRL shrugs…

                    GIRL

                    Me too. Let me know if I can
                    get you anything else.

        …and PASSES the bill to him, on a saucer, folded into
        the comb from her hair. He looks at it, and picks it
        up curiously. We see a SLOW ZOOM on his eyes as he
        reacts to the object and turns slowly around.

        The GIRL is wiping the table behind him; she turns
        slowly round to meet his gaze, and smiles.

        EXT. THE BEACH (CHURCH COVE)

        We see Luke and his new girlfriend on the beach as a
        MONTAGE of varying angles and shots. They chase each
        other, laugh, run away from the waves etc. She beckons
        him into the sea, he refuses and so on.
```

Fig. 6.9 *Extract from script*

Treatment for '*Lutey*'

Titles over black entice us briefly with a fragment from the legend of *Lutey*, whose decision to save a mermaid from death on land cursed his descendants and male heirs to be taken by the sea.

Luke, aged 17, is fishing in a rocky cove. His luck is not in. After casting repeatedly into a sea, which isn't relinquishing anything but a tatty little comb tangled in seaweed, he decides to pack up. He makes his way up to a weathered oak bench and puts his feet up in the sun. Meanwhile, he dreams…

…but Luke's dream, which begins with a colourful extravaganza of tropical fish, soon takes a more sinister turn. He finds himself on a beach, alone. He hears crying coming from a cave and enters to find a mysterious creature there – a mermaid. We hear over black, as she whispers to his ancestor her desire to return to the sea and hear his rejection of her love. Luke awakens suddenly and uncomfortably from his sleep to the shrieking of gulls.

He makes his way up to the beach café, where he is served by a girl of around his own age. He orders a coffee and sits looking out to sea, sulking slightly. Meanwhile, the girl flits between other customers, and his attention is increasingly drawn to her hair, which is held up with an elaborate comb.

He beckons the girl over and she enquires as to what she can get for him. He is tongue-tied and stammers a response. She smiles, looks down and as she looks up, we see that her eyes have changed colour and are pure silver. She hands him a saucer with his change, receipt and the comb.

We see Luke and his new girlfriend, laughing on the beach as he casts his rod into the sea again and she tries to distract him. Eventually, she succeeds. She takes his hand and they run down the beach together towards the sea; disconcertingly, she seems to flicker in and out of this final shot increasingly until we realise that Luke is walking into the sea alone. We have been tricked; the mermaid is still sitting on the beach and she turns to gaze at the camera as she fades from the screen to the crackle of a police radio.

Fig. 6.10 *Extract from sketchbook storyboard*

🔍 *Reflecting on one student's production experiences*

(Please note, this record is provided to give you an idea of the kind of experiences you may have when you are creating your linked production. There is no requirement for you to write a commentary on your production experiences for assessment)

My research topic was based on the BBC Film Network website and the future of short films. For my linked production, I set myself the challenge of making a short film that would be suitable for submission to the site. My first step was to write a treatment for the film.

I found the idea of creating a short film narrative based on a traditional tale as a screenwriting exercise in one of the books I was reading about short film-making. I also wanted to tell a tale with a supernatural element to it. The Lizard, a small part of Cornwall, is rich in folklore and is also a wild, eerie place. The tale of 'Lutey and the Mermaid' is essentially not dissimilar to many tales concerning such creatures. There are some familiar elements to the tale – the prominence of a comb as magical object, the granting of wishes and the cursing of the unfortunate Lutey, one of whose male descendants are lost at sea every nine years for evermore.

For my own treatment, I decided not to simply retell the story but to play with it a little. Would Lutey's descendants know who they were and their possible fate? Would a mermaid, as a supernatural being, really appear wearing a couple of scallop shells and warbling a sea shanty post 2000? The gender roles remained quite traditional in my film, and perhaps this was a missed opportunity. In the end, I suppose my purpose was less to surprise the audience, and more to entertain them with a modern twist on an old tale, which hopefully still has a chill of the supernatural about it.

The first two drafts of my treatment were far too complex for a five-minute film. I continued to pare down and simplify my story until I was left with the bare bones of a simple narrative, which I felt could be told in five minutes, in accordance with advice given in the book I read specifically about the writing of short films.

Even though my film included very little dialogue, I still wanted to produce a script (see Fig. for an extract). I had done quite a bit of reading about screenwriting and screen play format, and used a free copy of Scriptsmart Gold obtained from the BBC website (which is essentially an author template) to assist me with formatting the script as well as possible. It perhaps looks a little odd, but was a useful exercise, particularly in organising the limited dialogue for the café sequence.

Storyboarding definitely helped me to envisage the kinds of shots I wanted. Prior to undertaking storyboarding, I visited the locations I was planning to use and took a range of still photographs. I had to wait to get permissions to film at the café until quite near the date of the shoot, which was quite frustrating. I had two reserve locations in mind, but neither would have been as satisfactory. I found a cove which was perfect. As well as being located on the Lizard where the tale comes from, it presented me with a beautiful weathered and sculptural bench upon which Luke could lie down for his dream, dramatic rocky and wild backdrops, and an outside table at the café with an uninterruptible view of the scene even if the beach was busy.

The dream sequence was filmed partly in the college drama studio, using a strobe light, partly at a cove, which is rocky like the main location but tends to be quite quiet at that time of year. The cave revealed itself in a different part of my first location when the tide went out at the end of the morning shoot, luckily saving a move to another location I had in mind. I also included footage from Newquay Aquarium, who were quick to agree to the shoot and very helpful on the day. I recorded a number of separate sound files in the studio with actor and actress to give myself plenty of options for the sound mix, which I hoped would evolve with the editing of the dream sequence itself. For this reason, I scripted a number of phrases and interactions for the actors to say separately and then for me to edit and process in any way I liked.

It was never my intention that the mermaid costume would be seen too distinctly. The costume was made to order in silver-coated Lycra material. I had to wait some time for it to arrive before deciding how to use it. I wanted the waitress to be dressed in a contemporary way, but the black of her clothing, in addition to being appropriate for someone serving in a bar setting, could also signify the darkness and supernatural status of the character. I sourced a small but glittering comb, which could look contemporary but a little odd simultaneously, as well as catching the light. I wanted Luke to wear a colour that would signify vibrancy and life, but not glare from the screen. I found a T-shirt in deep red with a Japanese koi tattoo design on the back, linking his fascination with the fish to his youthful image. I wanted him to wear this with walking trousers and boots, appearing casual and relaxed – ordinary.

The film was made with the help of two production assistants, who had also made practical media productions themselves. I also had a separate crew member responsible for recording sound on a separate source and I directed, operated the camera and edited the film myself.

I used a second-hand Sony PD150p DV camera for filming and recorded in DV Cam mode, which is not as good as HD, but broadcast quality. I used a tripod for most shots, especially where a zoom was required since a zoom always magnifies camera shake. I also attempted to use a Merlin Steadicam, which proved difficult to handle, notably during the circling pan around Luke on the beach during his dream, and the shot where he is followed up the steps by something unseen. I abandoned this as a skill I need to work on more, and used the camera handheld for these shots and the final beach scene.

I used a Sennheiser shot-gun microphone on board the camera, but also used a Zoom HD-4 digital sound recorder as an entirely separate source for dialogue, rather than plugging it into the second XLR input on the camera. However, I was forced to use the dialogue recorded on the Sennheiser for the café sequence as the pole was so close to the echoey veranda roof. It doesn't matter how great your images are if the sound is poor. Despite the Rycote softie, I still experienced some issues with wind noise. Other dialogue was recorded in a sound studio directly onto a Mac, and edited and processed using Sound Studio software.

I experienced some technical problems with Final Cut Express near the start of the project and consequently I used iMovie 6 to edit it. In his book *Digital Film-making* (2007), Mike Figgis reports a conversation he had about this program as a tool with Terry Gilliam, making me feel more confident about its usefulness even within the industry. However, its use restricted me in a number of ways.

■ No facility to balance light through video filters across shots.

■ I was limited to the titles available in the program instead of having the flexibility of using Livetitle.

■ Some of the image mixing facilities I could have tried in Final Cut Express for the last sequence were not available in iMovie 6, as it only supports a single video track.

I wanted to use the dialogue in the film in an unconventional way in the dream/beach sequence, so it was not sequenced when written in the way in which a script might usually be. I composed the music using Garageband. I resisted using any loops with actual themes to them, as these are widely used in advertising, computer games and so on being copyright-free and could have unwanted intertextual connotations for the audience. For the credits, I chose an extract from an original acoustic track by a contemporary folk artist, called '*Bodies in the Water*', which I felt honoured both the folk origins of the story but also its modern setting. The gulls were recorded at a different location on a separate day and the cave sound effect was a paid-for download, unrestricted by copyright once purchased.

Embarrassingly, I reviewed some footage of Luke fishing in the cove at lunchtime on the shoot and mixed my tapes up, even though they were clearly labelled. I recorded over it and had to arrange another shoot just for about five shots of precious opening sequence the following weekend.

Investigating media

After reading the case study, discuss the following questions:

■ What kinds of pre-production planning went into the shoot?

■ What equipment was used during the production and how?

■ How was the shooting of the footage for the whole film broken down practically in terms of locations and team?

■ What post-production procedures took place?

■ What challenges did the project present and how were they overcome?

■ How could the team have divided the responsibilities differently if this had been a group project?

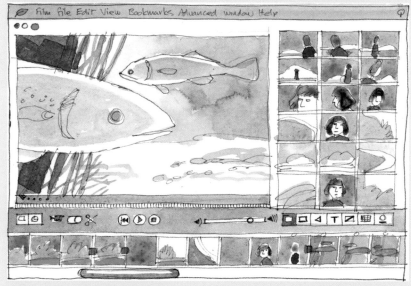

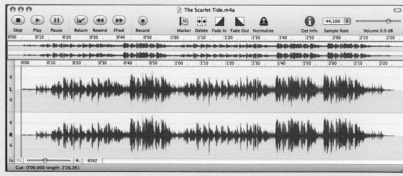

Fig. 6.12 *Editing the project using specialist video software (artist's impression) and audio software Sound Studio*

■ Presenting your work

It's important to present both your critical investigation and the accompanying work in its best light. If your critical investigation is submitted in written form, make sure it is word processed and that the font size and style are suitable for an academic submission. If the rest of your investigation is presented in an alternative format, such as an MP3 podcast or DVD commentary, it is worth while typing up a bibliography to show the breadth of your research.

When you have completed your practical work, back it up in an appropriate format, keeping a copy for yourself as well as submitting one to your tutor for marking. Clearly label the submitted copy with important information necessary to help identify it, such as your name, the title and type of product, your candidate number, subject and the year of examination. It may be worth repeating the same information on your own copy.

The specification states that suitable formats for submitting work include a DVD (domestic player format), video, print, website or MP3/Podcast (on a CD-ROM). Always use full colour printouts for print media if you have used colour in the design and a standard audio CD would also be suitable for any kind of audio work.

Undertaking a media practical production, whatever you choose to make, will have given you valuable life skills as well as technical ones. We hope you enjoy using them!

Chapter summary

In this chapter:

- how to research the practical skills needed for a linked production were discussed

- skills on how to plan a linked production effectively and as creatively as possible were explained

- the production and post-production processes, when working in each medium, were covered.

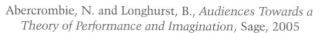

Bibliography

Abercrombie, N. and Longhurst, B., *Audiences Towards a Theory of Performance and Imagination*, Sage, 2005

Adorno, T. and Horkheimer, M. (known as the Frankfurt School), *The Culture Industry: Enlightenment and Mass Deception*, Verso, 1944 repr. 1986

Adorno, T., *The Culture Industry: selected essays on mass culture* (edited by J. Bernstein), Routledge, 1991

Alvarado, M., *Learning the Media*, Macmillan, 1987

Anderson, B., *Imagined Communities*, Verso, 1980 repr.1991

Anderson, C.A., 'An update on the effects of playing violent video games', *Journal of Adolescence*, 2004

Anderson, C.A. and Dill, K.E., 'Video games, aggressive thoughts, feelings and behavior in the laboratory and in life', *Journal of Personality and Social Psychology*, April 2000

Ang, I., *Watching Dallas: soap opera and the melodramatic imagination*, Methuen, 1985

Bandura, A., *The Young Child*, National Association for the Education of Young Children, 1982

Barthes, R., *Elements of Semiology*, Hill and Wang, 1967

Barthes, R., *The Death of the Author*, Manteia V., 1968

Barthes, R., *S/Z*, Hill and Wang, 1974

Baudrillard, J., *Simulations*, New York City Press, 1983

Blumler, J. and Katz, E. (eds), *The Uses of Mass Communication*, Beverly Hills, 1974

Buckingham, D., *Public Secrets, EastEnders and its Audience*, BFI, 1987

Burton, J. and Stevenson, E., *AQA Media Studies AS*, Nelson Thornes, 2008

Butler, J., *Gender Trouble*, Routledge, 1999

Cameron, D. and Frazer, E., *A Lust to Kill: a feminist investigation of sexual murder*, Polity Press, 1987

Castells, M., 'An introduction to the information age' in H. Mackay and T. O'Sullivan (eds) *The Media Reader: continuity and transformation*, Sage, 1999

Chomsky, N. and Herman, E.S., *Manufacturing Consent*, Pantheon Books, 1988

Cohen, S., *Folk Devils and Moral Panics*, Routledge, 1972 repr. 2002

Collins, J., 'Genericity in the nineties: eclectic irony and the new sincerity' in R. Collins, H. Radner and A. Preacher, *Film Theory Goes to the Movies*, Routledge, 1933

Collins, R., 'Media studies: alternative or oppositional practice?' in M. Alvarado and O. Boyd-Barratt (eds) *Media Education: an introduction*, BFI, 1992

Cooper, P. and Dancyger, K., *Writing the Short Film*, Focal Press, 2000

Corrigan, T. and White, P., *The Film Experience: an introduction*, Palgrave Macmillan, 2004

Couldry, N., 'Teaching us to fake it : the ritualized norms of television's "reality games"' in S. Murray and L. Ouelette (eds), *Reality TV: remaking television culture*, New York University Press, 2004

Corner, J., *Media Culture and Society* 'editorial' to special edition on reality TV January 1996

Curran, J., *Bending Reality: the state of the media*, Pluto Press, 1986

Curran, J. and Seaton, J., *Power Without Responsibility*, Routledge, 2003

Del Sola Poole, I., *Technologies of Freedom*, Harvard University Press, 1977

Dyer, R., *Stars*, BFI, 1979 repr. 1998

Dyer, R., 'The role of stereotypes' 1979 in P. Morris and S. Thornham (eds), *The Media Studies Reader*, New York University Press, 2000

Dyer, R., *Popular European Cinema*, Routledge, 1992

Dyer, R., *White: essays on race and culture*, Routledge, 1997

Dyer, R., *Heavenly Bodies*, Routledge, 2004

Figgis, M., *Digital Film-making*, Faber and Faber, 2007

Fiske, J., *Introduction to Communication Studies*, Methuen, 1982

Fiske, J., *Understanding Popular Culture*, Unwin Hyman, 1988

Frankfurt School, see Adorno, T. and Horkheimer, M.

Frensham, R., *Teach Yourself Screenwriting*, Hodder Headline, 2003

Gammon, L. and Marshment, M., *The Female Gaze*, The Women's Press, 1988

Gamson, M., *Claims to Fame: celebrity in contemporary America*, University of California Press, 1994

Gentile, D.A. and Anderson, C.A., 'Violent video games: effects on youth and public policy implications' in E. Dowd et al. (eds) *Handbook of Children, Culture and Violence*, Sage, 2006

Gerbner, G., *Toward a General Model of Communication*, Educational Technology Research and Development, 1956

Gerbner, G., Television and Social Behavior: Reports and Papers, National Institute of Mental Health, 1972

Giddens, A., *The Transformation of Intimacy*, Polity Press, 1992

Giddens, A., *Runaway World*, Taylor & Francis, 2003

Gitlin, T., *The Whole World is Watching*, University of California Press, 2003

Gledhill, C., *Stardom: industry of desire*, Routledge, 1991

Gledhill, C., 'The Case of the Soap Opera' in S. Hall, *Representation and Signifying Practice*, Sage, 1998

Goldhaber, M.H., 'What's the right economics for cyberspace?' *First Monday*, 1997

Gramsci, A., *Selections from Prison Notebooks*, Lawrence and Wishart, 1929–1935 translated 1971

Grist, L., *The Films of Martin Scorsese, 1963–77: authorship and context*, Macmillan, 2000

Gunter, B., *Poor Reception: misunderstanding and forgetting broadcast news*, Hillsdale, 1987

Gunter, B. and Svennevig, M., *Title of Book?*, University of Luton Press, 1987

Habermas, J., *Communication and the Evolution of Society*, Polity Press, 1991

Hall, S., 'Notes on deconstructing the popular' in R. Samuel (ed.) *People's History and Socialist Theory*, Routledge, 1981

Hall, S., *Culture Media Language*, Hutchinson, 1981

Hall, S., *Representation and Signifying Practice*, Sage, 1998

Hanson, M., 'A new era in video', *Guardian*, January 2008

Haraway, D., *Simians, Cyborgs and Women: the reinvention of nature*, Routledge, 1991

Higson, A., *English Heritage, English Cinema*, Oxford University Press, 2003

Hill, A., *Reality TV Audiences and Popular Factual Television*, Routledge, 2005

Kruger, S., Rayner, P. and Wall, P., *Media Studies: the Essential Introduction*, Routledge, 2001

Lyotard, J.F., *The Postmodern Condition: a report on knowledge*, Manchester University Press, 1984

Mackay, H., *Investigating the Information Society*, Routledge, 2001

McQuail, D., *Audience Analysis*, Sage, 1997

McRobbie, A., 'Notes on "what not to wear" and post-feminist symbolic violence' in L. Adkins and B. Skeggs (eds) *Feminism after Bourdieu*, Blackwell, 2004

Media Magazine, 'Why study the short film?' http://www.mediamagazine.org.uk/

Medurst, A., Lecture given at Chichester University, 1995

Miller, D., *Acknowledging Consumption*, Routledge, 1995

Modeleski, T., *Loving with a Vengeance: mass-produced fantasies for women*, Archon, 1982

Moores, S., 'Broadcasting and Its Audiences' in Mackay, H. (ed.) *Consumption and Everyday Life*, Sage, 1998

Morley, D., *The Nationwide Audience: structure and decoding*, BFI, 1980

Morley, D., 'Behind the rating' in J. Willis and T. Wollen (eds) *The Neglected Audience*, BFI, 1990

Mulvey, L., 'Visual pleasure and narrative cinema', *Screen*, 1975

Murdoch, G., 'Public service broadcasting' in 'An introduction to the information age' in H. Mackay and T. O'Sullivan (eds) *The Media Reader: continuity and transformation*, Sage, 1999

Neale, S., *Genre*, BFI, 1980

Neale, S., 'Questions of genre', *Screen*, 1991

Osgerby, B., 'The good the Bad and the Ugly'; post-war media representation of youth' in Briggs, M. Cobely, P. Cobley (eds) *The Media and Introduction*, Longman, 1998

Perkins, T., 'Rethinking stereotypes' in M. Barrett, P. Corrigan, A. Kuhn and J. Wolff (eds), *Ideology and Cultural Productions*, Croom Helm, 1979

Potter, W.J., *On Media Violence*, Sage, 1999

Propp, V., *The Morphology of the Folktale*, 2nd edition, University of Texas Press, 1928

Putnam, D., *The Undeclared War*, HarperCollins, 1997

Said, E., 'East isn't East: the impending end of the Age of Orientalism' *Times Literary Supplement* 1995

Saussure, F., *Course in General Linguistics*, Duckworth, 1983

Shuttac, J., *The Talking Cure: TV shows and women*, Routledge, 1997

Silverstone, R., *Television and Everyday Life*, Routledge, 1994

Spigel, L., *Make Room for TV*, University of Chicago Press, 1999

Springhall, J., *Youth, Popular Culture and Moral Panics*, St Martin's Press, 1998

Stacey, J., *Star Gazing: Hollywood cinema and female spectatorship*, Routledge, 1994

The Guardian Guide to Making Video, January 2008

Thompson, K., *Media and Cultural Regulation*, Sage, 1998

Todorov, T., *The Novel: an anthology of criticism and theory 1900–2000*, Blackwell, 1997

Glossary

A

Anthropomorphising: giving an inanimate or non-human subject human-like qualities to create a particular effect.

Auteur theory: suggests that the director is the author of the film and that films reflect his or her particular visual style, themes, values and ideologies.

B

Binary oppositions: when a text is divided into two clear groups of characters, situations, or values, for example, police and criminals.

Bollywood: the large Indian film industry whose output often exceeds that of the US film industry.

Bricolage: the process of creating a media text out of a series of artefacts, styles and signs from other media texts or cultural artefacts.

Britishness: the essence of what it means to be British. This is more often a media representation than an agreed shared set of values.

C

Censorship: the restriction and control of media content by powerful groups – whether governments or media producers.

Colourising: using a tool to change the colour range of a particular photo or set of photos, e.g. to have greyer tones, sepia, or be warmed using reds and oranges.

Connotation: the second order of meanings in which a wider range of associations may arise.

Constructionist view: a view of representation that suggests our knowledge of the world is constructed by media representations.

Cropping: removing unwanted areas of a photograph or focusing the reader's attention on a particular aspect of it by selecting where its borders are positioned.

Cross-cultural factors: the differences in culture between nations and groups within nations. Culture includes values, attitudes and everyday practices and lifestyles.

Cultural concern: an issue, concern or paranoia that a society or culture becomes preoccupied with or worried about.

Cultural imperialism: a process by which one country dominates other countries' media consumption and consequently dominates their values and ideologies.

Cyberspace: the virtual world of computers and telecommunications, which connects millions of individuals without reference to geographical places.

D

Denotation: the simplest, most obvious level of meaning of a sign, be it a word, image, object or sound.

Diaspora identity: the result of forced or voluntary migration where people experience both a sense of belonging to a cultural group that is 'other' to the dominant culture of their country of residence.

Digital revolution: the revolution in the production and distribution of media texts, which now rely on the digital codes used by computers and the Internet.

Discourse: a way of talking about discussing a subject that establishes 'common sense' or knowledge about that subject.

Dystopian: a perspective where everything is as bad as it can possibly be.

E

Economic context: the financial opportunities and constraints that govern a media text's production and distribution.

Elements: the basic units you want to include on the page layout. It . also applies to the composition of a photograph.

Enigma narrative: a narrative that involves the audience by setting questions or puzzles for them to solve.

F

FourDoc: a four-minute documentary to be shown online (www.channel4.com/fourdocs)or screened on Channel 4.

G

Gender trouble: any behaviour and representation that disrupts culturally accepted notions of gender.

Globalisation: the way in which in contemporary society distant countries are inter-related and connected together by trade, communication and cultural experiences.

H

Hegemony: the process in which a power relationship is accepted, consented to and seen as natural or as 'common sense'.

Heritage: media texts that are set in or portray the past, often in an idealised or romanticised way.

Hyper-reality: the fact that the distinction between the real world and the media world is disappearing.

Hypothesis: an informed assumption that you make about a topic area of your choice in order to focus your line of enquiry during your research.

Imagined community: a term developed by Benedict Anderson (1980), which refers to communities that predominantly exist in people's minds and gives them a sense of identity.

Inter-textuality: when a media text uses elements or references from other media texts.

Left wing: political views most often associated with the Labour party, suggesting a greater involvement by government in society and individuals' lives in order to prevent suffering and exploitation. Such views tend to be in favour of more welfare services and higher taxes to pay for them.

M

Meta-narratives: over-arching explanations of society; sometimes referred to as grand narratives.

Moral panic: a media-generated public outcry against a group, community or practice considered threatening and /or dangerous.

Myths: frequently told stories that a culture repeats in order to convey the dominant values and ideologies of that culture.

N

Narcissism: the identification with/ or erotic appeal of an idealised image of oneself.

News agenda: topics and issues focused upon by media news.

News values: the relative importance of certain stories over others.

O

Orientalism: a perspective that suggests the East and the Orient are represented as provoking both fear and fascination within Western culture.

P

Pastiche: creation of a media text out of elements of, or with reference to, other media texts in a mocking or caricatured way.

Political discourse: refers to the scope of discussion and debate that goes on within political circles, it includes, therefore, topics discussed in Parliament and by politicians and political journalists.

Polysemic: texts that are open to a range of different readings and interpretations.

Post-colonialism: a theory that suggests issues of race and the legacy of colonialism have a strong influence on media and media representations.

Principles of design: refers to balancing the elements in different ways so that they are aesthetically pleasing.

Psycho-analytic themes: based on the work of Sigmund Freud. He argued that human actions are often motivated by repressed sexual fears and desires.

Realism: media texts or representations that seem credible to an audience in terms of events, people, emotions or experiences, as opposed to a text that is seen to be merely fantasy.

Reflective view: view of representation that understands media representations as a reflection of lived reality.

Reflector discs: usually fold-away discs of silver and/or gold material, which can be used to create fill light and change skin tone or bounce another hand-held light off.

Right wing: political views most often associated with the Conservative party, stress the freedom of the individual and a more limited role for the government and consequently lower taxation.

Saturation: the amount and shades of colour used in a print media text and the resulting effect. High saturation is very bright, bold and unrealistic. Low saturation will have a more subtle effect.

Scopophilia: finding pleasure in looking at other people as objects.

Signified: the idea, meaning or concept that is represented by the signifier.

Signifier: the visible part of a sign, such as an image, letter, colour or diagram.

Simulacrum: a media text that makes no attempt to represent reality and merely represents other representations.

Sticky: a web designer's term that refers to web pages with dynamic content, which people want to come back to repeatedly.

Synoptic work: shows a breadth of view that demonstrates learning in different areas of media study.

T

Technological determinist: argues that technology dictates or determines the nature of society.

U

Utopian: belonging to or characteristic of an ideal perfect state or place.

V

Verisimilitude: 'seeming real' or 'like the truth'. Refers to what an audience expects from a text in terms of content, but also forms and conventions.

Virtual reality: an artificial 3D world generated by and shared between computers.

Vox-pops: Short for vox populi, meaning voice of the people. In news bulletins and documentaries, in particular, this technique involves editing together short clips of people's responses to the same question asked by an interviewer to give an impression of a range of public opinion. These can be very easily manipulated during the editing process to convey the desired view of the programme-maker.

Voyeurism: gaining pleasure from watching, especially secretly, other people's behaviour and bodies in sexual, intimate or emotional behaviour.